Death Penalty on Trial

Other books in ABC-CLIO's On Trial Series
Charles L. Zelden, Series Editor

Death Penalty
ON TRIAL

A Handbook with
Cases, Laws, and Documents

Gary P. Gershman

A B C ☉ C L I O

Santa Barbara, California • Denver, Colorado • Oxford, England

Library of Congress Cataloging-in-Publication Data
Gershman, Gary P.
 Death penalty on trial : a handbook with cases, laws, and documents / Gary P.
Gershman.
    p.   cm. — (ABC-CLIO's On trial series)
 Includes bibliographical references and index.
 ISBN 1-85109-606-X (hardback : alk. paper); 1-85109-611-6 (eBook)
 1. Capital punishment—United States—History.   I. Title. II. Series: On trial.
KF9227.C2G47 2005
345.73'0773—dc22

                                                                    2005001438

07 06 05 04 03 02 01 10 9 8 7 6 5 4 3 2 1

ABC-CLIO, Inc.
130 Cremona Drive, P.O. Box 1911
Santa Barbara, California 93116-1911

This book is printed on acid-free paper ∞.
Manufactured in the United States of America

Contents

Series Foreword

The volumes in the On Trial series explore the many ways in which the U.S. legal and political system has approached a wide range of complex and divisive legal issues over time—and in the process defined the current state of the law and politics on these issues. The intent is to give students and other general readers a framework for understanding how the law in all its various forms—constitutional, statutory, judicial, political, and customary—has shaped and reshaped the world in which we live today.

At the core of each volume in the series is a common proposition: that in certain key areas of American public life, we as a people and a nation are "on trial" as we struggle to cope with the contradictions, conflicts, and disparities within our society, politics, and culture. Who should decide if and when a woman can have an abortion? What rights, if any, should those with a different sexual orientation be able to claim under the Constitution? Is voting a basic right of citizenship, and if so, under what rules should we organize this right—especially when the application of any organizing rules inevitably results in excluding some citizens from the polls? And what about the many inconsistencies and conflicts associated with racial tensions in the country? These are just some of the complex and controversial issues that we as a people and a nation are struggling to answer—and must answer if we are to achieve an orderly and stable society. For the answers we find to these disputes shape the essence of who we are—as a people, community, and political system.

The concept of being "on trial" also has a second meaning fundamental to this series: the process of litigating important issues in a court of law. Litigation is an essential part of how we settle our differences and make choices as we struggle with the problems that confront us as a people and a nation. In the 1830s, Alexis de Tocqueville noted in his book *Democracy in America,* "There is hardly a political question in the United States which does not sooner or later turn into a judicial one" (Tocqueville 1835, 270). This insight is as true today as it was in the 1830s. In *The Litigious Society,* Jethro K. Lieberman notes: "To express amazement at American litigiousness is akin to professing astonishment at learning that the roots of most Americans lie in other lands. We have been a litigious nation as we have been an immigrant one. Indeed, the two are related" (Lieberman 1983, 13). Arriving in the United States with different backgrounds, customs, and lifestyle preferences, we inevitably clashed as our contrasting visions of life in the United States—its culture, society, and politics—collided. And it was to the courts and the law that we turned as a neutral forum for peaceably working out these differences. For, in the United States at least, it is the courthouse that provides the anvil on which our personal, societal, and political problems are hammered out.

The volumes in this series therefore take as their central purpose the important task of exploring the various ways—good and bad, effective and ineffective, complex and simple—in which litigation in the courts has shaped the evolution of particular legal controversies for which we as a people are "on trial." And, more important, the volumes do all this in a manner accessible to the general reader seeking to comprehend the topic as a whole.

These twin goals—analytical and educational—shape the structure and layout of the volumes in the series. Each book consists of two parts. The first provides an explanatory essay in four chapters. Chapter 1 introduces the issues, controversies, events, and participants associated with the legal controversy at hand. Chapter 2 explores the social, economic, political and/or historical background to this topic. Chapter 3 describes in detail the various court decisions and actions that have shaped the current status of the legal controversy under examination. In some cases that will be done through a close examination of a few representative cases; in others by a broader but less detailed narrative of the course of judicial action. Chapter 4 discusses the impact of these cases on U.S. law—their doctrinal legacy—as well as on U.S. society—their historical, sociological, and political legacy.

Part 2, in turn, provides selective supplementary materials designed to help readers more fully comprehend the topics covered in the chapters of Part 1. First are documents aimed at helping the reader better appreciate both the issues and the process by which adjudication shaped these matters. Selected documents might include court opinions (excerpted or whole), interviews, newspaper accounts, or selected secondary essays. Next comes an alphabetically formatted glossary providing entries on the people, laws, cases, and concepts important to an understanding of the topic. A chronology next provides the reader with an easily referenced listing of the major developments covered in the book, and a table of cases lists the major court decisions cited. And lastly, an annotated bibliography describes the key works in the field, directing a reader seeking a more detailed examination of the topic to the appropriate sources.

In closing, as you read the books in this series, keep in mind the purposefully controversial nature of the topics covered within. The authors in the series have not chosen easy or agreeable topics to explore. Much of what you read may trouble you, and should. Yet it is precisely these sorts of contentious topics that need the most historical analysis and scrutiny. For it is here that we are still "on trial"—and all too often, as regards these matters, the jury is still out.

Charles L. Zelden
Ft. Lauderdale, Florida

Preface

The death penalty is one of many explosive, emotional issues in the United States today. As with all of the topics in this series, it touches a nerve in most people. The issue of capital punishment, like many of the topics in the series, not only touches that nerve, it exposes it. Even those unsure about where they stand, are emotional as they contemplate what they would do if one of their loved ones was killed in a gruesome murder similar to those that proliferate this book.

Because of that heightened emotionalism, as with many such debates, arguments about the death penalty are difficult; they often emanate from two different starting points. Many proponents of the death penalty start from the point of view that capital punishment is a viable and acceptable state action. However, there is question whether it is a viable part of the U.S. criminal justice system. Opponents arrive at the debate with any question about the viability of capital punishment answered in the negative—it is not acceptable, ever. For those people the debate is already compromised. For the most part, the debate is among those who site between the polar extremes. There are individuals who support capital punishment, yet have serious reservations about it in terms of whom (juveniles, mentally retarded) we execute, whether it is fair, and so on. On the other hand, many people claim they are anti–death penalty, but they question that belief when faced with tragic events, such as those ranging from the Holocaust to September 11th.

It is with these latter two groups in mind that I wrote this book. The purpose of this book is not to argue one point of view or another but rather to provide a historical anchor and grounding for those who wish to learn about the death penalty and to give each side a better understanding of where the other side is coming from. In doing that, one of the first problems I struggled with was whether or not I should tell the reader my view on capital punishment, because the idea and purpose behind this book was not to argue a specific view-point—in part, my bias was not important. However, one of the things I realized while researching and reading other works, was, at times, the author's failure to reveal his or her viewpoint compromised points he or she tried to make. Thus, I decided it was important that I reveal my anti–death penalty bias. I have tried to be fair and even in the presentation—despite my own personal distaste for and rejection of capital punishment.

I hope the reader can embark on the same intellectual journey I did while writing my book. I discovered much about both arguments, including their strengths and their weaknesses. Often times I found myself nodding while reading an argument in favor of the death penalty and shaking my head in distaste while reading an argument against capital punishment. If the reader can come away with the same type of illumination and clarification that I did, not necessarily changing their mind, but with a more enlightened view toward capital punishment as a whole and a better understanding of its historical place and its evolution in the United States, then this volume is a success.

Acknowledgements

First and foremost, I must thank those who helped in the production of this volume—those who tirelessly perused my words, trying to help me get it right and hopefully minimizing my errors. This includes Alicia Merritt and Carla Roberts at ABC-CLIO, whom I must also thank for their patience with me as I approached (and passed) deadlines. To the other editors who corrected the numerous mistakes, I cannot overemphasize my appreciation. Next, I want to thank my colleague and friend and series editor, Charles Zelden, who sits in the office next to mine. It was his gentle prodding that got me to think about doing this volume, start it, and then finish it. Third, thank you to the various individuals who perused various sections and gave me helpful ideas for how to discuss a certain point or present an idea, most notably my brother Ian. An important part of this group of people are the friends and family who put up with me as I agonized over getting this or that done and my rantings and ravings as I struggled through various sections, including my family—my mother, my sister Jo and her husband, Danny, my sister-in-law Pam—and of course, my girlfriend Kim. Finally, thanks to my students who allowed me to test ideas and thoughts on them, and more importantly, were patient with me as I delayed returning papers and quizzes so that I could devote time to this volume.

Part One

1
Introduction

If we execute murderers and there is in fact no deterrent ef-
fect, we have killed a bunch of murderers. If we fail to exe-
cute murderers, and doing so would in fact have deterred
other murders, we have allowed the killing of a bunch of in-
nocent victims. I would much rather risk the former. This, to
me, is not a tough call.
　　　　　　　　　　　　　　　　　　—John McAdams
　　　Marquette University/Department of Political Science

The death penalty is pure violence, a barbaric and useless vi-
olence. Dangerous even, because it can only lead to other acts
of violence—as all violence does. The supreme punishment
ought to be a life sentence, and one without brutality.
　　　　　　　　—the Dalai Lama, *The Path to Tranquility*

"What a pity Bilbo did not stab the vile creature when he
had the chance!"
　　"Pity?" replies Gandalf. "It was pity that stayed his hand.
Pity, and mercy: Not to strike without need."
　　Frodo answers that he does not feel any pity for Gollum:
"He deserves death."
　　"Deserves death!" Gandalf responds. "I daresay he does.
Many that live deserve death. And some that die deserve life.
Can you give it to them? Then be not eager to deal out death

3

in the name of justice, fearing for your own safety. Even the
wise cannot see all ends."
                    —J. R. R. Tolkien, *Lord of the Rings*

To abolitionists who believed a life sentence preferable to an
execution:
    They read without a qualm, indeed they read with rejoic-
ing, the hideous irony of "killer gets life"; they sigh with re-
lief instead of horror. They do not see and suffer the cell, the
drill, the clothes, the stench, the food; they do not feel the sex-
ual racking of young and old bodies, the hateful promiscuity,
the insane monotony, the mass degradation, the impotent ha-
tred. They do not remember . . . that Joan of Arc, when of-
fered "life" preferred burning at the stake. . . . For my part, I
would choose death without hesitation. If that option is abol-
ished, a demand will one day be heard to claim it as a privi-
lege in the name of human dignity.
                    —Melvin Urofsky, *Letting Go*

A quick look at the chair, with its restraints hanging off the arm-rests, the hood for the defendant's head, evokes a visceral emotion. If a picture is worth a thousand words, maybe no picture, no image better sums up the debate over the death penalty than a picture of "Old Sparky"—the electric chair used by the State of Florida (until it was replaced in 1998). The chair is the symbol of arguments for and against the death penalty. It symbolizes the transition of the method of execution. Old Sparky evokes the images associated with capital punishment and reflects the brute horror of the penalty, the stated need for vengeance, where we have been, and where we are going.

Florida, using the electric chair, is notorious for its executions and for those it has almost executed. The Florida electric chair is THE symbol of the death penalty. It is the symbol of a state where politicians sought to be seen as tough on crime. Old Sparky was where Ted Bundy's life ended. On three different occasions following Bundy's death, flames shot out of the heads of those strapped into the chair. First was Jesse Tafero, a convicted cop killer who appeared to struggle against the horror for four minutes. Pablo Medina was the next man to face the roaring flames of Old Sparky. Allen Davis also faced horror, when his execution did not go smoothly.

Today, the electric chair has been replaced by lethal injection as the favored method of execution in Florida. Yet the debate does not stop, and Old Sparky's image, like that of the guillotine 200 years ago, persists and provides an important starting point for the discussion of capital punishment. No matter the method (electrocution, gas chamber, hanging, firing squad, or lethal injection), the state's taking of an individual's life is one of the most hotly contested legal battles in the United States.

Finding a Middle Ground

It would appear that the death penalty is simultaneously too much and not enough for society. The death penalty is one of the subjects in U.S. society that incite both rational and irrational debate. Emotions peak as individuals debate the efficacy and effectiveness of the ultimate penalty. It is precisely that emotionalism that often causes people to lose site of both the historical place the death penalty holds in U.S. history and the evolution of the debate over the death penalty. The polarizing nature of the debate often leaves participants without a common ground upon which to continue the argument.

This volume is an attempt to let some of the emotional air out of the balloon (if possible) and help create that common ground that will allow us to engage in a debate based on realities and facts, part of which is the emotional nature of the debate, and look realistically at the place the execution of criminals holds in American society in the twenty-first century. At the very least, it is hoped this text will help readers understand the arguments that envelop those who fight for and against capital punishment.

The essence of the death penalty debate rests on the basic question: Why do we choose to execute individuals? Yet sadly, most debate on the death penalty has often focused as much on the issue of how to execute as on the more intense and significant question of why, obscuring the real issues at hand. As seen in the debates about the electric chair, the gas chamber, hanging, the guillotine, and so on, each new method of execution was adopted as a mechanism to make the death penalty more humane, more palatable to society at large. The idea was for those who were being executed to die efficiently and quickly without undue suffering. Suffering suggested torture in modern society, and all but the most extreme capital punishment advocates decried using torture.

The death penalty thus highlights some of the many paradoxes that permeate U.S. society. A society that is steeped in individualism and prides itself on that characteristic, at the same time often focuses on the importance of community ideals and standards that create an environment more comfortable and more free for its citizens to live in. Consequently, the Court has often called for penalty to be individualized, so that its imposition is not arbitrary and capricious. Each illegal act is measured in its own right. Yet simultaneously, in weighing the individual nature of a particular crime the Court has attempted to establish uniform standards applicable to all similar cases and has looked to community values in doing so.

Execution is the ultimate form of retribution and vengeance an individual can impose, via the state, on another human being. In executing felons, the state acts for both the individuals injured and the community at large, satiating an apparent desire to eliminate certain individuals from the society—forever. But questions remain: Where does that authority to act on behalf of the individual and community stem from? Why do the government and the people persist in claiming that right? Should the state have this right?

On the other hand, the questions can be reversed: Why shouldn't the government have the right to eliminate from society, permanently, those whose acts endanger other members of the community? If in coming together to create a government, to guarantee our security, do we give up a portion of our personal liberties for the common good of all? Do we not forfeit the right to live when we violate the very laws we are meant to abide by as members of a community?

The answers to such moral questions are often not as cut and dried as both the proponents and opponents of capital punishment would have them seem. When one adds in the complications of application in a real-world context—say in the legal system of the United States—the complexities grow even larger.

The recent spate of death penalty cases and imposed moratoriums have reignited the death penalty debate in the United States—often confusing fact with fiction and leaving one questioning not only the background of executions in the United States but also why the United States, alone among the Western nations, still propagates such an extreme penalty.

To Kill or Not to Kill

One of these larger complexities involves the emotional side of the death penalty question. Since 1930, more than 4,500 people have been executed in the United States and some of these death penalty cases, in turn, have generated tremendous publicity—from detailed accounts of the oftentimes heinous crimes that induced the desire for the death penalty to the passion play that takes place in the public eye. The twentieth century is littered with examples of celebrated death penalty cases such as the Sacco and Vanzetti case in 1927; the Scottsboro Boys, the Bruno Hauptmann, and the Lindbergh cases in the 1930s; the Rosenbergs and the Caryl Chessman cases in the 1950s; to the more recent cases of serial killers Gary Gilmore and Ted Bundy; conspirator in the bombing of the Murrah Federal Building in Oklahoma City Timothy McVeigh; and Stanley "Tookie" Williams, founder of the notorious Crips, who is currently sitting on death row.

If this book had been written five years ago, much of the emotional trauma that permeates death penalty arguments would not be present. But with images of New York's World Trade Center crumbling to the ground and the sniper shootings in Washington, D.C., another shift in U.S. public opinion seems to be taking place. The question becomes will each of those incidents become just one more in the long list of events in U.S. history that have signified highwater (or low-water) marks in the imposition of the death penalty, or will they serve as important determinants in how, why, and when the death penalty is imposed on U.S. citizens?

Although anti–death penalty advocates often talk in terms of the Eighth Amendment and the constitutional proscription against cruel and unusual punishment, that argument is often tempered or directed by some more important threshold questions: Why do we execute some criminals and not others, and what purpose is served by capital punishment?

A variety of justifications for and against capital punishment have been put forth. Often the debates over these justifications become as heated as the debates over the death penalty itself.

One common source of disagreement between those supporting and those opposing the death penalty is whether or not the death penalty acts as a deterrent to crime. The basic idea here is that society has always lived by a system of negative reinforcement. Punish criminals, and would-be criminals will be discouraged from crime. This idea has been especially strong in the death penalty debate. The additional bonus with capital punishment, according to proponents, is that once a murderer is executed, he or she is forever precluded from murdering again.

Death penalty opponents dispute this rationale, arguing that the idea of deterrence has not been proven, nor can it be. What murderer, whether rational or not in the first place, would seriously consider the consequences of his actions (especially in the case of more heinous crimes) and then fail to follow through? Did Ted Bundy really consider the consequences of his acts? Opponents go on to argue that not only does the death penalty not deter, but it might even increase, the incidence of murder. Some researchers suggest that the state's sanctioning of killing by execution has a negative effect on society, by validating the taking of life. Finally, while it is true that capital punishment would forever remove the criminal from society, life imprisonment would have the same effect, in a far more humane manner, according to opponents.

It is probably most accurate to say that the statistics are inconclusive. There is no way of proving whether the death penalty is or is not a deterrent to crime. The arguments in the end are based on statistical information that has been skewed to fit a particular point of view. There is no way to determine whether the death penalty does or does not reduce the number of capital offenses that occur in society. Some societies without the death penalty have very low murder rates. Why? The reasons have nothing to do with capital punishment. Too many other factors (number of police, new laws, etc.) come into play. There is no question that the average rational person fears death. However, when talking about murderers, especially those who commit the types of crimes for which society would demand the death penalty, rationality is not an issue.

A second common argument in support of the death penalty is retribution. The basic argument here dates back to the biblical injunction of an "eye for an eye." One should receive a punishment that fits the crime committed. Take a life; lose your life. Retribution is a method of justice for the victims and their survivors. In contrast, opponents argue that life is always sacrosanct, any life. And the taking of a life by the state is just as wrong as the taking of a life by an individual. As noted above, the execution of individuals by the state endorses the taking of human life. Supporters argue this is fallacious for several reasons. First, by taking the murderer's life, the state is trying to show society that murder is an unacceptable crime, and whoever commits it will pay the ultimate price. Second, state-sanctioned executions do not legitimize murder. This argument is challenged by the notion that although the state imprisons people, it does not legitimize kidnapping. Finally, as an addendum to the previous argument, state executions and murder are very different and society is conscious of that difference. The former is illegal and undeserved, and the latter is a lawful, warranted punishment for committing an unlawful act.

Retribution is closely linked to the idea of vengeance or revenge. However, opponents argue that it is not appropriate for the state to be in the business of meting out revenge. Do we want the government engaging in what amounts to public bloodletting? To execute criminals, opponents argue, is to merely continue the cycle of violence. As a "civilized" society (another whole argument is defining what that means), we should treat our criminals in a more humane way. The question then arises as to what is meant by the word *humane*. This undergirds the arguments surrounding the meaning of cruel and unusual and plays an important part in how we choose to execute people. An important underlying question here concerns the function of the government and the prison system. Is it one of punishment purely? Is it to rehabilitate? How one sees the correctional system would determine how one answers this question. In the end, does society want vengeance as part of its process, or have we moved beyond that?

The third argument that comes into play revolves around the potential innocence of the convicted person. Opponents argue there is a danger of executing innocent people and cite cases to support that fact. The history of lynching supports this argument, because the majority of those hanged during the heyday of lynching in the late nineteenth and early twentieth centuries were innocent blacks in the South. Lynchings also acted as a mechanism by which the legal system was manipulated to guarantee that blacks who were accused of (though oftentimes not guilty of) rape or murder received the death penalty, rather than some lesser penalty.

Proponents of the death penalty argue that the system is rife with safeguards that make such an outcome statistically very small. The essence of this argument is the old saw about criminal justice. Is it better to let ten guilty men go free so one innocent man does not suffer or to let one innocent man suffer in order to protect society from ten guilty men?

Opponents argue such a great risk should not be taken. Even the smallest chance that an innocent man could be executed should be enough to give one pause. In contrast to the procedures in place for other criminal penalties, with the death penalty, there is no chance to correct a wrong once an individual has been put to death. Recent evidence suggests that mistakes have been made, and new revelations using DNA evidence and the Ohio Moratorium on executions suggest the system is far less perfect than previously thought and therefore should be abandoned. Opponents claim that the system seems unreliable, citing the profound number of errors that have been made in capital trials that have resulted in new trials, the majority of whose defendants did not receive the death penalty upon retrial. There is no question that life is fraught with risk, opponents say. However, one of the keys to life is risk management, and here is a risk that can easily be minimized, if not eliminated, through life imprisonment.

Proponents argue this is an acceptable risk. The odds of executing an innocent person are miniscule. They agree that punishing any innocent person is wrong, but that does not mean the system should be eliminated because we might infrequently incarcerate innocent people. As the system becomes more and more refined, the chance of innocent people being executed becomes smaller and smaller. (Proponents often argue there is no proof that an innocent person has ever been convicted, although this is a weak strand of the argument, because the argument rests on the fact that if it has happened a couple of times, it does not matter in the overall scheme of things.) Finally, proponents argue, the fact that we find inconsistencies and mistakes proves that the system does work. The fact that on appeal and retrial many do not receive the death penalty and some are even found innocent shows the system, while cumbersome, does function correctly.

A fourth argument centers around the question of whether the death penalty is arbitrary and, as a consequence, discriminates on the basis of race, socioeconomic status, and so on. This is perhaps the most objective of the arguments over the use of the death penalty. (Although as can be seen in the case law, numbers can be manipulated, and the same numbers that show an arbitrary application of the death penalty can be used to show that it is applied fairly and evenly.)

Opponents argue the death penalty is inherently unfair and should not ever be used. It is arbitrary because it does not necessarily execute the most heinous offenders, instead those individuals who have less adequate counsel, are poorer, are from a racial minority, live in certain states, and so on, are the ones that are more likely to be executed. As U.S. jurisprudence in the twentieth century has shown, the wealthy with their phalanx of high-priced lawyers get "better justice" than the poor. In addition, besides the question of class, race is a huge factor. There is no question that black men in the South receive the death penalty in disproportionate numbers to whites. To make it worse, opponents cite statistics that show that black men who kill whites are executed at a higher rate than either blacks or whites who kill blacks. This racial impropriety alone should strike down the death penalty. Finally why should the same crime call for the death penalty in one place but not in others? The answer to that question lies in prosecutor discretion.

In contrast, proponents say the death penalty is fair. The fact that the administration of the death penalty varies from place to place reflects the diversity of the nation and the basis of the U.S. criminal justice system within the context of federalism. Every crime is unique, and every jurisdiction has the right to administer justice within the demands of its own community. Because the Supreme Court demands individual attention to each case and rejects the idea of a mandatory death penalty, the differences among jurisdictions celebrate the system of justice rather than compromise it.

Supporters argue as well that the racial statistics are false. They claim that more crimes are committed by blacks than by whites, therefore more blacks get executed. Period. The fact that not everyone who deserves to be executed gets executed does not make the penalty unfair. All those who speed do not get caught, yet we do not eliminate speeding laws. Rather, the goal should be to make sure, in as many cases as possible, that those folks who deserve to be executed are.

Other arguments also dance around the controversy. For example, economic concerns come into play. Supporters of the death penalty argue this is a cost-effective way to deal with the most sordid elements of society. However, as opponents argue, it can cost more to execute an individual than to incarcerate him for life. The key factor here is that the cost of the appeals process, which the Supreme Court has made mandatory in death penalty cases, can drag on for years. The result has been that supporters have pushed for more streamlined processes that will cut costs. In addition, supporters argue this is a false statistic, because it doesn't take into consideration the cost that mainstream prisoners incur by making numerous appeals to the judicial system. Thus, whether one is executed, serves a life sentence, or something less, appeals are part of the process and do not add or subtract from the cost. In the end, this is probably a poor argument for both sides, because if the concern is justice, what does the cost matter?

Finally there is the question of whether the death penalty is a cruel and unusual form of punishment. As will be seen in the chapters that follow, this often serves as a central question to all death penalty litigation. The Court for the most part says it is not, per se. Rather they have focused on the how, for what, and who of this question to resolve it. Opponents argue the infliction of death is cruel and unusual because of how it is instituted and who receives the penalty. Issues of race and class play heavily in this argument.

What constitutes "cruel and unusual" is totally subjective. Some have argued it is more cruel and unusual to put a person in a small cell, on lockdown for twenty-three hours a day, and forever tell them what to do, than to terminate their life. If "cruel and unusual" is related to suffering and torture, surely there is far more suffering to be experienced in a lifetime in prison than in the quick, harsh face of execution.

Conclusion

The story of the death penalty is a paradoxical one. Few come to the argument with an open mind, and most tend to twist history to support their argument. As will be seen by the evolution of capital punishment in the Western world, in the United States and in U.S. jurisprudence the history of the death penalty has never followed a straight line. The vagaries of society, twists of public opinion, and the happenstance of events have all seriously affected when or if criminals will be executed.

References

Bedau, Hugo. 1997. *The Death Penalty in America: Current Controversies.* New York: Oxford University Press.

Bedau, Hugo Adams. 2004. *Debating the Death Penalty: Should America Have Capital Punishment: The Experts on Both Sides Make Their Best Cases.* New York: Oxford University Press.

Berns, Walter. 1979. *For Capital Punishment: Crime and the Morality of the Death Penalty.* Basic Books: New York.

Bohm, Robert. 1999. *Deathquest: An Introduction to the Theory and Practice of Capital Punishment in the United States.* Cincinnati: Anderson Publishing Co.

Bosco, Antoinette. 2001. *Choosing Mercy: A Mother of Murder Victims Pleads to End the Death Penalty.* Maryknoll, NY: Orbis Books.

Brennan, William J. 1986. "The 1986 Oliver Wendell Holmes, Jr. Lecture: Constitutional Adjudication and the Death Penalty: A View from the Court." *Harvard Law Review* 100 (December): 313.

Day, Nancy. 2000. *The Death Penalty for Teens: A Pro/Con Issue (Hot Pro/Con Issues).* Berkeley Heights, NJ: Enslow.

Dicks, Shirley. 1995. *Congregation of the Condemned: Voices against the Death Penalty.* Reprint edition. Amherst, NY: Prometheus Books.

Gerber, Rudolph J. 1996. "Death Is Not Worth It." *Arizona State Law Journal* 28 (Spring): 335.

Prejean, Helen. 1997. *Dead Man Walking.* New York: Newmarket Press.

2
Historical Background

Capital Punishment in the Ancient World

There is no question that modern America has cornered the market on the death penalty in the Western world. But, capital punishment has a long and complex record in world history. From the beginning of organized government and society, and even before that, rulers were quick to impose the most extreme penalty on their citizens. In an ancient world that was harsh and brutal in its existence, the imposition of a penalty of death seemed normal. In societies that were filled with stories of divine retribution and vengeful gods, it made sense.

To understand the place of the death penalty in U.S. society, it is important to understand the long legacy of capital punishment in world history. The United States is not distinctive in having a history of executions; rather it is unique in the fact that the United States, alone among Western "civilized" nations, still applies the death penalty on a wide scale.

The history of capital punishment begins with the beginning of the world. No sooner had the world been created and peopled, than capital punishment made an appearance. Probably the first example of capital punishment in human history can be found in the flood story. The flood story is a common tale in early Western civilization, and examples of it can be found in not just the Old Testament but also in Greek, Roman, Babylonian, Sumerian, and other societies. The flood was a classic case of the gods/God enacting retribution on humans for engaging in immoral activities. The debate over why the divinity in question inflicted such a harsh penalty mirrors the modern debate over the death penalty. Was it out of spite and vengeance that a divine being, God or gods, unleashed the flood upon the earth's inhabitants? Was it to send a message? Was it to serve as a deterrent? In any case, with the divine setting the example, human society quickly followed suit.

Whether to appease the gods or to satiate their own needs for vengeance and retribution, ancient civilizations regularly practiced the death penalty. In Babylon, King Hammurabi codified the law (one of the important roots of Western society and law) and established a code of transgressions and subsequent punishments. Hammurabi's code imposed the death penalty for twenty-five different crimes. The deeds for which one could be punished were wide ranging. Ironically and in contrast to modern law, under the Babylonians murderers were not necessarily subject to execution, but other acts, such as the fraudulent sale of beer, carried the death penalty.

Ancient cultures like the Hittites, Egyptians, Greeks, and Romans all included the death penalty in their legal codes. The first death penalty (gods not withstanding) in recorded history was in Egypt. (To suggest this was the first time a person was executed for their misdeeds would be misleading. This is merely the first written account. Codes such as those noted above suggest that capital punishment was very prevalent in societies striving to maintain strict order. The reality of early life was that punishment was swift and harsh.) In that first recorded case in Egypt, the guilty party, a member of the Egyptian nobility, was accused of the improper practice of magic. He was ordered to take his own life. In a superstitious society like ancient Egypt, such an action was seen as offensive to both the gods and the people, and fear of divine retribution made it a capital offense. Like Babylon, Egypt had a wide range of capital crimes that included offenses that seem to border on the bizarre in modern times, like the unauthorized disclosure of sacred burial places. (As will be discussed later, two important evolutions in capital punishment have been the determination of who can be executed and which crimes are categorized as capital. As the focus of society changed and the demands of society changed, so did those crimes that were seen as warranting death. The lack of a formal prison system reinforced the need for severe penalties, including the death penalty.)

In the Mediterranean world, the most extreme use of the death penalty was probably under the Athenian leader Draco. Draco, who promulgated Athens's first written laws, also included almost every offense imaginable as punishable by death (hence the word *Draconian,* referring to repressive legal measures). Punishment for the most trifling of transgressions was most severe.

In all of these societies, death was inflicted in cruel and barbarous ways. (Note this is obviously a qualification of what modern Western societies denotes as "cruel." Suffice it to say at this point that no matter one's position on the death penalty, all of the ancient methods were well beyond the pale of even the most ardent modern supporter of capital punishment.) Methods of execution often emphasized a slow, painful death rather than the quick, painless ways associated with modern times such as lethal injection. It was in reaction to these painful ancient methods that more modern systems like the guillotine, electric chair, and gas chamber were developed. All of them were instituted in the hopes of making capital punishment more "humane." Ancient methods included drowning, stoning, beating to death, and impalement. Roman society provided one of the best examples of these extreme and painful methods. For the crime of patricide, the guilty party was put in a sack with a dog, a rooster, a viper, and an ape and then submerged into water. The resulting terror of the condemned and the ensuing chaos and agony is almost beyond imagination.

Roman society mirrored prior civilizations and its contemporaries. The two most famous executions in ancient times were those of Socrates and Jesus. Socrates was given a choice: death by the state or by his own hand. Rather than submitting to a state execution, he chose to drink poison for the crime of flouting social mores and corrupting the young. Jesus, crucified by the Romans, was executed for political crimes and challenging the emperor's authority and divinity. Crucifixion was a standard form of execution, copied by other societies, and used to set an example of the painful horror that would befall those who challenged the royal authority. In both cases, the men were executed to set an example and reinforce government control.

As society "progressed," the methods of execution expanded. Often, as shown by the Roman punishment for patricide, specific forms of execution accompanied specific crimes. Many societies had punishment structures that mimicked the biblical notion of an eye for an eye. In Rome, a convicted arsonist would be burned alive. In addition, the execution itself was frequently combined with torture so the defendant would confess his guilt before he died. The ancient and even medieval world was offended by executing an innocent man, so the admission of guilt was wrung from them before their death. History saw criminals having molten lead poured on them, being starved to death in dungeons, being torn to death with red-hot pincers, and having their bodies sawed into pieces. Vestal virgins who violated their vows were sometimes buried alive. Obviously, under torture, many innocents confessed, but the executioners managed to relieve their consciences. This was reminiscent of the ancient tradition (seen in many myths) where a man might be cast adrift at sea to let the gods take their vengeance as they saw fit. What befell the poor soul then had nothing to do with the society that had cast him adrift, rather their destiny was the will of the gods.

As the penalties became more extensive, so too did the crimes that carried the punishment of death. Among new crimes that were punishable by death were a diverse group that included from publishing libelous material and insulting songs to disturbing the peace. Other possible capital crimes were destroying your neighbor's crops, malicious arson of a house or stack of corn, cheating someone in business, perjury, and murder of a free person. (In slave societies, killing one's own slave was comparable to destroying one's own property. Killing another's slave usually entitled the slaveholder to restitution; but in societies that took theft very seriously, because killing of a slave deprived one of his goods, death was a possibility. However, oftentimes, slaves were seen as not only less than human but less than property.)

As can be seen, the range of transgressions for which one might lose their life was far ranging. The philosophy was that the death penalty helped keep order in a society fraught with disorder. Executions were always public. The early idea was that public execution struck fear into the hearts of the citizenry and deterred those who might consider committing such a crime. Two historical examples that reinforced this belief were Spartacus and Antigone. Spartacus sparked a slave revolt in 73 B.C.E. in Rome. With the collapse of the revolt, the Romans crucified 6,000 slaves, as an example for other would-be rebels in the empire. The Greek tragedy *Antigone*, emphasized the death penalty was an important mechanism to restore authority when it seemed governmental controls were breaking down. It was a mechanism to deter those who would challenge the existing hierarchy.

It is questionable whether it was any more or less of a deterrent back then than it is now. Many of the crimes were committed by the poor and desperate, who did not care about the outcome if they were caught. They were at the end of their options. The tale of Robin Hood is not that far-fetched in the sense that many men were sentenced to death for killing the king's deer, a penalty they were fully aware of, but ignored, because they were desperate to feed themselves and their families.

Thus the Western tradition of the death penalty has longtime antecedents, and the United States' embracing of that tradition found its roots in England's adaptation of those traditions. The death penalty had a rich tradition in Great Britain. Well before England's invasion by the Romans, the death penalty was a fixture on English shores. A common form of execution was pushing the guilty party into a quagmire. The long, slow death that ensued mirrored the forms of punishment enacted on the European continent. By the tenth century, hanging was the favored form of execution in Great Britain.

One of the brief innovations William the Conqueror brought with him across the channel was a personal abhorrence for the taking of life, except of course, in war. However, the source of his revulsion to the death penalty remains unknown. It was clear he did not reject it because it was cruel, because he regularly had criminals mutilated for their crimes. But William was an exception, and by the Middle Ages the death penalty was not only prevalent throughout Europe but, especially in England, it was fused with torture and applied in a widespread manner.

In England, the death penalty was imposed for minor as well as major crimes. Oftentimes, men were not only hanged but also drawn and quartered, which imposed an element of humiliation into the capital process. How the individual died was often as important as why one was executed. Early America maintained this distinction when, after the Aaron Burr–Alexander Hamilton duel, Hamilton was almost denied a proper burial, reflecting society's growing aversion to dueling. Gender and class also called for different forms of execution.

Women were treated differently, and in most cases were burned. Burning was a sentence reserved for women, particularly witches, who most often were women. In most cases, the woman was supposed to be strangled before being burned. Unfortunately, the intent did not often match the action. Oftentimes, the executioners, who were habitually incompetent or drunk, failed to strangle the woman, causing her an agonizing death as the flames slowly consumed her.

Variations of forms of execution were also identified for different social classes. For example, beheading, because of its quick and apparent painlessness, was reserved for the upper classes. Lower classes were executed in a sloppier and more painful manner.

By the end of the fifteenth century, English law recognized eight capital crimes: treason, petty treason, murder (killing a person with "malice"), larceny, robbery, burglary, rape, and arson. Under the Tudors and Stuarts, additional crimes were added to the list. By the time of the English settlement in North America in the seventeenth and early eighteenth centuries, the expansive list included more than 350 different crimes. It was known as the Bloody Code. One of the great ironies of this time period was that as the code expanded the number of executions decreased. During this era, observers saw a direct correlation between the enforcement of the code and the reduction in crime. As in earlier societies, people viewed capital punishment as a deterrent to crime. However, in truth, the lower number of executions probably reflected a rising reluctance of judges and juries to convict people of minor offenses that carried the death penalty. Finally, at this time, as well as later, lower numbers of executions also reflected the exportation of criminals to either America (in the seventeenth and eighteenth centuries) or Australia. Thus a rich and varied heritage of capital punishment accompanied the first colonists across the water to North America.

Early America and the Death Penalty

The Atlantic crossing brought fortune seekers from England and Europe, the riffraff of the English jails, and indentured servants. With this wide variety of people came a need to impose some form of order. Early America saw a dire need for discipline. New England's rigid religiosity and John Smith's militaristic approach to colonial life reflected these needs. Those two different approaches emphasized the fact that in the American colonies there was no uniform criminal law and the influence of English law was inconsistent at best. With each colony under its own charter, and given a certain amount of independence, a sporadic and choppy criminal law emerged. The evolution of the U.S. version of the death penalty reflected this.

Colonies varied in their use and application of the death penalty. In New England, religion played an important role and influenced the early law. Massachusetts law placed twelve transgressions on the capital list: idolatry, witchcraft, blasphemy, murder, manslaughter, poisoning, bestiality, sodomy, adultery, man-stealing, false witness in a capital trial, and rebellion. Paralleling the early emphasis on the Bible and John Winthrop's allusions to Massachusetts Bay as a new Jerusalem, all capital sentences were accompanied by a piece of Old Testament liturgy as justification and authority. However, as the community expanded beyond the chosen few and the religious nature of the colony changed and wavered, biblical justifications for execution rapidly faded, and by 1700, a variety of crimes, from rape to petty theft, were added to the list as a vehicle to solve social ills rather than to complete some religious mission.

To the south, Virginia had the first recorded execution in the American colonies in 1608, when Virginian officials executed George Kendall for treason for spying for the Spanish. (Some historians suggest there is a question as to the legality of the sentence. In that case, the first recorded *legal* execution of a criminal is recorded as being that of Daniel Frank in 1622 for the crime of theft.)

Early Virginia struggled mightily against the elements, the natives, and societal disorder. In 1612, Virginia Governor Sir Thomas Dale enacted the "Divine, Moral and Martial Laws." These statutes provided for extensive use of the death penalty. These laws included the death penalty for crimes such as killing chickens, stealing grapes, and trading with the Indians. (Improper trading with the Indians could cause tremendous disruption. Bacon's rebellion, several decades later, erupted, in part, from Governor Berkley's Indian policy.) This fit into the harsh life of Virginia and the desperate attempt there to maintain order and discipline in the hopes of surviving. Life in colonial America was tough; survival was difficult, especially in Virginia's early years. In light of those difficulties, it is not surprising that harsh rules of law were imposed on all aspects of life in the attempt to maintain social order and a cohesive community.

Like New England, Virginia did not ignore religion. Note the code talked about morality. Failure to attend church was punishable by a week in the stocks and bread and water for the first offense, two weeks for the second, and death with the third absence. It is not known whether anyone failed to miss three times. Eventually this strict code was softened in an attempt to induce more settlers to come to the tidewater. But the legal code reflected that hard life that the early colonists in Virginia faced and the need to maintain order and discipline in the struggles to make the colony survive. Other southern colonies followed suit.

New York mirrored its sister colonies and imposed a rigid system. In 1655, it passed a series of laws called the Duke's Laws. These laws demanded the death penalty for the denial of the "true God," premeditated murder, killing by ambush, death by poison, sodomy, buggery, kidnapping, perjury in a capital trial, rebellion, and hitting one's mother or father.

In contrast, South Jersey and Pennsylvania saw at best a limited application of the death penalty. In fact, the original charter of South Jersey included no death penalty for any crimes, and it was not until the end of the seventeenth century that an execution took place there. Pennsylvania, with its Quaker traditions, was very similar and limited capital punishment to crimes of treason and murder.

These lenient attitudes seen in some of the middle colonies were only temporary. By the early eighteenth century, under pressure from the Crown, colonial legislatures adopted harsher measures. By the time of the Revolution, some parity existed and most of the colonies had similar penal codes with similar penalties. Death was the standard penalty for murder, treason, piracy, arson, rape, robber, burglary, and sodomy. Some states pushed the boundaries and included counterfeiting, horse-theft, and slave rebellion among the capital crimes.

As the American Revolution approached, other changes were taking place in the world. The political change that would follow the break from England was part of the philosophical revolution racing through Europe, most notably the Enlightenment. Enlightenment ideas were marked by a growing emphasis on reason and humanity. This philosophical change in approach to humanity and society helped transform the way Americans and Europeans viewed capital punishment. Great men such as Voltaire and Montesquieu protested the extensive use of and brutal manner in which it was administered. By 1764, the Italian jurist Cesare Beccaria published his famous *Essay on Crimes and Punishments*. It was widely published and read on both sides of the Atlantic.

In that work, Beccaria criticized the use of torture, the imposition of harsh penalties for minor offenses, and what he considered the generally antiquated state of the criminal law. He argued it was the certainty of punishment, any punishment, that created the deterrent. The drastic nature of the punishment, that is, execution, did not help deter criminal activity. It is important to understand that Beccaria did not push for light penalties, or a soft penal system. Instead, rather than execution, he pushed for incarceration and hard labor for capital crimes. Beccaria's emphasis was on the method, not the fact of punishment itself. He rejected capital punishment as a mechanism that a civilized society should employ, but did not find long years at hard labor and being locked up as inhumane. The advent of the guillotine in the eighteenth century reflected much of this desire for humanity and changed thinking concerning the death penalty. The guillotine was instituted for two reasons. It reflected the changing approaches to dealing with the ills of society for humane reasons and ones related to class. Both of these reasons were evident during the French Revolution.

Many methods of execution were used across France in the early eighteenth century. Like the rest of Europe and the world, these forms of punishment could be painful, bloody, and grotesque. Hanging and burning were common. A favored, painful form of drawing and quartering was tying the criminal to four horses and then sending the horses in four different directions. Beheading was reserved for the upper classes and was often accomplished by an executioner wielding an axe or sword. The more painful and bloody methods of execution were often performed in a public manner as a warning to potential criminals.

The violent irrational actions by the state became the focus of many eighteenth-century thinkers. As the writings of Voltaire and other writers of the day spread, opposition to the death penalty grew. The opposition growing out of ideas that were part of the core of the Enlightenment based its argument at first on humanitarian concerns. Voltaire and his comrades argued not that execution was wrong but rather that there had to be a "better" way to do it. One of those who advocated a better way was Dr. Joseph-Ignace Guillotin, the inventor of the guillotine.

The guillotine combined the desire for humanitarian execution with a means to make capital punishment the same for all. It was designed to administer a fast and painless death. Prior to the advent of the guillotine and a French decree in 1791 that declared the guillotine was to be the form of execution used for all French capital criminals, beheading was usually reserved for the rich or powerful. France's guillotine was available to all. It became an important symbol of the French Revolution, as a mark of the egalitarian (all faced the guillotine, regardless of age, sex, or wealth) and humanitarian nature of the Revolution.

This European, especially French, protest and move toward more humane methods of execution, found root in England and America, too. It served as the theoretical foundation for the major reforms of criminal law that took place in the eighteenth and nineteenth centuries. In England, Jeremy Bentham was the main proponent of more humane executions; in the United States, Benjamin Rush championed this cause.

Rush was an important member of the Philadelphia Society for Alleviating the Miseries of Public Prisons. As a member of that group, and an important player in U.S. society, he played a pivotal role in the development of the U.S. penitentiary system. The Walnut Street Jail in Philadelphia was the United States' first modern penitentiary.

The emergence of organized prison systems had a big impact on capital punishment. For the first time society had an alternative. As noted before, prior to this development, many societies, including colonial America and later, the United States, often relied on the death penalty because there was no effective alternative form of punishment. However, prisons, funded by the state, run by professionals, provided a viable option. Prisons enabled society to impose a penalty on criminals and satiate the public's need for retribution or vengeance without resorting to the extreme penalty of death. In addition, as the penal system grew, prison shifted from being facilities focused purely on punishment to ones that could also, in theory, rehabilitate. The U.S. penal system became not just a system of punishment, but one of correction and reform. Early attempts at rehabilitation often went astray, resulting in prisoner suicides, but the attempts at rehabilitation marked the change in emphasis on why and when people were punished. As these changes occurred they often mirrored changing approaches to capital punishment. When society felt criminals were products of nurture not nature and could be and should be changed, rehabilitation was emphasized and capital punishment was de-emphasized. As society felt a need to exact a price from those who committed crimes and emphasize criminal behavior as a fact of nature, a genetic failure, and did not see any need to try and give mercy, the death penalty was inflicted more. Thus, many of these reforms were indicative of not just anti–death advocate agitation, but a perceived need to curb excesses in the criminal judicial system rather than a widespread anti–death penalty animus.

With the end of the American Revolution and the break from England, it did not take long for death penalty reforms in the context of evolving American law to surface. Revolutionary and postrevolutionary America were filled with legal reform and constitutional revision at the national and state levels. From 1776 to 1800, figures like Thomas Jefferson embarked on an attempt to revise Virginia's laws, which would limit the death penalty to cases of murder and treason. The House of Burgesses defeated the law, but only after a raucous debate, and by only one vote. The Virginia codification of rights and liberties heavily influenced the federal government as it grappled with the new Constitution and the creation of the Bill of Rights.

The ratification of the Bill of Rights in 1791 included the Eighth Amendment, which prohibited the imposition of *cruel and unusual* punishment. What those words meant was never defined. Some questioned many of the terms in the amendment, such as *excessive bail* and *cruel and unusual*. Legislators claimed that the words were too indefinite, and although it spoke to the right idea—humanity—there was a question concerning the amendment's impact. There was also a fear that such a measure would hamstring the government when it came to passing laws. But the debate was sparse, and the clause passed. Nowhere in the debates is it hinted that capital punishment was to be eliminated. The death penalty was pretty much accepted at the time, and it was acknowledged that it was not cruel and unusual.

By 1793, owing much to the influence of Rush, Pennsylvania revised its legal code, recognizing degrees of murder, some not necessarily deserving the death sentence. Rush argued the death penalty was contrary to reason. He claimed it reduced the sanctity of life, thereby increasing the violence and the number of murders in society. By imprisoning rather than executing, greater control was exerted over the criminal elements of society. Finally, capital punishment was a tool of monarchies and tyrannies, not of democratic societies such as Pennsylvania strove to be. Rush's argument held sway in a complex society filled with both Quaker pacifists and death penalty supporters.

By 1833, public executions were becoming chaotic. Until this point, all executions in the United States were public. They were arranged so many people could see them, and they included carnival-like spectacles with rowdy crowds. The Clint Eastwood movie, *Hang 'em High,* while giving a cynical look at the hangings of the day, paints a good picture of the social event a good hanging became. Hangings drew large crowds, and alcohol flowed freely. The sight of the hanging (or whatever form of execution) only served to rile up the crowds, often resulting in riots and at times more uncontrolled bloodlettings. The "bread-and-circus" atmosphere began to become repugnant, as violence increased and local authorities found it more and more difficult to control the mobs. Rhode Island and New York were the first two states to take executions out of the public eye and perform them in private.

These changes, especially in New York, also reflected other reforms of the time period. The 1830s and 1840s was a time of religious revivalism and attempts to remold society. Much of this reform was centered in upstate New York. The Second Great Awakening, the rise of transcendentalist thought, and efforts to reform society dominated these two decades. Temperance, antislavery attitudes, educational reform, prison reform, and the like, all took place in this time period and were a part of the effort to perfect society and make the world a better place. A rapidly expanding United States was being confronted with the problems of industrialization and urbanization, which translated into rising crime rates.

Some argued the path to societal reform was through institutional change. Reform of hospitals, asylums, and prisons reflected attempts to fix these societal problems. The only way to reduce capital punishment was to effect quality prison reform. Many prison reformers felt even the most hardened criminals could be rehabilitated. Their attempts fell woefully short, and soon American prisons and asylums, rather than become mechanisms to create positive change in society and individuals, became dumping grounds for the dregs of American society.

The reforms were spurred in part by the abolitionist movement, with its appeal for the humane treatment of slaves. Society focused on other issues: from the women's movement to the end of the death penalty. The cause was picked up by numerous public figures, for example, Walt Whitman and Horace Greeley.

By the middle of the nineteenth century more changes were taking place. In addition to many states turning away from public executions, one, Michigan, abolished the death penalty all together. Other reforms reflected the need to ensure consistency in the application of the death penalty. Local authorities made the decision as to who got executed and who did not, which led to great disparity in the way the death penalty was enforced among counties in many states. In response, some states, such as Vermont, moved the power to execute prisoners from local to state authority in an attempt to bring more parity. But transition was slow, and even in the middle of the twentieth century, some states still left executions up to the local authorities.

The growing death penalty abolition movement spurred much of the growing controversy around executions. Opposition to capital punishment, nascent at times, grew and shrank in accordance to other societal issues and problems. Just as the death penalty was (and is) a basic fact of the U.S. legal system, so was the debate that enveloped it. That debate has varied over the past hundred years—often deriving its impetus from other historical events that have merged to create issues about the penalty.

As Michigan abolished capital punishment in 1837, other states followed suit. But as was often the case in many reform movements, they lost their impetus because of other outside events. By the 1840s U.S. reformist zeal, distracted by westward expansion, the Mexican War, the California Gold Rush, and growing sectional strife, was being directed toward other causes. Temperance and the women's movement both played second fiddle to the growing antislavery movement.

By the beginning of the twentieth century, riding on the wave of Progressive reform, was a growing anti–death penalty movement. But the movement experienced only temporary success, because a majority of citizens seemed to still favor execution. States recognized the public's desire to execute its criminals, and responded. Proponents argued that it was better for the organized machinery of the state to perform an execution than a lawless mob, which often ended up harming innocent victims. The assumption, of course, was that the state did not make mistakes. It was the possibility of mistakes (putting innocent people to death) that began to fuel a more fervent objection to the death penalty.

The Death Penalty and the Early Twentieth Century

The twentieth century also saw change in the form of execution. Beginning with New York, states began to adopt electrocution, rather than hanging, as the preferred mode of execution. By the 1920s, after the "successes" of poison gas on the battlefields of World War I, lethal gas was introduced as a means to execute criminals. Much like the use of the guillotine in the eighteenth century, the modern methods of execution developed in the early 1900s reflected society's desire to make executions fair and more humane. The use of these more efficient methods also meant that greater numbers of people could be executed, and during the Depression, the number of executions in the United States had reached an all time high of 199 per year in 1935.

The major drive in the early days of the anti–death penalty movement, besides of course abolition, was to decrease the number of offenses that were considered capital crimes and push for discretionary capital sentences. Early opponents believed that if the decision to execute were left to the judgment of courts, especially juries, the number of executions would decline. However, these early protagonists seriously misjudged society, and juries had no problems imposing the death penalty. From Reconstruction to World War II, the extraordinary number of lynchings that took place in the United States confirmed that America's bloodlust was not diminished, it had just taken a different form.

A more exhaustive discussion of capital punishment would look at execution outside the normal legal channels. Lynching plays an important part in U.S. history. It was a vehicle by which communities imposed order, as in the South, and expressed their own sense of right and wrong when they felt the wheels of justice turned too slowly, as in the West. However, the focus of this text is the death penalty as a formalized mechanism in the U.S. legal system.

Like the reform movements of the antebellum period, opposition to the death penalty grew in the Progressive era. The number of federal offenses that were considered capital crimes diminished, so that only four remained. The Progressives felt they had an ability to change the world, because they believed that evils in society were the result of nurture not nature. Therefore, they reasoned, if drinking were eliminated, society would improve. If the environment were changed, people would not find it necessary to resort to crime, and therefore would not have to be expunged from society.

The increasing application of scientific principles to social problems, sociological jurisprudence, and so forth, were reflected in the growth of new fields such as penology. This scientific approach to understanding criminal behavior contributed to the general inclination toward criminal law reform. These pushes for reform in the legal world were only a subset of the Progressive drive to reform laws overall—in the workplace, in government, and elsewhere.

Reflecting this growing sentiment, by 1917 twelve states had repealed the death penalty. This was a combined result of the influence of the Progressive movement and the reaction of U.S. society to the carnage of World War I. The millions of deaths on European battlefields for no good cause helped engender revulsion to the taking of life. But this aversion was short lived, and not long after the war, states began to reinstate the death penalty.

The Russian Revolution, growing xenophobia, the Red Scare, and the ensuing Palmer Raids all helped to resurrect pro–death penalty sentiments. As the United States entered the 1920s, the growing desire to return to the simpler, easier times of the 1890s manifested itself in increasing societal tensions. As Prohibition took hold, so did a rising crime rate and a need to stem it.

As science advanced, the argument against the death penalty for humanitarian reasons lost its starch. The development of more humane ways to execute individuals made capital punishment seem "okay." In 1924, cyanide gas was introduced as a more humane way to execute than electrocution. The original idea was that while the criminal slept, gas would be pumped into his cell, so he would painlessly and quietly pass on. This was not practical, so the gas chamber was developed to facilitate executions using gas.

In the 1920s a growing amount of literature suggested capital punishment was an important social measure. As Progressive idealism, which emphasized the importance of nurture over nature, faded, more people thought it was necessary to eliminate those who had forfeited their right to participate in society through the commission of heinous acts.

In the 1920s, the death penalty debate was marked by events that either built support for the death penalty or generated opposition to it. Not surprisingly, public support for capital punishment has been greatest in the aftermath of particularly horrid or brazen crimes. For example, in the wake of the 9/11 tragedy and the destruction of the World Trade Center, death penalty opponents were hard pressed to gain advocates for its abolishment. Conversely, controversial executions have led to an upsurge in abolitionist activity, as proponents' arguments become undercut by extraordinary circumstances, such as possible innocence or the sympathetic nature of the convicted, which usually surrounds such executions.

Two notable examples of controversial executions from that time period highlighted these trends and helped engender opposition.

First, the United States was both fascinated and repulsed by the trial of Nathan Leopold and Richard Loeb and Clarence Darrow's impassioned plea to give the two murderers a life sentence rather than the death penalty. Second, Nicola Sacco and Bartolomeo Vanzetti, supported by such illustrious men as Felix Frankfurter, became victims of an obviously political trial and miscarriage of justice. Both cases, owing to the eloquent support put forth by legal advocates, helped sway public opinion against the death penalty.

Some cases, like the murder of Albert Snyder, which saw the execution of Ruth Snyder and Judd Gray, aided both sides of the argument. Ruth was both a sympathetic and repelling individual. Her decline into insanity and eventual execution, stirred up tremendous debate. A photograph secretly taken of her dying made the front pages of the papers, forcing people to face the realities of the death penalty. Some nodded in satisfaction, others were repulsed.

But other cases helped swing the pendulum back. The Saint Valentine's Day Massacre of 1929 typified the bloody gangland killings of the day, brutal and horrible. Dressed as policemen, Chicago thugs rounded up members of a rival gang, lined them up against a wall, and shot them in cold blood in front of onlookers. Then, they walked over to the prone bodies and made sure the job was done by shooting each body again. The heinous nature of the crime was exacerbated by the fact that no one was ever brought to justice for it. Other highly publicized crimes increased public sentiment for the death penalty. The Lindbergh kidnapping and the subsequent trial and execution of Bruno Hauptmann in 1932 helped make kidnapping a capital offense at both state and federal levels. These two crimes and the overall violence of the 1920s and proliferation of lawlessness and gangsterism provided incentive for some states to reinstate the death penalty.

By World War II, forty-two of the forty-eight states had a death penalty. There was no real debate over it in the immediate postwar period, as the United States became focused on far more important things, from the escalating Cold War to involvement in Korea. The Rosenbergs case raised the issue again, but in a different context. Accused of selling secrets to the Soviets, they were the first U.S. citizens executed for espionage. In the case of the two supposed spies, it wasn't the death penalty that many people protested. The question was whether they should have been executed at all. And their executions, especially Ethel's, reignited the debate once again. The image of the Rosenbergs' two small children staring forlornly out of a car window fired people's emotions, and by the late 1950s sentiment began to swing the other way again.

At the end of the decade the case of Caryl Chessman prompted yet another resurgence of the debate. Chessman's case probably prompted as much anti–capital punishment response as any case in U.S. history. Chessman was arrested in Los Angeles as the Red-Light Bandit. The bandit would approach victims parked in isolated spots, flash a red light, similar to those used by the police, and then rob, and, in the case of women, sexually abuse, the victims.

Upon his arrest, Chessman signed a confession. He later recanted, arguing that the police had forced the original confession out of him. But the physical evidence was against him and eyewitness testimony resulted in a conviction on seventeen counts, including robbery and kidnapping. The jury determined that one of the kidnapping counts had resulted in the victim sustaining bodily harm. California had passed a law after the Lindbergh kidnapping that made bodily harm in the commission of a kidnapping a capital crime. In those cases, the defendant could get either life without parole or the death penalty. The jury sentenced Chessman to death in the gas chamber.

Rather than go quietly to his death, Chessman began a decade-long struggle to escape execution. During his time in San Quentin, he wrote four books, and his case became an international cause. By the time he died, there were many who argued he was innocent. The profound support for him from people like Eleanor Roosevelt, Pablo Cassals, Robert Frost, and Billy Graham did not help. Despite eight stays of execution he was finally put to death in the San Quentin gas chamber in May 1960. However, the sympathetic figure of Chessman did little to dissipate the growing discontent Americans felt concerning the rising crime rates. Throughout the 1960s, different events, from rioting to the Sharon Tate murders, evoked emotional battles over the efficacy of the death penalty. It was beginning to be questioned on practical, moral, and numerous other grounds.

The ensuing turmoil of the 1960s, the liberal Warren Court, and the head-on conflict between conservative and liberal forces in the United States provided new fuel for the debate, new arguments for both sides, and a controversy that probably, along with abortion, remains one of the most divisive issues in U.S. society today.

The Roots of the Debate:
Early Ideas about the Eighth Amendment

In the twentieth century, the death penalty argument has centered on the Eighth Amendment, which guarantees, among other things, that cruel and unusual punishment shall not be inflicted. Although at times, the Supreme Court has sidestepped the key question, in the end, it was the questions surrounding that amendment that formed the core of the debate: Does the death penalty violate the requirements of the Eighth Amendment? Is it inherently cruel and unusual punishment? Although other issues of fairness and equity that focused on Fifth, Sixth, and Fourteenth Amendment issues arose, the fundamental question in death penalty litigation has always been whether the execution of criminals is in line with the requirements of the Eighth Amendment. Proponents have rejected that line of reasoning, and underlying all arguments of death penalty opponents has been that, at its core, capital punishment in modern society is cruel and unusual.

The history of the phrase *cruel and unusual punishment* in Anglo-American law goes back to 1689 and the English Bill of Rights, where it first appeared in a form that would resurface in America. It was copied into the Virginia Declaration of Rights in 1776 and written into the Northwest Ordinance of 1787. By the time the Constitution was ratified in 1788, it was a common phrase in constitutional documents at the state level throughout the United States. During the first Congress, there was almost no debate over the amendment or the phrase. The death penalty was an accepted form of punishment in early America, and the idea that it offended the senses of justice and decency was outside the pale. Therefore, to the framers, execution was seen as a normal part of the criminal justice system. It was the avoidance of particularly cruel forms of punishment that was to be achieved.

Historically the phrase *cruel and unusual* appears to have been used in three different ways. First, the death penalty supported the idea that a penalty should be proportionate to the crime. The worst crimes deserved the worst punishments. The prevalence of crime in early societies and the lack of any kind of prison system or desire to show leniency toward criminals, especially violent ones, contributed to the widespread use of the death penalty. However, the insertion of the phrase into the English Bill of Rights reflected the need to temper punishment for some lesser crimes. In that case, it was a reaction to judicial imposition of penalties for political crimes that far exceeded the severity of the crimes.

A second use of the phrase was in the context of punishments that were seen as unauthorized by law and therefore beyond the court's authority. Critics attacked the harsh penalties of the late seventeenth century in England, not only because the punishments were often excessive, but critics claimed them to be illegal and outside the scope of the court's authority. This limit on judicial and executive authority reflected the late-seventeenth century notions of government and parliamentary authority. This idea was picked up in the construction of the U.S. Constitution in its checks-and-balances system.

Finally, the late-eighteenth-century interpretation of *cruel and unusual* challenged not execution per se, but the method by which one was executed. Some forms were so painful as to be considered "out of bounds." These growing concerns bore fruit in the increasing use of the guillotine in Europe and the push for more humane methods of execution and imprisonment generally.

Importantly, none of these definitions said capital punishment, per se, was cruel and unusual. Only in its application, when barbarous or torturous, could it be seen as such. So, the execution of robbers, rapists (well into the twentieth century), and others continued. Thus the early debate over capital punishment had nothing to do with the idea of *cruel and unusual.* Rather it would appear the phrase was intended as a way to prevent the adoption of radical forms of punishment that were prevalent in Europe. Americans prided themselves on the progressive nature of their legal and judicial systems in comparison to those of Europe.

Eighth Amendment issues began to arise as states changed their methods of execution. For example, a case in Utah in the late nineteenth century focused on the ability of the court to affix the method of execution. The Utah legislature had passed a law that stated that defendants were to be executed by firing squad, hanging, or beheading. In the case in question, the court chose a firing squad as the method of execution. The Supreme Court acknowledged that cruel and unusual punishments were forbidden by the Constitution; however, the Court saw a firing squad as a common form of execution, and not cruel and unusual, and therefore an acceptable choice. The Court emphasized that the Eighth Amendment referred to torture and other more egregious examples of execution, for example, when a prisoner was drawn or dragged to the place of execution, as often happened in cases of treason, or when he was disemboweled alive, beheaded, or quartered. The Court also mentioned traditional European penalties, such as public dissection and burning the prisoner alive, both of which were the kind of thing the Eighth Amendment was aimed at. By comparison, simple execution by firing squad was deemed neither cruel nor unusual.

Reference to the Eighth Amendment again appeared about thirty years later in 1910 in *Weems v. United States.* In *Weems* a U.S. official in the Philippines was convicted of falsifying a minor government record. He was sentenced to fifteen years at hard labor and had to pay a fine. In that case, the Court ruled the sentence amounted to cruel and unusual punishment because it was so disproportionate to the crime.

In *Weems,* the Court directly approached the question of what constituted cruel and unusual punishment. It struggled a bit with the phrase, because this was one of the first times the Court had reason to define that phrase and what it meant. (Remember that prior to the twentieth century, the Bill of Rights did not apply to the states. Thus, although many states had state constitutional proscriptions against the infliction of cruel and unusual punishment, the Supreme Court had had little reason to interpret the phrase, except in the rare federal case.) The sparse history of the use of that phrase at the Constitutional Convention left little for the justices to draw on. The result was a broad open-ended discussion of what was meant by "cruel and unusual." The ambiguity and general nature of the decision in *Weems* left the issue wide open for the remainder of the century. In his opinion, Justice McKenna spoke in broad terms that later justices picked up. He emphasized the idea that the Eighth Amendment had a fluid meaning, which adjusted to the times. He viewed the amendment as progressive. It was not constrained to the definition established in 1689 or 1787, but was to adapt its meaning to an ever-changing society, to changing public opinion. As public opinion became "enlightened by humane justice," the definition of what was cruel and unusual would change. This had to be the case in order for the amendment to have any real meaning. A static interpretation would allow those very types of actions the framers had sought to avoid—and U.S. society was attempting to turn its back on—to transpire.

Justice McKenna focused on and quoted from previous commentaries. He emphasized that *cruel,* in terms of the Eighth Amendment, referred to punishment that involved "torture or a lingering death." The key here was that death itself was not cruel, rather it was the methodology that determined whether the execution could be deemed cruel or not. There had to be something inhuman and barbarous about the method, something that amounted to more than just an execution. The aversion to torture, which had previously been such an integral part of the penalty, was obvious. He referred to statements by Justices Field, Harlan, and Brewer in interpreting a state case. Their comments broadened the definition of cruel and unusual to include punishments that were disproportionate to the offense. Disproportionate meant a penalty that was too severe or too long. By no means was the Eighth Amendment a bar to death by hanging or electrocution, because, especially in the early twentieth century, these were seen as normal and humane methods of execution.

In fact, McKenna argued that the Eighth Amendment was not really a bar on legislatures or the Congress but rather a restriction on the courts to ensure that they would be reasonable in their imposition of penalties for various crimes. It was a warning for courts not to abuse their discretion. Since judges, then, as now, often had great leeway in the penalty phase, it was important to rein in the renegade judge, whether too lenient or too strict. Then, as now, oftentimes the debate focused on the process—the means, rather than the end.

But McKenna spoke for a divided court. *Weems* featured a strong dissent. It argued that the majority decision went outside the historical scope of the Eighth Amendment in coming to its interpretation. It argued the Court's ruling limited Congress's ability to define what was a crime and to punish that crime by acting as a super legislature. This focus was very different from the majority's argument. This was the era of the Lochner Court. Similar to the various cases where the Court had second-guessed local legislatures, again the Court was treading where it should not and assuming a legislative role that did not belong to it. The dissent argued if the phrase *cruel and unusual* had any meaning it was a narrow one that was limited to the "atrocious, sanguinary and inhuman punishments which had been inflicted in the past upon the persons of criminals." That was not what had happened in *Weems.*

Overall, the dissent criticized the majority for reading far too much into the amendment, ignoring the views of the framers, and going well beyond the original ideas embodied in the Eighth Amendment. It was this distancing from the original intent that would provide a foothold and springboard for argument in the latter half of the twentieth century. As the Court began to focus on this type of interpretation, made more prevalent as the Bill of Rights began to be incorporated into the Fourteenth Amendment, the Eighth Amendment seemed a place ripe to bear fruit from this expansive notion.

Postwar United States and Cruel and Unusual

Three and a half decades passed before the Court had the opportunity to again review what was cruel and unusual. In *Louisiana v. Resweber* (1947) the defendant, Willie Francis, was sentenced to be electrocuted. Officials strapped him into the electric chair and turned on the charge. However, owing to a technical problem, not enough current flowed, the shock was inadequate, and the defendant did not die. Even so, the current was so strong that his lips puffed out, he bucked in the chair, raising it off the floor, and a loud groan escaped his lips. The current was applied two more times, and again the defendant didn't die. The guards removed him from the chair and returned him to his cell. The state then issued another warrant for his execution, while the chair was fixed so it could deliver a lethal charge.

In discussing Francis's appeal, based on the Eighth Amendment, the Court relied heavily on *Weems* and ruled this was not a case of cruel and unusual punishment. They did acknowledge the added suffering the prisoner was forced to endure, but that in itself did not make the punishment cruel or unusual. Quoting *Weems*, the Court repeated language regarding the traditional humanity of modern Anglo-American law that forbids the infliction of unnecessary pain in the execution of a death sentence.

At first glance, this would seem to be the very thing the Eighth Amendment was intended to prevent—the needless and unnecessary infliction of pain, suffering, and emotional turmoil for the condemned—for there was no doubt that Francis had suffered. But the Court seemed to disregard that aspect of the situation. Instead it emphasized that the cruelty against which the Constitution protected a convicted man was cruelty inherent in the method of punishment. Obviously some suffering was involved in any execution, no matter the method used, no matter how humane. In the Court's eyes, the fact that an unforeseeable accident prevented a prompt execution did not add an element of cruelty to that or any subsequent execution. In this case, the state did not act intentionally. It did not purposely inflict unnecessary pain, nor had it intended to. The Eighth Amendment forbade the *intentional* infliction of pain and suffering. Here, despite the unfortunate circumstances, Louisiana had not intended for Willie Francis to suffer unduly, had not intended to torture him or to make the situation less humane. None of the things that happened were supposed to be part of the execution. Francis was merely an unfortunate victim of an accident.

The Court noted that unfortunate things like this happened, and what Francis suffered was no different than the mental anguish and physical pain he might have suffered in any other accidental occurrence, such as a fire in the cell block. The idea of holding a state responsible for violating the Eighth Amendment, because of an accident—something outside its control—made no sense. The prisoner could not escape execution as a result of an innocent mistake. To release him from his sentence of execution would be a miscarriage of justice and a decision at odds with those of the trial court and the principles of the Constitution. Although there was no question that the incident was unfortunate, it could not be determined *cruel* in the sense that word was defined in the Eighth Amendment.

In his concurrence, Felix Frankfurtrer spoke to the general principles of fairness and justice that marked many prior cases. He spoke in terms of "immutable principles of justice which inhere in the very idea of free government," and the "fundamental principles of liberty and justice, which lie at the base of all our civil and political institutions." He saw the failed execution as an "innocent misadventure." To require the state to grant clemency would offend those principles noted above. He noted that despite the degree of one's repugnance to the "State's insistence on its pound of flesh," that distaste did not equal a violation. As he often noted in his opinions, personal views and dislikes had no place in the Court.

The case was a 5 to 4 decision, and the dissenters objected strenuously, and in laying the groundwork for subsequent arguments, raised one of the essential problems with Eighth Amendment jurisprudence and interpreting the death penalty. Justice Burton's dissenting opinion focused on the procedure. It did not look at what the state had intended or what should have happened. Rather, what did happen created a living nightmare for Willie Francis. The act itself, repeated attempts at execution, was what made the penalty torturous. This dissenting opinion was in direct contrast to the majority opinion, which focused on the way it should have worked.

Maybe more than any other aspect of constitutional interpretation, determination of what is cruel and unusual is totally subjective. Reminiscent of Justice Potter Stewart's comment about hard-core pornography, "I know it when I see it," the idea of when an execution is cruel or unusual depends on the individual case and on the person viewing it. Defining *cruel, torture,* or *unusual,* outside the most extreme circumstance, leaves much room for interpretation.

The dissenting justices declared that in the case of Willie Francis, intent was not the issue. The fact that the state did not intend to create a traumatic situation did not lessen the torture endured by Willie Francis. For the dissent there was no question: This was torture. Burton compared the repeated attempts to electrocute Francis with burning a person at the stake. No one disputed that being burned at the stake was cruel and unusual punishment. Why? Because it was acknowledged that the person tied to the stake suffered greatly as the flames slowly licked their way up the body, and in an excruciating manner burned him or her to death. Burton claimed that this, in essence, was what happened in Francis's case.

In addition, how many times must the state attempt an execution before it is deemed cruel and unusual? Here the dissent suggested if five times was considered cruel, then why not four, or three, and so on? There was no fear of setting a precedent here, because every case involving issues of cruel and unusual punishment and violations of due process was unique and had to be judged on the particular facts of the case.

The dissent also emphasized past opinions, reiterating the idea that what was considered fair today, might be deemed cruel tomorrow. For the dissent, the Eighth Amendment "more than any other provision in the Constitution" focused on what it called the "humanitarian instincts of the judiciary." It was the conscience of the justices that guided them in determining what was cruel and unusual, not static notions of the intent of the framers, outmoded notions of justice, or failure to look at the reality of what was going on.

The implication here was that the death penalty could possibly be deemed cruel and unusual. As society's standards changed, what was acceptable today could possibly be repugnant tomorrow. But, the Court was not willing to go down that path for thirty-five more years. The problem was that, in comparison to other decisions that helped shape U.S. social policy, such as *Brown v. Board of Education* and *Roe v. Wade,* where the majority of Americans supported the freedoms of education and choice, respectively, in the Francis case, the majority of Americans still supported the death penalty in some form. Was it the function of the Court to give substantive meaning to and read the nuance of public opinion into the words of the Constitution? Historically, at times, the Court, much to the chagrin of some of its members, has taken an important interest in the status of the law and the apparent attitudes of the public in looking at death penalty cases. The words of the dissent in *Resweber* supported this line of thinking.

Ten years later, the Court again had an opportunity to examine the idea of cruel and unusual in a case that, while not dealing with the death penalty, would have serious implications for it down the road. An American, Albert Trop, was convicted of desertion during World War II. The punishment was the revocation of his citizenship. The Court in *Trop v. Dulles* (1958) argued that, although 100 or 200 years ago, revocation of one's citizenship would have qualified as cruel and unusual punishment, in modern times it did not. This language seemed very reminiscent of the dissent in *Resweber.*

The Court looked at the sentence not in any historical context of the Eighth Amendment, but in terms of what modern society thought. It explicitly acknowledged the validity of the death penalty as a historically valid institution. It then noted that the definition of the phrase *cruel and unusual* was not static. It was important that the Eighth Amendment "draw its meaning from the evolving standards of decency that mark the progress of a maturing society." Thus, cruel and unusual meant whatever the society of the day said it was. The standard now became if the punishment "exceeded the limits of civilized standards." Importantly, the dissenters agreed with the majority's analysis; however, they disagreed that the revocation of Trop's citizenship was cruel and unusual. Justice Frankfurter's dissent noted that what Trop did was tantamount to being a traitor, and death was an acceptable punishment for traitors. It then made no sense that revocation of citizenship, a less severe penalty, violated the Eighth Amendment.

By the 1960s judicial, legal, and political arguments were coming to a head. The capital cases provided the focus for all of them. In the postwar period, the purpose for the prison system and hence the death penalty was being discussed regularly. Retribution as the basis for punishment was not a popular idea. There was a growing debate over the function of prisons. Did they truly rehabilitate and reform prisoners, or did they function purely to punish? A look at prisons across the United States, from Parchman to Attica, and at chain gangs in the South, seemed to suggest the latter.

The Model Penal Code of 1962 fed the growing fire. Much of the language in the code was based on the idea that pure retribution, an eye-for-an-eye-type mentality, was inhumane and morally unacceptable. The Model Penal Code acknowledged the importance of vengeance but emphasized the importance of first deterring criminal conduct. Whether this deterrence was proactive or retroactive did not matter. What did matter was looking at the prisons and trying to identify what prisoners needed while incarcerated.

Also, by the 1960s the movement for abolishment of the death penalty had grown stronger. Until the late 1950s, supporters of capital punishment outnumbered opponents 2 to 1. However, the numbers began to change as famous people began to speak out against the death penalty.

As much as anything, Albert Camus's "Reflections on a Guillotine," gave people pause. Winner of the Nobel Prize in Literature, Camus made an impassioned plea for the abolition of the death penalty. Looking both to the past and the future, Camus implored the "civilized" world to abandon execution as a means of dealing with criminals.

Camus argued, without the abolition of the death penalty, there was no hope for a society to be based on reason. The continued execution of prisoners would propel society down the decline it already seemed to be on. To assert that a man must be cut off from society, that is, executed, because he is absolutely evil, amounted to arguing that society was absolutely good. With the horrors of World War II still vivid in everyone's mind, the idea that society was absolutely good was just not believable. Rather, the reverse might seem more true. Society had decayed, had become so immoral and criminal, because it respected nothing but its own preservation. Therefore, it sacrificed itself under the standard of a twisted idea. The problem with execution was that when some put others to death, life ceased being sacred. When life was not sacred, the impact for society at large was tragic.

Supporting the philosophers were cases like the Rosenbergs and Caryl Chessman, which drew attention to the United States. As the death penalty began to dwindle and disappear worldwide, it became a political and legal bombshell in the United States.

Growing disenchantment with the death penalty became apparent as the number of executions began to drop. These declining numbers reflected numerous trends in society. Discretionary juries seemed to be less willing to impose the death penalty, which influenced a push to exclude those who opposed the death penalty from serving on juries. The result was the number of death sentences exceeded actual executions.

A growing number of appeals helped drop the execution rate, almost grinding it to a halt. These appeals were part of a strategy by anti–death penalty activists to block the system. By the mid-1960s a growing crime rate was paralleled by a growing prison population. Added to that mix were Supreme Court decisions and Warren Court liberalism, with its apparent procriminal stance, all of which seemed to fuel the appeal process.

Increasing appeals, fewer executions, and a death row population, which had quadrupled from 1955 to 1969, created a volatile mix, and the legal landscape and the United States were ripe for a battle over the death penalty.

References

Banner, Stuart. 2003. *The Death Penalty: An American History.* Cambridge, MA: Harvard University Press.

Bowers, William J. 1984. *Legal Homicide: Death as Punishment in America, 1864–1982.* Boston, MA: Northeastern University Press.

Camus, Albert. 1961. "Reflections on a Guillotine." In J. O'Brien (trans.), *Resistance, Rebellion, and Death.* London: H. Hamilton.

Chessman, Caryl. 1954. *Cell 2455, Death Row.* Englewood Cliffs, NJ: Prentice Hall.

———. 1955. *Trial by Ordeal.* Englewood Cliffs, NJ: Prentice Hall

———. 1957. *The Face of Justice.* Englewood Cliffs, NJ: Prentice Hall.

Gilreath, Shannon D. 2003. "Cruel and Unusual Punishment and the Eighth Amendment As a Mandate for Human Dignity: Another Look at Original Intent." *San Diego Justice Journal* 25 (Summer): 559.

Grossman, Mark, and Mike Dixon-Kennedy. 1998. *Encyclopedia of Capital Punishment.* Santa Barbara, CA: ABC-CLIO.

Harding, Roberta M. 1996. "The Gallows to the Gurney: Analyzing the (Un)Constitutionality of the Methods of Execution." *Boston University Public International Law Journal* 6 (Fall): 153.

Kirchmeier, Jeffery L. 2000. "Let's Make a Deal: Waiving the Eighth Amendment by Selecting a Cruel and Unusual Punishment." *Conneticut Law Review* 32 (Winter): 615.

Macready, Dawn. 2000. "The 'Shocking' Truth about the Electric Chair: An Analysis of the Unconstitutionality of Electrocution." *Ohio Northern University Law Review* 26: 781.

Radin, Margaret J. 1978. "The Jurisprudence of Death: Evolving Standards for the Cruel and Unusual Punishments Clause." *University of Pennsylvania Law Review* 126: 989.

Randa, Laura E., ed. 1997. *Society's Final Solution: A History and Discussion of the Death Penalty.* Lanham, MD: University Presses of America.

Steelwater, Eliza. 2003. *The Hangman's Knot: Lynching, Legal Execution and America's Struggle with the Death Penalty.* Boulder, CO: Westview Press.

3
Cases

Getting to *Furman*

The Court laid the foundation for challenging capital punishment at the end of the 1962–1963 term. Justice Arthur Goldberg, only to be on the Court for a few more years, circulated an unpublished memorandum to the other members of the Court. He brought to the attention of his fellow justices the fact that a number of death penalty cases were on the docket, but none of those cases challenged the constitutionality of the punishment.

He acknowledged that the Court had affirmed capital punishment, but only implicitly. Goldberg noted that the Court had never tackled the question head-on or decided whether or not, especially in light of the growing worldwide trend toward abolition, under what conditions the Constitution might bar the death penalty. However, at first, only Justice Brennan would join Goldberg to challenge the issue of capital punishment generally or take the more extreme step of striking it down.

Goldberg's frustration was evident as he filed a dissent from a denial of certiorari in *Rudolph v. Alabama* in 1963. Some critics credit Goldberg's opinion in *Rudolph* with sending a signal to attorneys that the time was ripe to begin challenging the death penalty. Justices Douglas and Brennan joined Goldberg in asking the Court to look at whether capital punishment violated the Eighth and Fourteenth Amendments of the United States Constitution.

Goldberg made three basic points. First, in light of the growing tendency throughout the country and the world against punishing rape by death (*Rudolph* was a rapist), he cited *Trop v. Dulles* and talked about the "evolving standards of decency that mark the progress of [our] maturing society," and the language in *Weems* that spoke of "standards of decency more or less universally accepted."

Second, he raised the issue, which would be confirmed in *Coker v. Georgia*, of whether in a crime that did not involve the taking of a human life, for example, rape, the death penalty was consistent with the principle stated in *Weems* that asserted punishments could not be excessive.

Finally, Goldberg argued punishing rapists by executing them did not serve the aims of society more effectively than incarceration, and was therefore unnecessarily cruel.

Goldberg's challenge to his fellow justices would not be accepted for several years, in fact not until he had moved off the Court. His focus on the language of *Trop* and *Weems* would carry his legacy forward and help set the agenda and the parameters of the ensuing debate.

However, despite Goldberg's plea, the Court was reluctant to tackle the death penalty, and it took five more years for a challenge to reach the Supreme Court. That case, *United States v. Jackson* (1967), involved the federal kidnapping statute. This law resembled many state statutes that were being challenged in death penalty litigation. The kidnapping statute, like the state laws, eliminated the death penalty as a possible punishment when the defendant chose a nonjury trial or pled guilty. Death penalty opponents complained this was unfair because the defendant was penalized for opting for a jury trial. Trial by jury, especially in capital cases, seemed to be the preferred form of trial, because statistics showed there was a greater chance for acquittal. In addition, trial by jury was a constitutionally guaranteed right. This put a lot of pressure on defendants to choose a course, which more likely found them guilty (a nonjury trial) or had them plead guilty if they chose to put their fate in the hands of a jury. This appeared to be an unfair choice that offended the notions of justice and due process.

On those grounds of apparent unfairness, the Supreme Court declared the kidnapping act unconstitutional, because it placed an unfair burden on the defendant. The law forced the defendant to make an unreasonable choice, because asserting his or her constitutional right to a trial by jury would decrease the defendant's chances of acquittal. The act of declaring one's constitutional rights should not be accompanied by additional burdens. Rather, the system should make it easier for one to assert his or her rights, not create possible pitfalls in the attempt to exercise those rights.

This concern for the ability to claim one's rights reflected the trend of the Court in the 1960s during the criminal due process revolution of the Warren Court. That Court, and for a while its successor, was very conscious of making sure not only that guaranteed rights were fulfilled, but access to those rights, or the ability to realize those rights, was not impeded. Landmark cases such as *Gideon v. Wainwright* (1963) (right to counsel) and *Miranda v. Arizona* (1966) (notification of rights) emphasized this philosophy. The justices reiterated this message in *Jackson.*

Justice Stewart's majority opinion held that the death penalty provision of the kidnapping statute was invalid because it imposed an unreasonable burden upon an accused's ability to exercise his Fifth Amendment right not to plead guilty and his Sixth Amendment right to demand a jury trial. Stewart noted the congressional objectives of the kidnapping act were laudable. By passing the act, Congress had tried to develop a system that more evenly and fairly applied the death penalty. The problem was, in its attempt to do so, Congress created a system that had a chilling effect on basic constitutional rights. For Stewart, there was no question that the statute compromised an individual's ability to have a fair trail and be fairly judged for the death penalty. It did not matter that congressional goals were positive, because the end did not justify the means.

The implications of *Jackson* were hazy. In his opinion, Stewart was careful to note there was no problem with the act as a whole—making interstate kidnapping a federal capital crime. Rather, he noted it was the procedural provisions, which allowed for the death penalty, that were struck down. In contrast, the dissent moved past the purely procedural aspects to the real core of the controversy. The objection from the dissenters, Justices White and Black, helped fuel the later controversy over how the death penalty should be applied, if at all. Because the majority at no point challenged Congress's ability to impose the death penalty, but merely the procedure, death penalty opponents did not seem to have much hope.

Witherspoon v. Illinois followed *Jackson.* Similar to *Jackson,* the focus in *Witherspoon* was on the Sixth Amendment rights that seemed to be denied. *Witherspoon* was a narrow decision that overturned only the specific application of the death penalty, and not the conviction, on the grounds that the state cannot exclude people from jury who *might* not apply the death penalty. This was in contrast to the previously accepted idea that excluding those who were opposed to the death penalty per se, did not create an unrepresentative jury. Such a jury was as likely to acquit as to convict. Again, a small technicality that seemed to deny the defendant a fair jury trial was the pivotal point in the case rather than the far broader issue of the death penalty itself.

Witherspoon's narrow holding focused on jury selection. Like *Jackson,* it implicitly acknowledged the validity of the death penalty, while raising another issue that seemed to strike at the basic fairness of the system that executed individuals. Underlying these early debates was a point soon to be picked up by some of the justices: If the death penalty was unfair in these cases, wasn't it always unfair, and therefore inherently cruel and unusual?

This reflected the growing number of opponents who believed the key to the debate and the definition of cruel and unusual was a question of fairness. The idea was that the Court needed to move past antiquated notions of torture and the like to more modern ideas. To be unfair in modern society meant to be cruel. But the time was not ripe for this argument, and the question of what constituted fair and unfair was still (and is still) a hotly contested debate.

Under the Illinois scheme, in a murder trial during voir dire, the prosecution could remove any prospective jurors by challenging anyone who had *misgivings* about capital punishment. This meant even those people who might vote to impose the death penalty, but had reservations, could be excluded. In *Witherspoon,* the resulting jury found the defendant guilty and imposed the death penalty. The defendant challenged the conviction on the grounds that the "stacking" of the jury in such a manner denied him his right to a fair trial. By creating a system that favored "hanging" juries, it was more likely the defendant would be convicted, let alone sentenced to death.

Stewart, again writing for the majority, emphasized the issue was a narrow one. It did not involve the right of the prosecution to challenge for cause those prospective jurors who said they could never impose the death penalty or would refuse to even consider it at all.

In a footnote, the Court emphasized a juror does not have to say prior to the case whether or not he would vote for the death penalty. All that can be asked is that he or she approach the case with an open mind and not be committed to vote against the death penalty no matter what the facts and circumstances of the case turned out to be. However, nothing prohibits the state from executing someone whose jury was composed of no one who would automatically vote against capital punishment, regardless of the evidence, or would be prevented from making an impartial decision about the defendant's guilt because of the possibility of execution.

Such exclusion was not the same as just excluding individuals merely because they *might* not be able to impose the death penalty. The problem here was the Illinois scheme authorized the prosecution to exclude all who said that they were opposed to capital punishment and all who indicated that they had conscientious scruples against inflicting it without ever investigating what those principles meant. For example, despite their personal feelings against the death penalty, did that mean they could not convict the defendant or possibly vote to execute them?

In *Witherspoon,* the jurors were being excluded because of a very tenuous "maybe." The verdict of guilt was maintained. (No showing was made that such a jury was prejudiced toward a finding of guilty.) However, the imposition of the death penalty was overturned because the Illinois structure fell short of the impartiality a defendant was entitled to. When the state excluded anyone who had any reservations about the death penalty, it was no longer neutral. In the attempt to create a jury that might impose the death penalty, it created one that was *more* likely to execute. It was obviously unfair to let an individual be judged by a jury with a predilection for conviction. If that was unfair, then the same unfairness existed when a jury was organized so that a verdict of death was more than just a probability, but a likelihood. This was the makeup of the jury in *Witherspoon.* A hanging jury was at odds with the Constitution.

In a separate opinion, Justice Douglas argued first, there was no difference between those potential jurors who just expressed beliefs against capital punishment and those who were so opposed to the death sentence that they would never vote for it. The jury was supposed to represent a cross section of the community, and the community reflected a variety of beliefs about the death penalty. Second, Douglas argued such a contamination of the jury meant the guilty verdict itself was brought into question and therefore should be reversed. Douglas pushed the point noted previously, that the jury by its predilection for execution was more apt to find a guilty verdict, so that the ensuing verdict should be overturned and the whole process challenged.

Justices Black, Harlan, and White dissented. They claimed the state should not be forced to accept jurors who were biased against one of the critical issues in a trial. They dismissed the "maybe" element of the majority and suggested that the mere possibility that one may be opposed to the death penalty, and the fact that a finding of guilty would subject the defendant to the death penalty, meant those jurors were prejudiced and would inhibit the state's ability to prosecute. Black attacked the majority for employing legal subterfuge to get around the imposition of the death penalty. If they wanted to declare capital punishment unconstitutional, then they should do so. The result of playing games was an incredibly ambiguous opinion that did not resolve anything concrete. The only thing this case changed was the questions that could be asked of jurors in order to exclude them. In the end, the guidelines the Court announced would make no change in the composition of juries, but instead opened the door to challenges further down the road. The only thing the Court truly accomplished was to destroy the idea of an unbiased jury.

Despite Douglas's complaint, the guilty verdict was sustained because the Court noted it could not be concluded that the exclusion of jurors opposed to capital punishment resulted in an unrepresentative jury on the issue of guilt or substantially increased the risk of conviction.

White took Black's argument another step. He claimed that the majority opinion was tainted with their personal distaste for the death penalty, and questions concerning what constitutes appropriate penalties should be left to the legislative branch.

By the time of *Witherspoon*, it was becoming very evident that arguments about capital punishment in U.S. society would hinge not purely on issues of the law. By the late 1960s, it was apparent Americans had mixed attitudes about capital punishment. With people like Charles Manson, Sirhan Sirhan, and James Earl Ray sitting in prison, many Americans asked why not execute these people? The arguments against and for the death penalty would resemble the concerns of many of the other civil liberty cases on the dockets in the 1960s: What was the best way to effectuate those rights guaranteed by the Bill of Rights. If allowing the death penalty was constitutional, what was the best way to implement it? For proponents, the path was clear: Establish a mechanism of execution that was fair. Opponents believed that if they could keep chipping away at the process and show its inherent unfairness and inconsistencies, perhaps they could get the Court to strike down capital punishment completely. They concluded and hoped there would always be questions of fairness and prejudice forcing the Court's hand. Conversely, supporters assumed there was a fair and equitable way to execute people and claimed the constitutionality of the penalty.

They could do this because, as the cases just discussed make evident, the Court focused more on procedural issues and did not directly challenge the death penalty itself. With a jury in place, the next issue to be tackled was what system should be used to apply the death penalty.

Opponents and some members of the Court perceived the unguided discretion given to juries to choose between life and death to be inconsistent with the tenets of due process. In addition, the majority viewed the single-verdict procedure, in place in many jurisdictions, to be unconstitutional, because in such cases, juries convicted and announced sentence in the same procedure. Such a system hamstrung defense lawyers concerning the decisions they were forced to make. This was in contrast to what was known as a bifurcated system, where in one phase of the trial, the jury determined guilt, and in a completely separate phase, the jury decided the type of punishment. The latter system gave the attorney more leeway in presenting character evidence and in deciding on whether or not to let the defendant take the stand.

The problem with the single-track version was it forced lawyers to make tactical decisions at the wrong places in the trial, compromising their ability to defend their clients. For example, suppose the lawyer thought the defendant would make a sympathetic witness at a sentencing hearing. Perhaps his background, his relationship with his family, and so on, would be mitigating evidence. Mitigating evidence is evidence that precludes the jury from applying the death penalty. However, mitigating factors usually speak to character. Once character issues have been introduced, the prosecution is allowed to delve deep. In the course of doing so, usually many negative characteristics (after all this is a murderer on trial) can be brought to light that might give the jury reason to rethink the defendant's guilt or innocence. A typical line of reasoning might be: Well, he was a bad person, so even if he did not commit this crime, he should be punished for all these other bad things he's done. Thus, the defense attorney was forced to

make an incredibly difficult and unfair choice that might determine
not only the type of penalty imposed but also whether or not a guilty
verdict would be returned. The attorney had the option of allowing
the defendant to testify (raising the specter of self-incrimination),
possibly hastening the verdict of guilt, in order to get mitigating evidence in before the sentencing phase, with the hope of softening the
penalty applied. (Of course, as previously noted, there was always
the chance the defendant's testimony would not only help the jury
find a guilty verdict but also enhance the prosecution's argument for
the death penalty.) On the other hand, if the defendant did not testify,
and was found guilty, the jury did not have the mitigating evidence to
consider, and would probably impose a harsher penalty.

It was this issue the Court tackled three years later in *McGautha
v. California* (which was joined with another case, *Crampton v.
Ohio*). These cases attacked the single-track scheme seen in earlier
cases, the constitutionality of which the Court had refused to rule
upon. A Court in transition (Harry Blackmun and Warren Burger,
Nixon appointees, now sat in place of Abe Fortas and Earl Warren,
and new appointments, including William Rehnquist, were on the
horizon) refused to overturn the system. Justice Harlan wrote the
opinion and was joined by four others. He noted that the lack of specific guidelines for the jury did not make the death penalty process
unfair and a single-track system was not unconstitutional. Three justices (Douglas, Brennan, and Marshall) argued that a bifurcated
scheme was mandated under the Constitution. Underlying their arguments was the idea that anything that led to execution was unfair,
thereby cruel and unusual, and hence unconstitutional.

Harlan's opinion was in line with his general conservative view of
criminal procedural due process. He often focused on ideas like "implicit in the concept of ordered liberty." Instead of focusing on
specifics, it was the general tenor of what was going on that was important. In *McGautha*, Harlan said there might be "better" ways to
deal with capital cases, but that did not mean the method at hand was
unconstitutional. As he had noted in earlier cases, the state should
not be put in a "constitutional straitjacket." His goal was to make
sure that criminal trials, all criminal trials, were fundamentally fair.
There was no set or perfect way to guarantee this, and as long as the
process abided by these general dictates it was okay. His opinion in
McGautha followed this conservative and limited approach.

He empathized with the lawyers and observed that difficult judgments were what the practice of law was all about. Because a particular scheme forced the defendant and his lawyer to make difficult decisions on tactics did not mean it was unconstitutional. In addition, the Fifth-Amendment privilege against self-incrimination did not come into play when a defendant testified as a tactic. Under such circumstances, he was not being forced to testify against his will, but rather had freely decided to do so.

Harlan, as he often did, relied on history. He claimed the reason for giving juries discretion was to create and sustain a system that was more likely to have mercy, not less likely. Giving the jury discretion eliminated a wooden approach to the law and allowed jurors to take into consideration their feelings and impressions and possibly spare a defendant's life. Black concurred and reemphasized that the Eighth Amendment did not outlaw capital punishment.

The three dissenters (Marshall, Douglas, and Brennan) objected on two grounds. Douglas objected to the single-verdict procedure, claiming it put the defendant in the untenable position of being forced to surrender his Fifth Amendment rights against self-incrimination if he chose to take the stand, for example, to support a defense of insanity or to present mitigating circumstances for the penalty phase. Brennan objected to the unbridled discretion exercised by the jury, claiming such unguided decisionmaking violated due process. The scheme in play had serious procedural inadequacies. Brennan objected that the Court, in finding a conflict between the rule of law and the power of the state to kill, had resolved the dilemma in favor of the state's authority to execute. If anything, shouldn't the balance tilt the other way? he asked.

Thus the stage was set for the challenge presented in *Furman v. Georgia.* At this point in time it appeared two basic camps, with some slight variances, were emerging. On one side there were those who argued the death penalty was okay generally. Others, who agreed with this proposition, took a somewhat narrower view by focusing carefully on the process. In the end these two positions were not far apart. On the other side were those who conceded the death penalty might be constitutional if the procedure was fair, but the process never was and never could be fair, so the penalty was unconstitutional. Even more extreme, were those who argued the death penalty, per se, was unconstitutional. Justice Marshall was the greatest voice of this last position, seeing the death penalty in modern America as cruel and un-usual because it was unconscionable for the state to be executing its citizens.

Furman v. Georgia: Death Takes a Hiatus

By time *Furman* and its sister cases (*Jackson v. Georgia* and *Branch v. Texas*—rape cases—and *Aikens v. California,* along with *Furman*—a murder case) made their way to the Court, there were obviously problems with capital punishment in the United States.

Growing public opinion suggested Americans might be against the imposition of the death penalty. World opinion was coming to bear on the United States. (Note that prior to the 1970s the United States and Europe were not that far apart on where they stood on the death penalty. Most Western nations had a death penalty, but used it spar-ingly.) In addition, two celebrated cases over the previous two decades, the Rosenbergs and the Caryl Chessman cases, suggested that the civility of the death penalty was a myth. The image of the Rosenbergs being led to execution, compounded by the forlorn looks on the faces of their children, and the eloquent writings of Chessman from death row in California tweaked the emotional cen-ter of Americans.

On the other hand, by 1972, the United States was becoming more focused on law and order. Breakdowns in the 1960s, battles between the police and student protesters, rioters, and radical elements in so-ciety had created an atmosphere that suggested Americans were more willing to crack down hard on criminals. After the Attica State Prison uprising, most Americans sided with the guards, and follow-ing the killing of four students at Kent State, Americans' sympathies lay with the national guardsman, not the students. Richard Nixon was being reelected on a law and order campaign, and the United States was rejecting liberalism at the polls, as seen in the crushing de-feat of George McGovern, and in the growing animosity toward Warren Court decisions and their apparent leniency toward crimi-nals. It was in this climate that *Furman* appeared.

Looking at it in retrospect and viewing the disparate nature of the opinion, it makes sense. It reflects the changing tides in the United States and is not the anti–death penalty case that some critics would make it out to be. Rather it is a picture of a Court trying to come to grips with jurisprudential fluctuations, from basic philosophical issues to the very makeup of the Court. Unlike *Roe,* where the Court seemed to reinvigorate Warren Court liberalism and give those on the left hope, *Furman* was redrawing the line and giving clarity to a situation and in essence, as can now be seen, was an attempt by the Court to create a system by which people could be executed more fairly, without the arbitrary and capricious elements that seemed to taint the system.

In *Furman* and its companion cases the basic arguments were that capital punishment was an antiquated penalty that no longer had a place in modern society, and that racial disparity in death penalty cases denied equal protection guaranteed by the Fourteenth Amendment. This latter question was also couched in Eighth-Amendment terms.

Thus the challengers to the death penalty raised two basic issues—that the death penalty overall was unconstitutional, and that the process by which the death penalty was applied was unconstitutional, because it allowed juries absolute discretion with no guidance, therefore making the system arbitrary and capricious and fraught with inequities.

To support the argument that the death penalty was unconstitutional per se, the challengers noted the worldwide trend away from the use of the death penalty. They argued the penalty remained on the books only because of the rarity and arbitrariness with which it was applied. The infrequent application of the penalty made it more palatable. If a long trail of defendants were to lose their lives, very soon the U.S. public would lose their tolerance for such penalties. Public acceptability of the death penalty had been maintained only by allowing discretion in capital sentencing.

The arbitrary nature of the penalty was a natural by-product of a penalty that was so rarely applied. In the natural course of the criminal process, the number of similar cases and therefore similar penalties created a leveling or an equalization of the system. In the case of capital punishment, however, because it was so infrequently used, it was bound to be applied inconsistently in similar situations.

In addition to pointing out the natural inconsistencies, opponents of the death penalty quoted statistics that indicated that class and race played a huge part in the capricious nature of the penalty. If one was poor and black (and in the South), the chance of that person being executed greatly increased. To this day, geographical disparity has provided fuel for the opponents' argument against the death penalty.

They have noted that the same criminal acts committed in Texas and New Hampshire result in far different penalties.

Finally, the argument persisted that the death penalty was not a part of the regular criminal law machinery of Georgia or of the nation. It did not fit into the normal process. It was a freakish aberration, a rare extreme act of violence, visibly arbitrary, and most likely racially discriminatory. It was a penalty randomly applied, because if it were applied on a regular basis, the universally shared standards of public decency would be offended. As a civilized society, Americans would reject such an assault.

The death penalty was viewed as an anathema to a civilized society. One of the hallmarks of "civilized" society was the rejection of gross forms of punishment, including terror. For death penalty opponents, the death penalty was the ultimate terror. It was a sword of Damocles hanging over the heads of defendants; it was an act of terror, not an act of law. Capital punishment directly offended the basic underlying principle of the Eighth Amendment, which had been aimed at the elimination of torture and terror. Critics argued that because it was part of a system that helped enforce order through institutionalized terror, the death penalty was not an instrument of a democratic government but the product of a totalitarian regime. Therefore, to enforce the death penalty was to reject democratic principles and to embrace a political ideology antithetical to the basic rubric of American life.

The supporters of capital punishment rejected all these arguments. They started by denying that the current guidelines provided for an arbitrary system. They noted that plenty of guidelines existed for juries, and judges, when they decided to execute criminals. In fact, the instructions to juries were extensive. They were thorough, impartial, and completely inclusive. More importantly, they gave the jury a choice of alternative verdicts. Contrary to the suggestion made by the opposition, proponents claimed that the juries were not railroaded into applying the death penalty but were given much more guidance and leeway to be magnanimous than they were in noncapital criminal decisions. In essence, it was a guided decision weighted toward justice.

An underlying argument for supporters of the death penalty was that just because all criminals who deserved the death penalty were not executed, does not make it any more arbitrary than other forms of punishment. The fact that the police do not stop every person who speeds, does not mean speed limit laws are cruel and unusual punishment or unfair. Those who are caught are guilty and deserve punishment. Some who are guilty do not get caught; some who are caught pay a lesser fine. Such are the vagaries of our justice system.

The supporters of the death penalty as it was then applied in Georgia and other states asked what else could people want? What other guidelines could the trial court possibly give? As was noted in their brief, the idea of providing additional guidelines was "completely beyond the imagination." In the *Furman* case, the jury had the option, after finding the defendant guilty of murder, to return a verdict that recommended mercy and ask for life imprisonment. However, the jury felt that because of the heinous nature of the crime, life imprisonment was not acceptable, and they sentenced the defendant to die.

In contrast to the opponents, supporters felt capital cases were not that much different than ordinary criminal cases, and they believed that each case should stand or fall on its own merit. If the death penalty was arbitrary, all sentencing was arbitrary. Opponents saw inconsistent application of the death penalty as no different than situations where one individual is sentenced to twenty-five years and another to life for committing the same crime. There always had been and always would be disparities in the sentencing of apparently alike criminals. Those disparities did not negate the justice system. The only difference in capital cases was the extreme or severe nature of the penalty, but the rationale didn't change merely because death was involved. If the crime was heinous, allow the jury to affix the death penalty. If the jury felt there were mitigating circumstances, allow it to grant some relief to the defendant. This was the essence of the U.S. judicial system.

With all these arguments being presented, *Furman v. Georgia* and its sister cases came to the Court and focused on the Eighth Amendment question of cruel and unusual punishment. At oral argument each justice focused on various intricacies. One of the more interesting exchanges revolved around the due process clause. One justice focused on the wording that said there should be no deprivation of *life* or liberty, without due process. These words were not just semantics, the Court noted, rather the phrase put in question the viability of the death penalty in U.S. society.

With these words hanging in the air, and the members of the Court straying all over the place at oral argument, the resulting decision was the longest opinion in Court history to that time. In its decision, the

Court held that the imposition and carrying out of the death sentence, *as currently applied* in Georgia and other states, constituted cruel and unusual punishment, in violation of the Eighth Amendment. A majority failed to rule that the death penalty, per se, was unconstitutional. Furthermore, a majority of justices failed to reach consensus on any point except the judgment just noted. A brief per curiam opinion was issued, and nine concurrences were produced, each one using a different approach.

Justice Douglas focused on the discriminatory implications of the death penalty, concentrating on racial disparities in the imposition of the death penalty. He claimed that these racial inequities—more blacks than whites were executed—made the death penalty cruel and unusual. Douglas argued if a law functioned so that those who made more than $50,000 were for the most part exempt from the death penalty, and blacks, those who had not passed the fifth grade, people who made less than $3,000, and citizens who were unstable or unpopular were executed, the law would be unconstitutional. In essence the Georgia statute, because of its discretionary nature, did just that. It enabled the jury (or judge) to execute those who were not popular, not wealthy, not a member of the majority, and so on.

Justice Brennan took a very wide view of the Eighth Amendment. He repudiated the historical interpretation of the clause *cruel and unusual* as the Court had done in *Weems* and reiterated the point that the Eighth Amendment is to guard against arbitrary uses of power. Brennan chided his fellow justices and said that just because the legislature has the power to stipulate punishments, that did not mean the Court's responsibility had been abdicated. Rather, that was the very purpose of the Eighth Amendment. The problem was to create guidelines and establish the principles to guide society. And the primary guiding principle was whether the punishment in question degraded the dignity of human beings. He rejected the idea of the Eighth Amendment's prohibition against cruel and unusual punishment being limited to torture or only to those punishments that were considered cruel and unusual at the time the Eighth Amendment was adopted. He felt this was a static view of the Constitution. And in line with his general philosophy toward constitutional interpretation that suggested an evolving concept of justice and liberty and a need to look at modern applications of eighteenth-century words, Brennan argued it was a denial of human dignity for a state arbitrarily to subject a person to an unusually severe punishment. Especially when society had indicated that form of punishment was unacceptable. In addition, Brennan claimed because the death penalty was no more effective in curtailing crime than a lesser punishment, this made it excessive and, therefore, cruel and unusual.

In his concurrence, Justice Stewart attacked the death penalty statutes at issue as being arbitrary and capricious. He refused to go to what he called the ultimate question: Was the death penalty, per se, unconstitutional? He felt there were problems in the cases before the Court, and the randomness of the application of the death penalty in these cases made the death penalty, as applied, repugnant to the thinking of U.S. justices. The unique quality of the penalty made it essential that it be fairly applied. Instead, Stewart noted, it was "wantonly and . . . freakishly imposed," like getting struck by lightning. Yet despite these harsh words, Stewart conceded that the death penalty was not inconsistent with the Eighth Amendment by not addressing the ultimate question. The intimation was that under the right circumstances, Stewart would vote for imposition of the death penalty.

Justice White's concurrence stated from the start that he was not opposed to the death penalty per se. He could see its application in certain cases. However, in the cases before the Court, too much discretion, and the application of the penalty on such an infrequent basis, suggested the death penalty served no substantial purpose. An action by the state must have a purpose. If the action failed to serve that purpose, then it was void. And the death penalty failed to serve the stated purposes (at that time usually retribution and deterrence) because it was so rarely applied.

Justice Marshall wrote the longest opinion and took the most extreme view, stating that the death penalty violated the Eighth Amendment because it was an excessive and unnecessary punishment and because it was morally unacceptable to the people of the United States. Therefore under any circumstance, the death penalty was unconstitutional. Marshall wrote a long historical discussion about the death penalty and how that history had evolved. Underlying Marshall's opinion was the recognition of the racial and class disparities in the application of the penalty and, for the great champion of civil rights, this as much as any other reason meant the death penalty was unfair.

Thus, despite a majority voting to strike down the death penalty statute as it was currently applied in the United States, a majority refused to declare capital punishment unconstitutional per se. Only three Justices (Brennan, Douglas, and Marshall) were willing to go that far and declare the death penalty unconstitutional under the Eighth Amendment.

In addition to the five concurrences that saw no coalescing of arguments about how and why the death penalty should be eliminated from the justice system, the four dissenters also wrote opinions. The four dissents along with the lukewarm concurrences of Stewart and White suggested the death penalty's absence from the U.S. legal system would be for a limited time at best. The dissenters were much closer in their views about why the death penalty was acceptable in *Furman v. Georgia* and the accompanying cases, as well as generally.

Chief Justice Burger took a strict view of constitutional interpretation and looked at the very nature of the Eighth Amendment in that context. He noted cruel and unusual punishment had nothing to do with capital punishment and therefore did not bar the death penalty. The Eighth Amendment was not concerned with procedure. It did not speak to the process by which a state determined that a particular punishment was to be imposed in a particular case. The interpretation of the Eighth Amendment that was suggested in the concurrences went beyond the intention of the founders. To set aside the death sentences in *Furman* and its companion cases on the grounds that prevailing sentencing practices did not comply with the Eighth Amendment meant the Court was fundamentally misconceiving the nature of the Eighth Amendment guarantee. This was the job of the legislature, not the Court. To interpret the Constitution in such a manner flew directly in the face of history and recent cases. History suggested the phrase *cruel and unusual punishment* was adopted to prohibit torture or excessively cruel punishments.

Justice Blackmun started by noting his personal aversion to the death penalty. He picked up on a theme that saturated all the dissents: What had changed over the last year, two years, ten years, and so on, that all of a sudden the death penalty should be seen as contradicting the dictates of the Eighth Amendment? Arguments against capital punishment were fine. However, they belonged in legislative battles, or demands for executive clemency, not in the Supreme Court of the United States. The Court could not, under the guise of interpreting the Constitution, establish a policy that was best executed by the legislature.

Reiterating Burger's overall analysis, Justice Powell emphasized the historical nature of the death penalty as it related to the Eighth Amendment and claimed that the arguments against the death penalty contradicted constitutional history. He took a narrow view of the function of the Court and emphasized the need for self-restraint. None of the opinions supporting the Court's decision provided a constitutionally adequate foundation for the decision. The case against the constitutionality of the death penalty fell far short, especially when put up against affirmative references to capital punishment in the Constitution, Supreme Court precedents, the need for the Supreme Court to exercise self-restraint, and the duty of the Court to avoid policymaking and acting as a legislature.

Finally, Justice Rehnquist, as was a common theme from his first days on the Court to his current tenure, focused on judicial restraint. His opinion echoed other opinions, and he blasted his fellow members for the wide-ranging interpretations that threw the Court into the middle of social issues better left for the legislature to decide. He stated that even the most expansive reading of the leading constitutional cases did not remotely suggest that the Supreme Court had been granted what he called "a roving commission," by either the framers of the Constitution or the authors of the Fourteenth Amendment. As a Court, they had no right to invalidate laws on the basis of an ideology that had recently appeared on the Court's doorstep and had no roots in historical evolution.

For Rehnquist and his fellow dissenters, there was no question about the viability of the death penalty. To strike it down per se, flew in the face of constitutional precedent and led the Court down a path of social action that it should not go. Despite personal aversions to the infliction of capital punishment, decisions on whether to maintain capital punishment was a legislative matter, outside the purview of the Court. All their dissents emphasized these ideas to varying degrees. The Court's only concern was to make sure the process was fair.

In contrast, there was no real consistency in the majority concurrences. From radical thoughts on the death penalty to the more moderate view of the place of the death penalty in society, the majority ran the gamut.

It is important not to view *Furman* in a historical vacuum void of the social ebb and flow of the time. The decision, both the strong opposition by the dissents and the fractional nature of the majority, reflected not only a growing opposition to the death penalty, but also more general trends in U.S. culture and jurisprudence.

Decisions of the Warren Court and those of the early years of the Burger Court often focused around the idea of using the Constitution as a vehicle for social change. Note the plethora of criminal procedural cases and the attitudes of justices like Douglas, Marshall, and Brennan, and those of shorter tenure like Goldberg and Fortas, who saw the Court as a vehicle to effect such change. One year after *Furman, Roe v. Wade* was decided, one of the most evident examples of the Court getting involved in, as critics argued, imposing social policy. This attitude reflected the more, albeit dying, liberal nature of the Court. The trend was soon to be stopped as Nixon appointees began to dominate the Court and the resurgent conservatism that took over the White House and Congress began to manifest itself in the Court.

Furman also reflected part of the Court's attempt to standardize criminal procedure. Going back to the early 1960s the Court had made a decided effort to eliminate inconsistencies in the criminal law and make states abide by the same basic principles and rules. *Miranda v. Arizona, Mapp v. Ohio,* and *Gideon v. Wainwright* all reflected this trend, with the steady incorporation of the Bill of Rights into the Fourteenth Amendment. It was a conscious attempt to balance the adversarial system and make it fair, yet not hamstring the state in arresting, convicting, and punishing criminals. As the Burger Court began to garner steam, it began to reshape some of the decisions of the previous decade, pulling them back a bit and creating a new balance out of what it saw as the excesses of the Warren Court. *Furman* was decided right in the middle of this realignment.

Because *Furman* threw into question all death penalty statutes, its effect was to void all capital punishment laws as then written. They were all declared unconstitutional, and more than 600 people on death row were granted reprieves. Although a huge sigh of relief emerged from death rows across the nation, needless to say, the decision provoked widespread reaction. Abolitionists hailed it as the beginning of a new America. As is often the case, people read into a Supreme Court decision only what they want to be there. In *Furman,* many failed to see the intricacies of the opinion, the common threads that would seem to support the imposition of the penalty, and the changing attitudes of the United States away from leniency toward criminals. Conservative political elements focused on that changing tide.

President Nixon and California Governor Ronald Reagan, aspiring to be president, blasted the opinion and used it to feed the growing condemnation of the Supreme Court that had begun in the early 1960s with the likes of *Mapp* and *Miranda* and coming to a head with *Furman* and *Roe*.

The post-*Furman* jubilation was short lived. As can be seen in the fractionalized nature of the opinion and the failure of the justices to come to a consensus, the subject was ripe for rehearing.

In *Furman*, only Marshall and Brennan believed capital punishment in general was prohibited under the Eighth Amendment. The other opinions focused on procedural inequities that told the states, "fix the procedure and you can execute." As noted previously, the dissent reflected the ideas that capital punishment is okay, it is not the place of the Court to deal with societal issues—and this is what capital punishment was—and the legislatures and the people should be the ones to decide.

Gregg v. Georgia: Death Returns

By 1976, thirty-five states had rewritten their death penalty statutes to coincide with the apparent parameters laid out in *Furman*. Most of the statutes that had fallen by the wayside had been structures where juries had unfettered discretion to decide who should live and who should die and/or were single-trial systems. If there was one common theme in *Furman*, it was that any scheme that was arbitrary and capricious in the application of the death penalty would be declared unconstitutional. The more inconsistent or rare the application of the death penalty, the more likely it would be seen as arbitrary and capricious.

With the new laws in place, in 1976, the Supreme Court agreed to revisit the question of capital punishment. Shifts in the Court suggested a different result, and both sides of the argument held their breath. The Court took five cases in order to review the constitutionality of the death penalty. Two of the cases looked at statutory frameworks that dealt with mandatory imposition of the death penalty for certain crimes and were reviewed under *Woodson v. North Carolina*. The other three were grouped together under *Gregg v. Georgia* (*Profitt v. Florida, Jurek v. Texas*) and provided the vehicle to recommence the execution of individuals guilty of capital crimes in the United States.

Furman had left the door open for *Gregg* by not resolving the issue of whether the death penalty violated the Constitution. In *Furman*, most of the members of the Court had focused on fairness—there had to be clear standard procedures by which a person was convicted and then sentenced to death. As would become apparent in *Gregg*, bifurcated trials seemed to solve a lot of these problems.

Gregg provided a means for death penalty opponents to finish the argument started in *Furman* and ask the Court to declare the death penalty unconstitutional across the board.

For the proponents, this was the vehicle to show that the implementation of the death penalty could be fair and equitable and that, properly applied, it was not cruel and unusual punishment.

Gregg produced a 7 to 2 decision saying capital punishment was not cruel and unusual and did not violate the Eighth Amendment. The key to *Gregg* was that it picked up elements of *Furman* (and other cases) that had noted what was needed to make a death penalty statute constitutional. To be fair, not arbitrary and capricious, and therefore not violate either Eighth Amendment demands or more general questions of due process under the Fifth and Fourteenth Amendments, three elements were necessary.

First, there had to be clear standards for the judge or jury in their sentencing decisions. Unguided decisions, with no direction from the court, would be seen as arbitrary and unfair and therefore unconstitutional.

Second, the judge or jury had to consider any mitigating factors prior to sentencing. The sentencer was obligated to explore reasons not to execute. Failure to look at and consider mitigating factors was unfair. Without looking at these elements, the sentencer got only one picture of the defendant. It was essential, especially with a penalty this extreme, that all elements be considered in making the decision. In essence, the decision maker(s) had to go beyond just the hard facts of the crime and take into account the individual.

Finally, there had to be an automatic review of each death sentence in the state appellate court system. Review was necessary to make sure no mistakes had been made. Because of the extreme nature of the penalty, there had to be no indication of impropriety and the means by which the individual was to be executed had to be absolutely fair.

Providing all of these three were evident, the process was deemed fair and equitable and the execution could take place.

As with most death penalty cases, it is the heinous nature of the crime itself that argued for the death penalty. Few who read the facts that follow would argue Gregg was not a despicable character. However, it is for that very reason that this made an excellent test case. It was assumed that if an individual such as Gregg were treated fairly, then all criminal defendants, especially those who were not so "obviously deserving" of harsh punishment, would receive fair treatment.

In *Gregg v. Georgia,* the defendant, Troy Gregg, and a sixteen-year-old companion, Floyd Allen, were hitchhiking from Florida to North Carolina. During the trip, they were successful in getting a ride. Both the driver and the passenger in the car were drunk. After a while, the car broke down, and Fred Simmons, the driver, purchased a new one. When Simmons purchased the new car, he let Gregg and Allen see that he had a large amount of cash. They continued their drive through Georgia. At a certain point, Simmons and his friend, Bob Moore, declared they had to go to the bathroom, so they stopped the car in order to do so.

After the car stopped and Simmons and Moore had left the car, Gregg turned to Allen and said he was going to rob the other two men. Gregg got out of the car. He took a gun, leaned against the car to steady his aim, and shot the two as they were returning from relieving themselves. After they fell down, he circled behind them and shot each one in the back of the head, to make sure they were dead.

Gregg and his compatriot were later arrested in Asheville, North Carolina, with $107 in their possession, a new stereo, a new car stereo, the car that Simmons had purchased, and the gun that had been used to kill both victims. Gregg admitted to robbing the two men and then killing them. After being taken into custody, when asked why he killed them, Gregg said, "By God, I wanted them dead."

At the trial, Gregg pleaded self-defense, an instruction that was given to the jury. The jury returned guilty verdicts on the counts of murder and robbery.

A second sentencing proceeding then took place. No new evidence was presented at that second phase of the trial, and minimal arguments were made for or against the defendant. However, both attorneys did make extensive arguments about the propriety of capital punishment in regard to the specific charges.

The judge then instructed the jury that it had the option of recommending either death or life imprisonment on each count. In doing so, it could consider mitigating and aggravating circumstances. In addition the jury was instructed to sentence the defendant to death only if it found one of the following circumstances beyond a reasonable doubt: (1) the murder was carried out during the commission of another capital felony, that is, the robberies; (2) the victims were murdered so that Gregg could get their money and car; or (3) the murder was an "outrageously and wantonly vile, horrible and inhuman" act involving a depraved act. The jury recognized the first and second of these aggravating circumstances and returned a sentence of death. An immediate appeal to the Georgia Supreme Court took place, and it affirmed the jury's sentence.

The Georgia Supreme Court focused, in part, on whether the death sentences had resulted from an arbitrary and capricious action (like prejudice) on the part of the jury. In light of the heinous nature of the crime, the court found the penalty appropriate. However, the death sentences for the armed robbery convictions were voided. Rarely had juries in Georgia imposed the death penalty for that crime, so to do so here was considered excessive. In addition, because the jury had considered the robberies as aggravating circumstances for the murders, it could not create a circular argument and make the murders extenuating circumstances for the robberies.

The Georgia statute under which Gregg had been prosecuted was a new law, written in reaction to the Supreme Court decision in *Furman*. The suggestions made in *Furman* had been taken to heart, and the reservations expressed by some of the justices in that case were resolved. The resulting 7 to 2 decision once again firmly entrenched the death penalty in the U.S. justice system.

Gregg had challenged the death penalty under the new Georgia statute as "cruel and unusual" punishment under the Eighth and Fourteenth Amendments. The new statute, which had been amended following *Furman v. Georgia*, retained the death penalty for murder and five other crimes. The big difference in the new scheme was it established a bifurcated, or two-level, system. Under this system, in essence two trials were held. At the first trial, guilt or innocence was determined. If a guilty verdict was returned, a second trial or hearing was held, where the sentencer (be it judge or jury) was presented with additional extenuating or mitigating evidence. Under the plan, at least one of ten specified aggravating circumstances had to be found to exist beyond a reasonable doubt in order for the death penalty to be imposed. Those circumstances then had to be designated in writing. In jury cases, the trial judge was bound by the recommended sentence. The sentence was then automatically appealed and reviewed.

In its review of a death sentence the State Supreme Court had to consider three things as part of the appeal. First, it had to assess whether the sentence was influenced by passion, prejudice, or any other arbitrary factor. Was the jury so inflamed that the sentence was not proportionate to the crime committed? This was a tricky element. Obviously, in a death penalty case, the horror of the murder inflamed the jury. The important point here was to make sure the jury or judge focused on the facts of the case, the specific factors rather than emotional twinges.

Second, the State Supreme Court reviewed whether there was evidence supporting the finding of an aggravating circumstance. The final element was really a combination of the first two factors. The High Court focused on the sentence in relation to the crime and decided if the death sentence in the specific case coincided with penalties in similar cases. If the State Supreme Court affirmed the death sentence, it had to refer to similar cases that it had considered in coming to its decision.

Justice Potter Stewart, joined by Justices Powell and Stevens, wrote the main opinion. To the chagrin of death penalty opponents, he concluded that the punishment of death for the crime of murder does not, under all circumstances, violate the Eighth and Fourteenth Amendments. For Stewart, while the Eighth Amendment imposed some restrictions, historically, it had been interpreted in "a flexible and dynamic manner to accord with evolving standards of decency." The important thing that the Eighth Amendment did was forbid the use of punishment that was "excessive." Excess was defined as a punishment that involved unnecessary and unjustifiable infliction of pain or one that was inconsistent with the severity of the crime.

An important argument spoke to the idea of excessive. Stewart conceded that a legislature may not impose excessive punishment. However, the fact that less-severe alternatives exist does not mean the punishment chosen is automatically excessive. The mere existence of life imprisonment or long terms of incarceration, as alternatives to execution, could not mean the death penalty was per se, excessive.

The Court placed a strong emphasis on the fact that the framers of the Constitution accepted capital punishment. For a Court heavy with justices steeped in original intent and a more formalistic view of constitutional interpretation, this was important. Adding to this was the importance of precedent, and for nearly two centuries the Supreme Court had recognized the viability of capital punishment for the crime of murder, if not other crimes.

Stewart's opinion noted that the Court needed to consider not its own personal agenda but the desires of the people. The Court was not a vehicle for adopting social change, rather that was the function of the legislature. In cases such as this, it was important to look at what society thought and felt, which was represented by what the *elected* representatives of the people had done. This was how one determined what were "contemporary standards of decency." In this case, the fact that thirty-five states and the Congress had enacted new legislation to abide by the dictates of *Furman* and create a system that would fairly impose the death penalty, was important, if not controlling.

The reasons why the death penalty was imposed were not really important. The stated reasons of retribution and deterrence where legitimate reasons for these laws. The laws served a legitimate purpose, and it was not the function of the Court to explore the legislatures' purpose any further than that. In addition, it would be improper for the Court to second-guess, in this case the Georgia legislature, about the value and feasibility of the death penalty in certain cases.

Therefore, capital punishment for the crime of murder (and at this point the Court limited itself to the crime of murder), in light of the evidence and rationale presented by the state, could not be viewed as inconsistent.

Furman focused on making sure the death penalty was not imposed arbitrarily or capriciously. A carefully drafted statute would take care of the concerns of that case. In this case, the Georgia (and other states) system solved the procedural problems that *Furman* raised. It guaranteed the jury had ample information and guidance by creating a bifurcated proceeding. In the second proceeding, where sentencing took place, the jury received the necessary information and guidance and was forced to look at mitigating and aggravating circumstances. After this was done, automatic review by the State Supreme Court made sure the system was being fair and the penalty imposed was in line with the penalties normally imposed for like situations. By doing these things the system, rather than being arbitrary and capricious, was incredibly fair and evenhanded. Thus the Georgia statutory system was deemed constitutional.

In a concurrence, Justices White and Rehnquist and Chief Justice Burger elaborated on the Georgia scheme and why it passed constitutional muster. White noted the new scheme did everything *Furman* had asked. It not only guided the jury, but it also made the Georgia Supreme Court review the case and decide whether in fact the death penalty was being administered "in a discriminatory, standardless, or rare fashion." White argued if the State Supreme Court did what it was supposed to do, there could be no unfairness, because all impositions of the death penalty that did not meet the guidelines imposed would be dismissed. And in the case at hand the Georgia Supreme Court did what it was supposed to do. Gregg's failure to show that the State Supreme Court had failed to act properly made his argument fail. The point was, the death penalty was acceptable as long as the procedure followed was correct, and in this case it was perfect.

White also talked about the question of prosecutorial discretion. The state had the option of whom they could seek the death penalty for. The fact that all capital crimes did not result in the death penalty did not mean the process and the system were arbitrary. The criminal justice system functioned in a way that gave prosecutors leeway in terms of who, how, and when to prosecute. As long as they did not abuse that discretion in making the determination it was fine. As will be seen, White realized the growing paradox that was becoming an issue. The very things that created a system that allowed for individual determinations suggested arbitrary behavior. The fact that prosecutors did not charge all possible cases as capital crimes did not mean that the prosecutors acted in a random or arbitrary manner. Rather, this was the way prosecutors worked, and these were the type of decisions they had to make on a daily basis in their capacity as prosecutors.

Finally, White rejected out of hand the general idea that the death penalty was cruel and unusual. He discussed the idea that juries always had the option of choosing life imprisonment. The law required juries to be unanimous, and mandatory review guaranteed the sentence was not reached in an arbitrary fashion. Justice Blackmun, in a short statement, merely concurred and did not elaborate.

Both Justices Brennan and Marshall dissented. The two dissenters voiced strong opinions, attacking all facets of the opinion. Justice Brennan again asserted that the standards of decency had changed. It was the Court's duty as the "ultimate arbiter of the meaning of our Constitution" to decide when certain punishments have moved beyond the pale and were no longer acceptable in modern society. When certain punishments, in a modern sense, were the equivalent of the rack and screw, they ceased to be acceptable.

He repeated his ideas from *Furman* and emphasized that modern moral concepts meant people had to be treated in a manner "consistent with their intrinsic worth as human beings." Punishment could not demean or debase what it meant to be human. It was the duty of the Court to decide whether the death penalty did such a thing and compromised our humanity. In essence, Brennan concluded that it is the Court's duty to regulate morality.

Justice Brennan cited Chief Justice Warren in *Trop v. Dulles,* noting that the Eighth Amendment and the notion of "cruel and unusual punishment must draw its meaning from the evolving standards of decency that mark the progress of a maturing society." Brennan charged that the majority contradicted this statement by focusing their energies not on the death penalty itself, but rather on the process by which the state took the life of a capital defendant. Brennan argued *Furman* had demanded the Court look at the death penalty itself and whether it was an acceptable form of punishment in modern U.S. society. He felt the majority had ignored this, and by looking purely at the procedural safeguards, they had implicitly accepted capital punishment without actually reviewing the penalty itself.

When looking at the historical evolution of society and the law, for Brennan the thing that stood out was the imposition of a higher moral standard. As Western society progressed, morality had grown increasingly important in determining standards by which society functioned. The Constitution, born in the Age of Reason, acknowledged this. To view the death penalty in a kind of static morality did an injustice to the Constitution and to those men who designed it. Society was an evolving, growing entity, like the Constitution, moving toward a civilization that was more equitable and steeped in a greater good.

Maintaining the death penalty contradicted that societal evolution, Brennan argued the Court's function, as the ultimate arbiter of the Constitution, was to look at society and that what he called "moral concepts" required the Court "to hold that the law has progressed to the point where we should declare that the punishment of death, like punishments on the rack, the screw and the wheel, is no longer morally tolerable in our civilized society." For Brennan, it was the act of state-sanctioned execution, no matter the form, that was reprehensible. Proper procedure and a fair application did not mute the immorality of the act.

Justice Marshall repeated his objections from *Furman.* In *Furman,* Marshall had concluded the death penalty was unconstitutional because it was an excessive form of punishment, and if the American people fully understood its implications, they would reject it as immoral.

Marshall argued despite the passing of new death penalty statutes in the wake of *Furman,* they did not reflect an informed citizenry. In fact, Marshall noted, even in the wake of the new statutes, surveys showed the majority of Americans were uninformed and knew little about the death penalty. He still felt an informed public would find capital punishment "shocking, unjust and unacceptable."

However, even if the public was informed and found the penalty acceptable, there was no question it was excessive. And, an excessive penalty was unconstitutional, even if the majority found it palatable. Marshall focused on the question of whether there was a less-severe penalty that would accomplish the legitimate purpose of punishment. For Marshall, life imprisonment served that purpose.

The only reasons that could make the death penalty acceptable, for Marshall, were deterrence and retribution. As Marshall acknowledged then, and most scholars of the death penalty acknowledge now, capital punishment has little to do with deterrence. (Think about the case of *Gregg*. Did the existence of a death penalty in Georgia deter Gregg from committing the cold-blooded murders described previously? It is reasonable to assume that it never entered his thought process? Those who engage in such vile actions as Furman or Gregg are not concerned with the consequences of their actions.)

Although some modern proponents of the death penalty still argue that the death penalty has a deterrent effect, it is a difficult connection to make. But Marshall adamantly denied the deterrence effect, blasting studies that suggested there was such a connection. Justice Marshall argued that the new statutes that had been enacted in the wake of *Furman* did not reflect an informed public. He said the Court erred in accepting certain studies, most notably one in *Furman*, by Isaac Ehrlich, which had claimed the death penalty acted as a deterrent. It does not stop revenge killings; it does not stop anything. Marshall claimed it was not a necessary means to stop the killing in society. Because it did not do what it was purported to do, it had to be excessive, and therefore unconstitutional.

Marshall's retribution argument was a little more difficult. He argued that although retribution is an important component of the criminal justice system, the system does not require approval of retribution as a general justification for punishment. The question was whether retribution provided a moral justification for capital punishment.

Marshall attacked Stewart's statement that labeled retribution as a key component of the criminal justice system. Stewart argued that when people believed there were no consequences for actions taken, anarchy ensued. In essence, Stewart argued deterrence and retribution were linked together and were vital parts of the reasoning for making the death penalty acceptable. Marshall said that was fallacious reasoning, and restating Brennan's argument, noted that this did not mean that life imprisonment did not serve that purpose as well.

In addition was the argument that the death penalty served some higher purpose; that is, the taking of a murderer's life was morally good. Marshall suggested Stewart's argument was circular—and that merely because society demanded an execution did not justify that execution.

In the end, Marshall made arguments reminiscent of the ones he made in *Brown v. Board of Education* that declared segregation illegal. In *Brown*, where people might not have been ready to end segregation and integrate society, it was the duty of the Court to do what was right and move society forward. It had the same opportunity concerning the death penalty, but failed to seize its chance.

The Fallout: Post-*Gregg*

After the *Gregg* decision, capital punishment states passed new laws similar to Georgia's and began sentencing more people to death. In Georgia, the last serious challenge to the death penalty would be decided eleven years later in *McCleskey v. Kemp* (1987).

Gregg reflected the pinnacle of Burger Court liberalism and the beginning of the move away from Warren Court influences. The disappearance of Douglas and Black was beginning to be felt. Like *Roe*, *Gregg* reflected the divisiveness of the Court and its inability to come to a coherent resolution of judicial issues that would bind and guide future Courts. It reflected the evolving transition of the Court from heightened liberalism and expansive reading of the Constitution of the Warren Court days—especially in dealing with criminal procedure due process issues. It is important to remember that despite the progressive reading of the Bill of Rights by the Warren Court, it was not until four years after Earl Warren's retirement that the death penalty was finally declared unconstitutional, albeit for a limited time.

The barring of capital punishment for a limited amount of time and its quick reemergence with *Gregg* reflected the way many of the justices viewed Eighth Amendment issues. In many ways the majority of the Court viewed the death penalty as a procedural issue and not as a fundamental rights issue. As the Court grew more conservative and strove to reshape the procedural issues expounded upon in the 1960s, viewing the death penalty as a procedural problem left it ripe for reassessment, review, and, in the end, very limited reform. The growing conservatism of the Court and the United States would reshape Warren Court decisions and early Burger Court decisions, during the later years of the Burger Court, with the renewed conservative leadership brought in by Ronald Reagan and under William Rehnquist's leadership as chief justice.

Despite the strong words of Brennan and Marshall, it was apparent their argument was a losing one. The other seven justices all acknowledged the rationale of the death penalty to some extent and were not willing to excoriate it from the U.S. criminal justice system. Whatever the reasoning, whether for retribution or deterrence, they believed it was an acceptable penalty for murder. The only questions that seemed to hang in the air, with the rationales proffered in *Gregg*, were Could death be imposed on nonmurder cases, and was a bifurcated scheme, with a separate sentencing phase, a necessity? This latter question was to be answered in a case that was decided simultaneously with *Gregg*.

Woodson v. North Carolina was the other major case to be decided with *Gregg*. *Woodson* resulted from the finding that North Carolina's death penalty statute, in line with the ruling in *Furman*, granted the jury too much discretion in determining who would live and who would die. Unrestricted discretion was seen as arbitrary and capricious. To eliminate this problem, North Carolina rewrote their statute post-*Furman* and created a system that allowed the jury no discretion whatsoever and created a scheme by which the death penalty became mandatory for first-degree murder.

Mandatory schemes were seen as a vehicle to quell jury discretion in line with the complaints in *Furman*. States argued mandatory schemes would prevent the very thing the Court in *Furman* had complained about—random selection of defendants for execution with no rhyme or reason as to why one died and one lived. Defense lawyers argued that mandatory schemes eliminated what the Court in *Furman* seemed to have suggested was important—the use of mitigating circumstances and the individualization of the process, resulting in what they still said would be indiscriminate sentencing patterns. They reiterated arguments made in *Furman* and *Gregg*, that there was no way to really create a logical structure that would eliminate the concerns of the Court, and therefore capital punishment should be declared unconstitutional.

In a somewhat hollow victory for death penalty opponents, the Court struck down the North Carolina statute and other statutes like it because mandatory schemes such as that one did not create standards to guide and regularize the imposition of the death penalty. Also, with such standards there needed to be a system that could rationally review the process.

Woodson was a narrow 5 to 4 majority. As was becoming common in many death penalty cases, historical trends and societal shifts were important. In *Woodson,* the Court noted the trend had been away from mandatory schemes since the nineteenth century; it was seen as inconsistent with the phrase that was to mark many death penalty cases—"evolving standards of decency." The consideration of mitigating circumstances and other specific aspects of the defendant was an important hurdle this scheme failed to leap.

One of the great ironies of this overall train of reasoning is that the very aspects the Court saw as making the penalty more equitable, can be argued to have made it more arbitrary. If the same crime warrants different penalties based on the individual who committed that crime, isn't there a certain arbitrary nature to determination of penalty? Sentencing by its very nature carries an arbitrary quality.

Woodson stemmed from the post-*Furman* attempt by the North Carolina legislature to revise their sentencing procedures. The North Carolina Supreme Court had held unconstitutional the provision of the North Carolina death penalty statute that gave the jury unbridled discretion to return a verdict of guilty of first-degree murder without capital punishment. However, they also ruled that the offending provision was severable so that the statute survived as a mandatory death penalty law. In response, the North Carolina legislature enacted a new statute making the death penalty mandatory for first-degree murder. First-degree murder included not only premeditated murder, but any murder that occurred in the course of committing or attempting to commit a felony.

In *Woodson,* four men were convicted. Each one faced the death penalty for the murder of a cashier during a robbery of a convenience store. Woodson, one of the participants, had remained in the car throughout the robbery. He didn't enter the store; he didn't fire the gun. Woodson also claimed he had been coerced into participating and had been seriously drunk. In fact, he argued, it took one of his fellow robbers—the man who fired the lethal shot—threatening to kill him and striking him in the face to get him to come along. The other two robbers pleaded guilty to lesser charges so as to avoid the death penalty and testified for the prosecution. Woodson wanted to do the same, but was not allowed to. In the end, Woodson was found guilty and sentenced to death under North Carolina's mandatory death penalty law.

The United States Supreme Court ruled the system was unconstitutional. Although they were unable to agree on an opinion, five members of the Court agreed that the imposition of the mandatory death sentence violated the prohibition against the infliction of cruel and unusual punishment under the Eighth and Fourteenth Amendments.

Justice Stewart was again in the driver's seat and wrote the plurality opinion. Joined by Justices Powell and Stevens, he first and foremost noted the striking down of this law did not mean the death penalty under all circumstances violated the Eighth Amendment. Second, he reiterated his line of reasoning from previous cases that the Eighth Amendment's purpose was a more limited one—to "assure that the state's power to punish was exercised within the limits of civilized standards." Third, despite the history of mandatory death sentences, it had become apparent in modern times that such a scheme had a chilling effect on juries and tended to result in them failing to convict. Fourth, by creating a mandatory death penalty, the state had failed to really consider the main concern of *Furman*. In essence, by creating a mandatory system, the state had maintained a single system and failed to bifurcate the sentencing procedure. The jury was forced to consider the penalty while they voted on guilt. *Furman* had been clear this was unacceptable. Finally, the North Carolina statute did not pass muster because one of those elements that went toward considering "the fundamental respect for human dignity" that *Furman* emphasized, was negated when a mandatory death penalty was imposed and the individual defendant's record, character, and mitigating circumstances were not taken into account.

The problem, as Stewart saw it, was that mandatory sentences did not eliminate arbitrary behavior. They only masked the problems that were inherent in a system where juries exercised discretion without guidance or direction. Mandatory sentences gave juries no guidance about who should be executed and who should live.

In a trial where there was a mandatory death sentence, juries did not get to consider individual character traits or particularities of the specific crime when deciding on the individual's fate. This is exactly what *Furman* noted juries must do. Rather, in these cases, juries treated everyone exactly the same, when the nuances of the situation were the key, for no two situations were exactly alike. It created a system that looked at defendants not as unique individuals but as "members of a faceless, undifferentiated mass to be subjected to the blind infliction of the death penalty."

History showed such a system resulted in juries that betrayed their oath and duty. Because they had no choice, or discretion, juries would find obviously guilty defendants—defendants who they acknowledged were guilty—not guilty, because they felt, although the individual should be punished, death was far too extreme a penalty for the particular situation. Stewart's historical analysis suggested that most jurors deemed death as an inappropriate penalty for most first-degree murder situations.

Justices Brennan and Marshall repeated their opinions from *Gregg,* helping create a majority, but refused to sign Stewart's opinion that acknowledged that the death penalty was constitutional.

In dissent, Justice White argued that a mandatory death penalty removed the arbitrary and capricious nature of the procedure, which *Furman* had objected to. How was this unfair? Certain elements had to be met. They were met; the defendant was sentenced to death.

Justice Rehnquist also dissented and objected to what he felt was the plurality's misstatement of the history of mandatory death penalties. The fact that some jurors might not convict because they did not want to see the defendant executed had nothing to do with constitutionality. It did not make the system unfair. How was a system unfair that might execute fewer people? Also, Rehnquist did not understand the emphasis on the need to explore the individual nature of the defendant. Why was it necessary to explore relevant aspects and any mitigating factors? In this case, death was not cruel and unusual based on the facts. Thus, why let the defendant off the hook? Finally, fear of arbitrary decisions was rectified by appellate review.

Woodson and *Gregg* together laid out parameters for future litigation on the death penalty. They acknowledged the constitutionality of capital punishment as long as certain guidelines were followed.

The bifurcated trial that had been emphasized by states to get over the objections of *Furman* fit into the Court's rejection of the mandatory scheme in *Woodson.* There needed to be a trial and then a separate guided jury discretionary phase.

Gregg coupled with *Woodson* would have appeared to close the door on death penalty litigation. The core element of the question—

the constitutionality of the penalty per se—was no longer an issue. Despite the claims of the vocal minority, the majority of the Court felt it was valid. As time would show, the questions left revolved around now how to apply it, and in applying it, who should or should not be executed.

The Court's reasoning seemed to inherently reject opponents of the death penalty's argument that the penalty itself was inherently unfair. Unlike *Brown v. Board of Education,* which had scuttled the entire system of separate but equal, because the very idea of separate was unequal, *Gregg* and its progeny did not reject the foundations of the death penalty. In essence, it rebuilt the house with the same foundation. *Brown* had said we need a new house with a new foundation.

Thus the subsequent cases, while narrowing the scope of the death penalty, did not chop away at the basic premise and principle that under the right circumstances the death penalty is an acceptable form of punishment in U.S. society. *Woodson* established this by attacking the process of the system, not the penalty itself.

By this point in time, there were two basic strands of jurisprudence. Generally, those who steeped their arguments in history and historical process tended to reject capital punishment, per se. The growing reliance on the evolution of society and what the civilized world was doing, found these justices looking at the evolving nature of the Constitution in a historical context. However, as the Court grew more conservative, fewer and fewer justices picked up this ideology. And, those that did, like Justice Scalia, turn history around and focus on what was acceptable in the eighteenth century and do not view the standards as changing and adaptable to the twenty-first century.

In contrast, those justices who focused on criminal procedure and the essential idea of fairness were all right with the death penalty. Despite their personal abhorrence for it in many cases, the modern justices, such as Rehnquist, and Scalia, more recently, focused on most death penalty issues as problems for legislatures, and not the courts, to resolve. The only function of the Court is to make sure that what the legislature has done—the process—is in line with basic constitutional principles.

Thus, post-*Gregg,* the death penalty debate took on a different dimension. Although opponents still argued for the eradication of the penalty as violating the Eighth Amendment of the Constitution, and, using the arguments of *Furman* and *Gregg,* they tweaked the debate with more up-to-date statistics and more scientific arguments, the core arguments remained the same. As *Gregg* and *Woodson* suggested, the ensuing legal battles and the evolution of capital punishment in the United States have tended to focus on two things: who gets executed (included in this are the crimes for which they die) and the process by which they get executed. For proponents, this meant the viability of the death penalty was a settled issue and now it just needed tweaking. For opponents, these represented the last two avenues to go down to slowly eliminate the penalty from the U.S. justice system.

Three subsequent cases, two in the next two years and one a decade later, reinforced this pattern.

The question of process was raised again, in two cases of the same name. In *Roberts v. Louisiana* (1976), the Louisiana statute dictated a mandatory death penalty for certain crimes. Louisiana argued they had created a system that avoided the pitfalls of *Furman* and avoided the imposition of the death penalty by arbitrary or capricious methods. Boiled down, the new statute gave the jury four options in a first-degree murder case: guilty, guilty of second-degree murder, guilty of manslaughter, and not guilty. The judge had to instruct the jury on all four charges, even if the defendant did not request it.

The jury had to decide if two elements existed: specific intent to kill and an armed robbery. If both elements existed, automatically it was first-degree murder and the death penalty kicked in. If only one condition existed, the crime was then second-degree murder, and the mandatory punishment for that crime, imprisonment at hard labor for life, applied. The jury could not ask for an alternative penalty if they found the defendant guilty of first-degree murder.

Justice Stewart (joined by Powell and Stevens) rejected the idea that the death penalty was unconstitutional, per se, under the Eighth Amendment. However, they struck down the statute because the jury had no guidelines. In addition, if it wanted to find the individual guilty of first-degree murder, but did not want to execute him, it was forced to violate its oath and find a lesser offense. Such a system smacked of the very arbitrariness the Court had rejected in *Furman*, *Gregg*, and *Woodson*.

Justices Brennan and Marshall reiterated their previous argument that the death penalty was unconstitutional per se.

The dissent, written by Justice White and joined by Rehnquist, Blackmun, and Chief Justice Burger, relied on *Furman*. White noted the catch-22 mentality of Stewart's decision. He noted the Court rejected the Louisiana—and North Carolina in *Woodson*—statutes because they removed any discretion from the jury. But, simultaneously, it rejected the very same statutes because they asked for the jury to use discretion in resolving the issues. The use of discretion by the jury flew in the face of the standards established by *Furman*. Either the statute gave too much discretion, or did not give enough. It could not do both concurrently.

A year later, a similar mandatory scheme was invalidated. In the second *Roberts v. Louisiana* (1977), Roberts was convicted and sentenced to death for the first-degree murder of a police officer. He received capital punishment because under Louisiana law the death penalty was mandatory for the intentional killing of an on-duty fireman or policeman. The United States Supreme Court reversed the Louisiana Supreme Court's upholding the death penalty.

The per curiam opinion joined by Justices Brennan, Stewart, Marshall, Powell, and Stevens voided the Louisiana death penalty procedure. This was no different than the previous case, despite the fact it was a police officer's death at issue here. A scheme that did not look at mitigating factors or the specifics of the crime committed could not stand up under the rules established.

Justice Rehnquist complained this was a very specific circumstance—the premeditated murder of a policeman. That fact alone was an aggravating circumstance that no particular situation or characteristic of the defendant could mitigate. The state had to be allowed to protect its own, and no purpose was served by undermining the state's duty to maintain order so all citizens could be secure and enjoy their own liberty.

The last piece of the puzzle was completed a decade later in *McCleskey v. Kemp* (1987). In *McCleskey* the Court was faced with a challenge that went to who was being executed, and that "who" made the penalty cruel and unusual, because it was argued, the only reason McCleskey was receiving the death penalty was because of his race. Using various studies, death penalty opponents argued that African-Americans were disproportionately more likely to be executed than whites, and those who killed whites as opposed to blacks, were more likely to die at the hands of the state. Warren McCleskey was an African-American man who was found guilty of two counts of armed robbery and one count of murder. His victim was white. McCleskey's argument rested heavily on studies conducted in Georgia in the 1970s. Three professors (David C. Baldus, George Woodworth, and Charles Pulaski) looked at more than 2,000 cases. McCleskey relied on their conclusion that argued defendants charged with killing white victims were far more likely to receive a death sentence then those charged with killing blacks. Also, according to the study, African-American defendants were more likely to receive the death penalty, no matter who they killed. Finally, of the people who were given the death sentence most were black defendants who killed white victims.

Using these statistics, McCleskey charged that Georgia's death penalty statute discriminated on the basis of race and was therefore unconstitutional as a violation of equal protection and therefore the Eighth Amendment. If blacks faced a higher chance and rate of execution because of their race, didn't that directly challenge *Furman*'s admonition against arbitrary and capricious behavior? For what could be more arbitrary than executing individuals on the basis of their race? This was an important part of Justice Douglas's argument in *Furman* and received new life here.

At oral argument, it was emphasized that despite the attempts by Georgia to make the system fair, and fairly apply it, it was obvious the system did not work, because a disproportionate number of blacks found their way to execution.

When asked if the case reflected racial bias on the part of the prosecutor, McCleskey's lawyers said yes. One only had to look at the cases. Blacks who killed blacks had a far greater chance of pleading out, but blacks who killed whites tended to find their way to stiffer sentences and death row. But the lawyers also argued that bias on the part of the specific prosecutor was not important, but rather, the system's wide discrepancies that were apparent under Baldus's study were the key.

Georgia countered that what appeared on its face to be a discrepancy was really evidence of the differences among the cases. Cases with white victims tended to be more "serious" cases. The state argued that black victim cases were often the result of family disputes, drunken brawls, lovers' squabbles, and the like, whereas cases with white victims resulted from armed robberies, property disputes, and so on.

McCleskey rejected an important line of argument about racism put forth by opponents of the death penalty. It reaffirmed the ideas of *Gregg* that changes in the death penalty, most notably abolition, needed to come from the legislature and not the Court, and it exhibited Justice Blackmun's shift from the pro– to the anti–death penalty position.

Justice Powell, writing for the majority, claimed that just because more blacks than whites suffered the death penalty, that did not mean discrimination had taken place. Statistics alone could not prove discrimination. Racial animus or intent to discriminate on the part of the prosecutor and/or jury had to be proven. In reaching this conclusion, Powell emphasized the holdings in *Furman* and *Gregg*.

He argued *Furman* stood for the proposition that when a death penalty is imposed in an irrational manner, it is excessive and therefore cruel and unusual under the Eighth Amendment. The infrequency with which the death penalty was imposed in Georgia in the early 1970s made it irrational when it was imposed. He combined that with his claim that *Furman* left open whether the death penalty was under all circumstances cruel and unusual. *Gregg* settled that question, stating that as long as history and public acceptance supported the imposition of the penalty for a particular crime and there was justification, it was constitutional.

Furthermore, *Gregg* stood for the proposition that as long as there was a fair process, one in which the jury had some discretion, the process was constitutional. There had to be rational criteria and the ability to consider aggravating and mitigating circumstances. Just because juries' actions are not predictable does not mean they are arbitrary or capricious. McCleskey's argument criticized the discretion and leeway the jury had. The very discretion, which made the system fair, was seen to undercut the system.

Powell feared that McCleskey's arguments, taken to their conclusion, would have grave impact on the criminal justice system. He saw a Pandora's box being opened that would cast a shadow on all types of criminal penalties across the board. The race issue could be used any time there was a discrepancy in sentencing of any other group, whether it was an issue of race, religion, or gender. For Powell, McCleskey's argument was even more far-fetched because it related to the race of his victim. The correlations were too tenuous to declare an entire system as violating the Constitution. To call such a minor discrepancy arbitrary meant that any characteristic, for example, facial characteristics, could be used to create a suggestion of capricious action, bringing the justice system to a halt.

In the end, Powell rejected the statistics. Different numbers did not equal different treatment. At best, the Baldus study showed a possible likelihood, not intentional discrimination. There was no insidious attempt by the State of Georgia to make sure that those who killed whites suffered greater penalties than those who killed blacks. Therefore, the system was not arbitrary or capricious. Just because others in similar situations were not executed, does not mean the system was unfair. That was the essence of the discretion in the system.

The dissents challenged Powell's interpretation of the studies and what they meant. Brennan invoked the notion that the death penalty was always cruel and unusual. In addition, he said the Baldus study proved exactly what the Court was hoping to avoid in *Furman* and *Gregg:* the use of unacceptable factors (e.g., race) to decide an individual's fate. Brennan emphasized that this case was unique because in the past, defendants had challenged the system on speculation, not on hard statistical evidence. In addition, in Georgia, this very type of system did exist at one time, so to suggest that remnants of that system had been wiped clean was ludicrous.

Blackmun, in a departure from his past decision, voted against the death penalty. Although he focused on Fourteenth-Amendment considerations of racial discrimination and equal protection, there was no question he had changed sides. So, although the death penalty opponents had a new supporter in Blackmun, who could not, in light of the Baldus study, see the penalty as fair any longer, the conservative wing of the Court was further entrenching the penalty.

Thus, the Supreme Court resolved that the death penalty was constitutional. Even apparent discrepancies, like those seen in *McCleskey,* without showing intentional discrimination, failed to undermine the idea. Lurking in the background were the ideas of "cruel and unusual" and evolving notions of decency, but as the modern Court strove to streamline the process, the death penalty battles focused more and more on limiting the possible pool of executable people. The Court strove to identify what crimes (rape, murder, treason) would call for the death penalty, and who (juveniles, the mentally challenged, etc.) could be executed.

For opponents, the tact appeared to be that if the available pool became so limited, it would be obvious that the death penalty was beyond the pale of acceptability to U.S. society and extended beyond what was decent, and therefore must be eliminated from the U.S. legal system.

But, on the contrary, as the pool continued to shrink, the support for the death penalty appeared to grow.

References

Acker, James R., Robert M. Bohm, and Charles S. Lanier. 1998. *America's Experiment with Capital Punishment: Reflections on the Past, Present, and Future of the Ultimate Penal Sanction.* Durham, NC: Carolina Academic Press.

Baird, Robert, and Stuart Rosenbaum, eds. 1995. *Punishment and the Death Penalty: The Current Debate.* Amherst, NY: Prometheus Books.

Baldus, David C., George C. Woodworth, and Charles A. Pulaski. 1990. *Equal Justice and the Death Penalty: A Legal and Empirical Analysis.* Boston: Northeastern University Press.

Banks, Jeffery M. 2003. "In Re Stanford: Do Evolving Standards of Decency under Eighth Amendment Jurisprudence Render Capital Punishment Inapposite for Juvenile Offenders?" *South Dakota Law Review* 48: 327.

Barsanti, Jason E. 2004. "NOTE: *Ring v. Arizona:* The Sixth and Eighth Amendments Collide: Out of the Wreckage Emerges a Constitutional Safeguard for Capital Defendants." *Pepperdine Law Review* 31: 519.

Bedau, Hugo Adams. 2004. *Killing as Punishment: Reflections on the Death Penalty in America.* Boston: Northeastern University Press.

———. 2004. *Debating the Death Penalty: Should America Have Capital Punishment: The Experts on Both Sides Make Their Best Cases.* New York: Oxford University Press.

Berger, Raoul. 1982. *Death Penalties: The Supreme Court's Obstacle Course.* Cambridge, MA: Harvard University Press.

Bilionis, Louis D. 2000. "The Unusualness of Capital Punishment." *Ohio Northern University Law Review* 26: 601.

Cochran, Jill M. 2004. "NOTE: Courting Death: 30 Years Since Furman, Is the Death Penalty Any Less Discriminatory? Looking at the Problem of Jury Discretion in Capital Sentencing." *Valparaiso University Law Review* (Summer) 38: 1399.

Foley, Michael A. 2003. *Arbitrary and Capricious: The Supreme Court, the Constitution and the Death Penalty.* Westport, CT: Praeger.

Forrester, Nathan A. 2003. "Two Views on the Impact of *Ring v. Arizona* on Capital Sentencing: Judge versus Jury: The Continuing Validity of Alabama's Capital Sentencing Regime after *Ring v. Arizona.*" *Alabama Law Review* 54 (Summer): 1157.

Graff, Bryan. 2003. "Executing Juvenile Offenders: A Reexamination of *Stanford v. Kentucky* in Light of *Atkins v. Virginia.*" *Georgia State University Law Review* 20 (Winter): 485.

Greenwald, Helene B. 1983. "COMMENT: Capital Punishment for Minors: An Eighth Amendment Analysis." *Journal of Criminal Law and Criminology* 74 (Winter): 1471.

Grossman, Mark, and Mike Dixon-Kennedy. 1998. *Encyclopedia of Capital Punishment.* Santa Barbara, CA: ABC-CLIO.

Hall, Timothy S. 2002. "Legal Fictions and Moral Reasoning: Capital Punishment and the Mentally Retarded Defendant after *Penry v. Johnson.*" *Akron Law Review* 35: 327.

Higginbotham, Patrick E. 1991. "Juries and the Death Penalty." *Case Western Reserve Law Review* 41: 1047.

King, Rachel. 1997. *Don't Kill in Our Names: Families of Murder Victims Speak out against the Death Penalty.* Lanham, MD: University Presses of America.

Latzer, Barry. 2002. *Death Penalty Cases, Second Edition.* Amsterdam: Butterworth-Heinemann.

Lifton, Robert J., and Greg Mitchell. 2000. *Who Owns Death? Capital Punishment, the American Conscience, and the End of the Death Penalty.* New York: Morrow.

Nelson, Lane, and Burk Foster. 2000. *Death Watch: A Death Penalty Anthology.* Upper Saddle River, NJ: Prentice Hall.

Nigel, Alan I. 1994. "Justices William J. Brennan and Thurgood Marshall on Capital Punishment: Its Constitutionality, Morality, Deterrent Effect, and Interpretation by the Court." *Notre Dame Journal of Law, Ethics, and Public Policy* 8: 11, 66.

Palmer, Louis J., Jr. 2001. *Encyclopedia of Capital Punishment in the United States.* Jefferson, NC: McFarland.

Patterson, Chaka M. 1995. "Race and the Death Penalty: The Tension between Individualized Justice and Racially Neutral Standards." *Texas Wesleyan Law Review* 2 (Summer): 45.

Radelet, Michael L. 1989. *Facing the Death Penalty: Essays on a Cruel and Unusual Punishment.* Philadelphia, PA: Temple University Press.

Robinson, Tracey E. 2004. "By Popular Demand?" *George Mason University Civil Rights Law Journal* 14 (Winter): 107.

Steffans, Bradley, et al. 2001. Furman v. Georgia: *Fairness and the Death Penalty.* San Diego, CA: Lucent Books.

Streib, Victor L. 2003. *Death Penalty in a Nutshell.* St. Paul, MN: Thomson/West.

Trail, Rebecca. 2002. "NOTE: The Future of Capital Punishment in the United States: Effects of the International Trend towards Abolition of the Death Penalty." *Suffolk Transnational Law Review* 26 (Winter): 105.

4
Impact and Legacy

Gauging *Gregg:* Who Can Die for What

McCleskey helped establish the parameters of the death penalty. In the post-*Gregg* world, it became more and more evident that the death penalty in some form was here to stay. As the twenty-first century moves on and images of 9/11, the World Trade Center, snipers on the highway, and the like permeate our society, it would seem there is no reason for society or the Court to retreat from this basic premise.

Immediately following *Gregg,* in two cases, the Court helped narrow the death penalty to only murder cases. After much argument, the Court developed the rationale that the death penalty, when used as a punishment for crimes not involving murder, was seen as cruel and unusual punishment because in such crimes it was excessive and disproportionate.

In *Coker v. Georgia* (1977), Georgia was faced with what to do with an individual who, while serving time in prison for a host of crimes, including rape, murder, and kidnapping, escaped. While on the lam, he committed a series of new crimes, including rape, and was, upon his capture and trial, sentenced to death.

The key to the majority opinion, written by Justice White, was that the Eighth Amendment did not bar the death penalty in all cases. Reiterating the ruling in *Gregg,* he noted the death penalty was not "inherently barbaric." Rather, the Eighth Amendment forbade punishments that were "excessive" or "barbaric." If the punishment was out of proportion in relation to the crime committed, it was beyond the bounds outlined by the Eighth Amendment. How did one define those terms? An excessive punishment was one that did not really punish the individual for the crime committed, but was one rooted in pain and suffering.

White emphasized it was important that the subjective attitudes of the justices not come into play and that the Court rely on objective factors. Those factors, which later would be molded into what the Court calls the "evolving standard of decency," focused on public attitudes as reflected in history, precedent, legislative attitudes, and the responses of juries to similar situations.

As is often the situation in death penalty cases, in trying to assess public attitudes, the Court played with the statistics, and the majority and dissent came to very different conclusions as a result. White said despite the fact that death as a penalty for rape was on the books in some jurisdictions, juries repeatedly failed to apply it. This reflected growing public disenchantment with this penalty for rape—growing legislative and jury reluctance. He saw the jury as an important indicator of contemporary values.

These two factors taken together convinced White and four of his brethren that capital punishment was an inappropriate penalty in modern-day America. White ended his opinion by arguing, if one considered that even where a killing was deliberate, minus aggravating circumstances, the defendant could not be executed, how could one accept the argument that a rapist (whether or not there were aggravating circumstances) could or should receive a more severe punishment, when death did not occur. Although the reasoning smacked of biblical "eye-for-an-eye" rationale, White argued that the threshold question for whether capital punishment should be allowed had to be: Did the defendant take a life? Under any other circumstances, imposition of the death penalty was excessive.

Chief Justice Burger's dissent ripped the majority for doing exactly what it said it would not do—being subjective. Burger lambasted the Court for not allowing the state legislatures to do the job they were elected to do and for imposing a new requirement on the death penalty—the taking of a life. Although he agreed that the Eighth Amendment barred disproportionate penalties, rape was as heinous a crime as there was—maybe even more so than murder. As such, how could one put it outside the boundaries of the death penalty? By taking the death penalty off the table for most crimes, the Court emasculated the state's ability, and its people's ability, to protect the citizens of the state.

Rather than focus on the particular case, the dissent looked at Coker's entire past as well as the current crime spree at issue. In *Coker v. Georgia* there was no question that the defendant was a reprehensible man. It was ridiculous to assume that the Eighth Amendment declared the death penalty to be excessive in the case of someone who, in three years, had raped three women, killed one, attempted to kill another, and broken out of prison so he could continue to wreak his havoc upon the public. If ever there was a person who warranted the death penalty, and, if ever death could be seen as a proportionate penalty, wasn't this the person and the case?

Burger noted that rape was "inherently one of the most egregious brutal acts one human being can inflict upon another." As such, it deserved the ultimate penalty, in certain cases. To not allow the state to deliver this penalty when it chose to do so distorted the federal system, replacing the state legislative process with the subjective opinions of the Court.

Finally, challenging White's final statement, Burger wanted to know why it was so important that the victim of a rape die in order for the death penalty to be applied. A crime where the victim lives on, scarred forever by the actions of the defendant, could often be far more horrible than a "simple" murder. In fact the aggravating circumstances that would make a murderer subject to the death penalty were all here. To suggest that one could do everything to a person but kill them, and still escape the death sentence, was to argue irrationally and turn the criminal justice system on its head.

Any question about whether Burger's final argument would carry any weight and the death penalty would end up being used in non-death cases, was laid to rest five years later in *Enmund v. Florida*. (The rare exception to this is at the federal level, which mandates the death penalty for crimes such as espionage and treason.) *Enmund* reiterated the basic premise of *Coker*. In the Florida case, Enmund sat in a car while his fellow criminals went into a farmhouse, robbed an elderly couple, and shot them to death. Because he waited outside and did not kill, attempt to kill, or have any intent to kill, he could not be sentenced to death. Such a penalty would have been disproportionate.

In the Florida case, the Court rejected the death penalty for people who were bystanders and did not actually kill, attempt to kill, or intend to kill. The U.S. Supreme Court overturned the Florida Supreme

Court, which ruled that because the evidence suggested that the defendant was in the car waiting to help his fellow robbers escape, that proved sufficient culpability. Under Florida law anyone who aided and abetted in a crime where a murder took place was guilty of first-degree murder. The 5 to 4 U.S. Supreme Court decision revealed the continuing deep divisions in the Court over the death penalty, pulling together many of the arguments that had highlighted previous cases, such as *Gregg, Woodson,* and *Coker.* Notably, only Justice Brennan, in a short concurrence, argued that the death penalty, per se, violated the Eighth Amendment.

The Process of Sentencing

In the wake of *Coker,* the argument in the post-*Gregg* era has become one of who dies and how they die. More and more, it is this latter issue, the process, that the Court focuses on. Death penalty opponents argue that whittling away at the process will reveal inequities (like they did in *Furman*), and the whole system will be thrown out. In contrast, advocates argue by honing the process and removing inequities, the system becomes better, more efficient, and thereby more entrenched in the judicial system.

The overriding principle the Court has used in determining death penalty cases after *Gregg* rests on two basic ideas. First is an evolving standard of decency. The oft-cited case here is *Trop.* The standards are determined by conceptions of modern society as reflected by objective evidence. The debate often focuses on how to interpret that evidence.

A second important argument, emphasized most often by Justice Scalia, when reviewing a death penalty case is "whether it constitutes one of those modes of punishment considered cruel and unusual at the time the Bill of Rights was adopted."

Although basically all members of the Court agree on the decency issue, in the end it is often the analysis of the issue—the manipulation of statistics, history, and so on—that results in a strongly divided Court.

One of the major strands of analysis following *Gregg* focused on what were aggravating and mitigating circumstances and how to properly include them in the decision about whether to execute. How the sentencer viewed the elements—in the case of a jury decision—and how the judge instructed the jury concerning such circumstances was pivotal.

The Court began to grapple with the two important parameters almost simultaneously. *Lockett v. Ohio* (1978) dealt with previous issues of juror exclusion and, more importantly, focused on the issues of aggravating and mitigating circumstances. In *Lockett,* a sharply divided Court tried to resolve thorny issues, only to apparently raise new ones in their attempts to solve the old ones. The Court upheld the basic nature of the death penalty but declared its application unconstitutional in this case.

In Ohio, the death penalty statute provided for a conviction of aggravated murder if at least one of seven aggravating circumstances was determined to have existed. However, the aggravating factors could be negated if the judge delivering the sentence determined one of a variety of mitigating circumstances existed. Generally, mitigating circumstances included psychological factors such as mental defect or incredible duress on the part of the defendant, or situations where the death had been the result of victim's instigation. In this case, there was no question the defendant met the aggravating circumstances requirement. However, at no point had the judge seriously considered mitigating circumstances so that the possibility of a non–death penalty could be considered.

Once again a variety of opinions came forth from the Court. Chief Justice Burger wrote the plurality opinion and was joined by three others. In addition to dismissing some procedural issues, he focused on the fact that the judge failed to consider mitigating factors. This was not acceptable. The sentencer, in this case, the judge, had to consider such evidence. His failure to do so meant the imposition of the death penalty in this case was unconstitutional. Burger reiterated the point raised in earlier cases that it was important, especially in death penalty cases, to treat each defendant as an individual. This could not be done unless mitigating factors (as well as aggravating) were considered, because these were the very issues that made a person an individual—their background, their family, and so on.

Although joining in the judgment, the concurrences objected to Burger's rationale for overruling the death penalty in this case. Justice Marshall, as always, objected to the death penalty per se. However, this argument seemed to have less force on the Court by this time. And although Justice Blackmun would eventually swing into this camp, the pro–death penalty attitude was becoming more entrenched in a majority of the Court. Although Blackmun only objected because the defendant had not actually pulled the trigger that committed the murder, he was not yet an anti–death penalty advocate. However, the seeds of his discontent could be seen as he questioned core elements of the process by which people were executed. Justice White picked this up and questioned how one could be sentenced to death without the requisite intent to commit the crime.

Lockett raised serious issues, and the scene of death penalty litigation returned to its old stomping grounds of Georgia two years later to try to hash out some of these issues. At issue in *Godfrey v. Georgia* (1980) was what constituted an aggravating circumstance. Noting the necessity to tailor the death penalty to the individual in *Lockett,* the Court was faced with a Georgia statute that noted execution of an individual was proper if the crime committed was "outrageously or wantonly vile, horrible or inhuman in that it involved torture, depravity of mind, or an aggravated battery to the victim." In this case, the defendant blamed his mother-in-law for his marital problems. He felt it was her fault his wife refused to reconsider their marriage and try to patch up their problems. He went to the trailer where family members, including his daughter, were staying. He shot his wife in the head with a shotgun. Death was instantaneous. He then entered the trailer, where he beat his daughter with the gun. Following this, he shot his mother-in-law, also killing her instantly. After finishing these acts, he called the sheriff's office and told them to come out there because he had just committed a "hideous crime."

The death penalty was overturned because the parameters were too broad and vague. Quoting both *Furman* and *Gregg,* Justice Stewart's opinion emphasized the need to establish a procedure that was both individualized and not arbitrary or capricious. The broad language used in the Georgia statute failed to meet any of those requirements. The problem here was that the core of the state's argument was that the actions taken by Godfrey were "outrageous and wantonly vile, horrible and inhuman." As Stewart pointed out, almost any murder fits that category. This would demand the execution of just about any person who commits murder. But an important strand of death penalty jurisprudence for a majority of the Court is that not all murders warrant the death penalty. The Georgia statute gave no guidelines and established no rules that individualized the application of the death penalty. In essence, the Court argued these murders were no more or less heinous than a "normal" murder, and therefore the imposition of the death penalty was arbitrary and capricious. As noted before, the jury had to have guidance when it was asked to determine if the death penalty was applicable.

Justices Marshall and Brennan noted this was the very problem with the death penalty. The objectivity and impartiality that had been contemplated in *Gregg* was impossible. Adding on to that, the effects of discrimination and poverty, it was impossible to evenly and fairly apply the death penalty.

Chief Justice Burger's dissent argued that nothing else could deserve the penalty more than this situation. In this case, the defendant himself acknowledged the horrendous nature of the crime when he called the police. In fact, he used words reminiscent of the Georgia statute. Burger emphasized it was not the function of the Court to second-guess a jury's judgment that this hideous intentional crime was not hideous enough. To do so would be to upend the jury system and deny the jury from making the very type of individualized decision it had made in this case.

Justices White and Rehnquist joined the chief justice in a separate dissent and emphasized this point. Who were they, the Court, to say that this was not a horrible enough crime to warrant execution? In addition to the defendant's own admission, the way he performed the crime, with a weapon meant to disfigure, taking time to reload, the clubbing of his daughter in the head, suggested something fairly "vile" or "inhuman." If this was not vile or inhuman—what was? The dissent accused the majority of covertly resurrecting arguments laid to rest in *Gregg*, that the government was not competent to administer the death penalty. The Court had stepped beyond its authority and intruded upon Georgia's ability to fairly execute someone who had committed horrible acts. For Rehnquist an underlying issue was also apparent here, notably questions of federalism and the Supreme Court not stepping on the toes of states in making legitimate policy decisions about their criminal justice system.

When or how then could one be executed? What constituted a horrible enough crime to warrant execution, and what circumstances, no matter how horrible the murder, could remove an individual from the death sentence?

Two years later, the Court faced this issue over mitigating circumstances, mixing in the question of executing juveniles. In *Eddings v. Oklahoma* (1982), in sentencing a sixteen-year-old to death, the trial court failed to consider mitigating circumstances, and thus the death penalty had to be overturned. In this case, Oklahoma proved its aggravating circumstances.

Eddings was sixteen years old when he ran away from home with several friends. They left in his brother's car, driving aimlessly, until they reached the Oklahoma turnpike. In the car were a shotgun and several rifles. At one point Eddings lost control of the car and was pulled over by a member of the Oklahoma Highway Patrol. When the officer walked up to the car, Eddings killed him with the shotgun.

Eddings presented as mitigating evidence that he was only sixteen when he committed the crime and that he suffered from an unhappy childhood and deep emotional disturbance. Included in information about his childhood were the facts that his parents had been divorced when he was four and his mother was an alcoholic and a prostitute. His father, who he lived with when his mother could no longer control him, could not keep him in line, even by using physical punishment.

The judge determined that although the aggravating circumstances had been proved, because Eddings did not prove the mitigating circumstances (his unhappy upbringing, emotional disturbance, etc.) the judge had no way to consider it and sentenced the defendant to death.

The key here for the majority was that by failing to consider some of the evidence, the judge failed to give the case the individualized attention mandated in prior cases. The Court relied directly on *Lockett* and emphasized that mitigating circumstances had to be considered and could not, as a matter of law, as had been done in this case, be excluded.

Pennsylvania assumed center stage next in *Blystone v. Pennsylvania* (1990), when its system of aggravating and mitigating circumstances was challenged. Abiding by the rules noted previously, Pennsylvania demanded a jury look at both aggravating and mitigating circumstances. However, if aggravating circumstances were found and no mitigating circumstances were shown, the mandatory imposition of the death penalty was deemed constitutional.

Pennsylvania's statute passed muster. At first glance it appeared to be a mandatory scheme, like the one previously rejected in *Woodson*. Instead, it went through a fairly exhausting checklist, which created a framework where, if certain individuals were found to have acted under certain circumstances and there was no evidence to suggest the mitigation of those circumstances, the defendant could be executed. The arbitrary and capricious elements shunned by the Court in previous cases were avoided. Both aggravating and mitigating circumstances were considered, and unanimity by the jury about an aggravating circumstance with no mitigating evidence was required. In addition, while specific aggravating circumstances were defined, unlimited mitigating evidence was available. Thus, the death penalty was imposed not just for the conviction of a certain type of murder, but only after all the evidence had been weighed. In this case, the aggravating evidence outweighed the mitigating material.

A strong majority opinion, written by then Chief Justice Rehnquist, reflecting the changing tenor of the Court, emphasized this statute carried the very individualized type of analysis the Court had previously called for.

Blystone had murdered a hitchhiker he picked up. Before he picked up the victim, who suffered from a learning disability, Blystone told his traveling companions he was going to pick up the hitchhiker and rob him. After robbing him of $13.00 and commenting on how scared the victim was, Blystone told his fellow passengers he was going to kill the hitchhiker. He laid the victim on the ground and fired six bullets into the back of his head, later bragging about the crime.

Blystone was convicted of a host of crimes, and the aggravating circumstance in this case, found by the jury, was that he committed the murder while committing a felony. No mitigating circumstances were found, and Blystone was sentenced to death.

Rehnquist noted this was not a mandatory death penalty that left no discretion to the jury and no consideration for the individual in question. Rather, in this case, guidance was given to the jury. It was directed to review all the evidence, not just the specific list of aggravating circumstances, but also any evidence that might be considered mitigating. In contrast to *Woodson*, the jury here could consider all aspects of the character and record of the defendant and specific circumstances of the crime. Thus, this was not an automatic death penalty, but rather an exploration of the complexity of the crime and individual, and only after jumping through a variety of hoops, could the jury impose the death penalty.

Blystone saw shifts in the Court. Justice O'Connor, who had previously voted against the imposition of the death penalty on procedural grounds, now seemed to be firmly in the pro-camp. Justices Blackmun and Stevens, while voting against the death penalty, refused to accept the absolute approach against the death penalty invoked by Marshall and Brennan. However, Blackmun's delicate balance of striking down death penalty statutes, but not ruling against the death penalty per se, was becoming more precarious. And, although he would soon shift to the anti–death penalty camp, it would be too little too late for anti–death penalty advocates, and as the Court shifted in its makeup, capital punishment became more firmly entrenched.

Eight years after *Blystone,* the emphasis placed on balancing mitigating circumstances equally against aggravating factors diminished. With Marshall, Brennan, and Blackmun all gone from the Court, a six-person majority emphasized the acceptability of the death penalty and the discretion given to the states in its imposition.

The Court reinforced this idea in a Virginia case, *Buchanan v. Angelone* (1998). Virginia's system did not mandate the judge to specifically instruct the jury about mitigating circumstances. Instead, a general instruction telling the jury to consider all the evidence at hand in deciding to impose the death penalty was fine. In *Buchanan,* the defense asked for an instruction to the jury that it explicitly consider the four issues raised as mitigating factors, rather than just the general statement. If the jury did not believe the mitigating evidence warranted it, the death penalty was not applicable.

In Virginia, one of the key aggravating circumstances the prosecution had to prove beyond a reasonable doubt was that the crime was "vile." The jury decided if this condition had been met and could— but did not have to—sentence the defendant to death. In this case, the jury specifically noted on its verdict form that it found the murder vile and it had weighed the mitigating evidence.

The dissent objected, claiming that the instructions to the jury misled the jury and pushed them toward a death sentence because of the failure to emphasize mitigating factors. Although the jury said they had considered mitigating factors, the dissent claimed they had not considered it in a balanced manner.

Chief Justice Rehnquist's majority opinion signaled a Court far more inclined to give the jury discretion and leeway in imposing the death penalty. Noting the jury form, the Court said it needed to respect the jury and could not second-guess its intentions or the fact that it said it had considered the evidence.

Who Can Die

It is the issue of what constitutes a mitigating circumstance that has seemed to envelope the Court in recent years. The two most notable examples of this are cases involving the mentally handicapped and juveniles. If one considers that modern death penalty jurisprudence emphasizes the individuality of the sentence and modern community standards, the drawing of a firm line for either of these groups of people seems contrary to the first standard yet in line with the second.

The Court has struggled with both groups of people. As often is the case with death penalty litigation, it is not the extreme case that causes the problem, but the borderline one. Thus, the individual who slaughters numerous innocents for no reason other than his own demented pleasure (the Ted Bundys of the world) with no mitigating circumstances does not cause as big a problem. Rather it is the individual who killed, but it is questionable as to why he or she did it, that tends to raise the debate. Thus, in cases involving the mentally challenged, when the individual is so seriously handicapped that he or she does not fit the class of people society wishes to execute, the decision is easy. It is drawing the line that defines what constitutes mentally challenged and thus absolving such a person of a crime and exempting him or her from capital punishment that becomes difficult. This same struggle appears in considering the execution of juveniles—when is an individual old enough, smart enough, cognizant enough, to deserve to be executed?

The debate over this issue for the most part is the debate over who should be executed. In other words, what segments of society, despite the fact that they have committed certain crimes, should be exempt from the death penalty because of their status? As the arguments have moved to the Supreme Court, justices on the bench sympathetic to the anti–death penalty argument grow fewer at the same time the society interest in execution becomes more polarized.

Leading up to the case of *Atkins v. Virginia* (2002), which declared it was unconstitutional to execute the mentally handicapped, the Court had ruled that it was proper to execute the mentally retarded. Such acts could not be seen as cruel and unusual punishment. In *Penry v. Lynaugh* (1989) the Court said mental retardation was an important mitigating factor that should be considered during sentencing.

Penry brutally raped, beat, and stabbed his victim with a pair of scissors in her home. Although she died a few hours later, Penry was arrested on the strength of her description. He was picked up while on parole for a previous rape. After being picked up he confessed to the crime, twice, and was charged with capital murder.

At his competency hearing, a clinical psychologist testified that Penry was mentally retarded because of organic brain damage, which was probably caused by a trauma to the brain at birth. He was determined to have an IQ between 50 and 63, which indicates mild to moderate retardation. Tests prior to the trial showed an IQ of 54 and the mental age of six and a half (although he was actually twenty-two). The psychologist testified, "there's a point at which anyone with [Penry's] IQ is always incompetent, but, you know, this man is more in the borderline range."

Justice O'Connor, focusing on an important strand of reasoning the Court used in deciding death penalty cases, noted there was no national consensus against executing defendants who were classified as mentally retarded. In 1989, at the time of *Penry*, only two states (Maryland and Georgia) specifically prohibited such executions. However, by the time the Court heard *Atkins* in 2002, sixteen more states had enacted legislation that made it illegal to execute the mentally handicapped.

In addition, in her *Penry* decision, O'Connor noted an oft-cited argument by Justice Scalia that the Eighth Amendment applied only to practices condemned at the time of the ratification of the Bill of Rights. She did recognize the common law prohibited punishment of "idiots." Because of the modern insanity defense, however, it was not likely these people (individuals who lacked all sense of reason and ability to distinguish between good and evil) would be executed. In this case the defendant did not fall into that class since he was competent to stand trial and the jury had rejected his insanity defense. Thus, unlike those classified as "idiots" at common law, to categorically announce that all those with mental retardation were exempt from execution was unacceptable. It was up to the jury to decide on an individual basis the culpability of the individual.

Rejecting the decision in *Penry*, a six-person majority ruled in *Atkins* that the execution of the mentally retarded constituted excessive punishment as prohibited by the Eighth Amendment.

Daryl Atkins was convicted of abduction, armed robbery, and capital murder, and was sentenced to death. Atkins and his companion abducted a man and drove him to an automated teller machine. They then drove off and shot him eight times, killing him.

At trial, both Atkins and his companion, William Jones, testified the other had done the shooting. The jury believed Jones, a more credible witness, and not Atkins, and Atkins was convicted of capital murder.

At the penalty phase, to get the death penalty, the state introduced victim impact evidence and proved two of the necessary aggravating circumstances. To prove the first aggravating circumstance—future dangerousness—Atkins's prior felony convictions and the testimony of four victims of earlier robberies and assaults were introduced. The prosecutor proved the second aggravating circumstance, "vileness of the offense," by the use of elements in the trial record, including pictures of the deceased's body and the autopsy report.

The defense relied on one witness, a forensic psychologist, to present mitigating evidence. The doctor had evaluated Atkins before trial and concluded that he was "mildly mentally retarded." He based his conclusion on the fact that Atkins, after taking a standard intelligence test, registered an IQ of 59. The doctor had also interviewed acquaintances of Atkins and reviewed school and court records.

The majority, authored by Justice Stevens, argued things had changed since *Penry*. First, there now was a national consensus that had developed against executing the mentally retarded. This was supported by religious and professional groups both in the United States and around the world. Second, considering the purposes of the death penalty—retribution and deterrence—those ends were not served by executing mentally retarded people. Third, people who were mentally retarded, because of the very nature of that handicap, could not be held accountable. Finally, it was more likely for a wrongful execution to occur in cases involving mentally handicapped people, because of their inability to present mitigating circumstances. In essence, the Court ruled mental retardation was a mitigating circumstance that negated any aggravating circumstance. Although it did not absolve the mentally challenged of their responsibility in committing the crime, it took the death penalty off the table. In the end "the evolving standards of decency" made the execution of the mentally retarded excessive and unconstitutional.

Obviously, the dissent reacted strongly. Justice Scalia and Chief Justice Rehnquist, both joined by Justice Thomas, wrote strongly worded dissents challenging the majority opinion.

Rehnquist objected to the Court's emphasis on foreign laws and other opinions. Only state legislatures and jury determinations should be focused on to determine contemporary standards. In addition, it was not the Court's place to second-guess statistical studies and empirical evidence submitted to the Court. This was a long-abandoned practice that raised the specter of judicial interference reminiscent of the early twentieth century and much condemned since then.

Justice Scalia went further in disparaging the majority. He questioned differentiating between the death penalty and other forms of punishment. Punishment was punishment, and making a distinction such as the Court had made moved it beyond the bounds of the text and history of the Constitution.

In this case, Scalia noted the jury had considered Atkins's retardation (he was classified as mildly mentally retarded with an IQ of 59) along with the testimony of a psychologist. After considering this mitigating evidence (and contrary evidence from the state's psychologist that challenged the previous psychologist's findings), the jury sentenced the defendant to death. In any case, the issue of the defendant's mental abilities was central to the case. As Scalia noted, however, his mental retardation was not enough to exempt him from the death penalty in light of both the brutality of this specific crime and his long history of violent criminal behavior.

Scalia argued Eighth Amendment jurisprudence and the question of cruel and unusual revolved around two issues. First and foremost, reiterating an important theme for him in death penalty litigation, something could not be considered cruel and unusual punishment if it was not considered such at the time of the adoption of the Eighth Amendment. Second, when considering any punishment, does that punishment in question violate "modern standards of decency"?

For Scalia, the majority did not even suggest in any way that the Eighth Amendment forbade the execution of the mildly mentally retarded in 1791. Only those classified as "idiots" received special exemption. Therefore, the only avenue open to the Court was to argue that execution of this class of people now fall outside the "evolving standards of decency that mark the progress of a maturing society." This was the language used in *Trop,* and the language the Court focused on in both the majority and the dissent.

In focusing on this latter phrase, Scalia said the majority missed an important reason for the death penalty, its social purpose. Capital punishment removed from society dangerous people and prevented them from ever committing such a crime again. To rule that mental retardation, per se, removed an individual's culpability was ridiculous. Only the sentencer could determine whether or not the mental handicap in question served as a mitigating factor in determining whether the defendant was culpable enough, just as other mitigating factors helped the jury (or judge) decide.

Despite the vociferous dissents, anti–death penalty advocates took heart, and simultaneously to the challenges of executing the mentally challenged, advocates were challenging state statutes that mandated the execution of juveniles. Should individuals convicted of committing a crime prior to their eighteenth birthday be subjected to execution for their crime?

As much as any aspect of death penalty litigation, this issue separates society. The juvenile becomes the perfect foil for all the arguments for and against the death penalty. Supporters focus on the crime itself. Its heinousness is not diminished by the age of the offender. If the purpose of the death penalty is retribution and the removal of certain people from society, why should whether they were eighteen, seventeen, sixteen, or whatever matter? On the other hand, opponents focus on the individual. If ever there was an example of a circumstance where an individual could change, it would be with one so young as to not really understand the consequences of his act.

The Court did not really look at the issue of juveniles until the early 1980s. As with cases dealing with the mentally handicapped, in *Eddings* (noted above) the issue of the defendant's age became one more mitigating factor in deciding whether to execute, and the Court did not consider whether the execution of criminals who had committed a crime prior to their eighteenth birthday was cruel and unusual.

Although on occasion the Court would hint at the issue, it refused to face the matter head-on. In *Burger v. Kemp* (1987), although a case decided on the basis of the Sixth Amendment right to counsel, Justice Powell's dissent raised the issue of the propriety of executing a seventeen-year-old. *Thompson v. Oklahoma* (1988) moved one step closer, as four justices ruled that because the defendant was only fifteen years old at the time of his crime, it would be cruel and unusual to execute him. However, Justice O'Connor's concurrence on narrow grounds failed to give the extra vote needed to declare such a process unconstitutional.

In *Thompson*, a fifteen-year-old, together with three adults, participated in the brutal murder of his brother-in-law. They shot him twice and then cut his throat, chest, and abdomen. The four murderers inflicted multiple bruises and a broken leg. After they were done, they chained the body to a concrete block and threw it into the river.

All four defendants were tried independently, each was found guilty, and each was sentenced to death. Thompson did not claim the punishment would have been excessive if he had been an adult; rather that because he was a minor at the time of the crime, he was exempt from the death penalty. At trial, it was established Thompson was competent and that there was not reasonable prospect of rehabilitation. During the penalty phase, the prosecutor pushed for two aggravating circumstances. The jury found the first factor—that the crime was heinous, atrocious, or cruel—to exist. However, the second consideration—future danger—was not recognized. The jury failed to concede that Thompson would continue to commit crimes that could be seen as a "continuing threat to society."

Justice Stevens's plurality opinion in *Thompson* took a similar tact to the argument that would eventually win in *Atkins.* In establishing evolving standards of decency, he looked at current legislation, the willingness of juries to impose the death penalty on juveniles even where it was acceptable, and the views of other organizations, both domestic and foreign, regarding juveniles and the death penalty. Looking at these things he said there has always been different ways of drawing the line between child and adult, but there was near unanimity (a point contested by the dissent) that states should treat children under sixteen as minors.

Stevens observed the Court was the ultimate arbiter of what cruel and unusual punishment meant and what its limits were in modern society. Those limits were created by who was executed and why they were executed. He looked at juveniles and issues of their culpability. What purpose was served by executing them? Were the social purposes emphasized in other cases served by killing them? Stevens emphasized juveniles had a long life ahead of them, and therefore there was hope. In addition, especially in the case of a fifteen-year-old, there was less culpability. Because, fifteen-year-olds do not (cannot?) act in a way that shows they understand the implications and consequences of their actions, deterrence could not be seen as a reason to execute.

In his dissent, Scalia first reexamined the facts of the case. As bloody as the description of the crime was, he went into far more detail to highlight the atrocious qualities of the case. When he moved on to the law, he emphasized the Eighth Amendment at the time of its adoption did not prohibit the execution of people who committed those kinds of actions. He also found no clear indication from the states that evolving notions of decency suggested it was against public policy to execute juveniles. He maintained it was nice that juries often refused to impose such a harsh penalty on young defendants, but that in itself did not suggest a new constitutional standard. He would not have had a problem with a rebuttable standard that fifteen-year-olds (or any age for that matter) could not be executed. But to enshrine it as an absolute into constitutional law was to play games with the document and create new doctrine.

The next year, the Court again tried to resolve the problem of juveniles, but in this case, *Stanford v. Kentucky,* at issue were a sixteen- and a seventeen-year-old youth. That one year made a crucial difference.

Thompson had held out hope that a new line might be drawn by limiting the execution of juveniles. *Stanford* seemed to shatter those hopes, upholding the death sentences for two juveniles. Scalia, long in the minority, got a chance to infuse his jurisprudence in a majority decision.

In *Stanford* (two cases—one involving a seventeen-year-old, and one involving a sixteen-year-old), as in most death penalty cases, the crimes committed were brutal. In the Kentucky case, Stanford (and his accomplice) had repeatedly raped and sodomized the victim during a robbery of the gas station where she worked. They then took her to a secluded area and he shot her in the face. They did all this for 300 cartons of cigarettes, a couple of gallons of gas, and some cash. In the second case, *Wilkins v. Missouri,* Wilkins in preparing for a robbery, planned on robbing and killing whoever was there, so he could not be identified. After robbing the store, he stabbed the mother of two repeatedly, even as she begged for her life. His haul consisted of some liquor, cigarettes, rolling papers, and $450.

In both cases, the juveniles were found competent to stand trial and were sentenced to death.

Both argued that to sentence juveniles under the age of eighteen to death was cruel and unusual punishment. Scalia repeated the same arguments he had used in *Thompson* and emphasized the common law notion of a rebuttable presumption of any criminal at the age of fourteen. However, these defendants were far closer to eighteen than fourteen, and to draw a hard-and-fast line was ludicrous. Why be rigid, he asked? Instead, allow for some flexibility and individuality in the decisionmaking process, which the Court traditionally emphasized, and allow for a presumption that could be overturned by the prosecution and subsequently defended by the defense. It was ridiculous to draw a hard-and-fast line, and cases should be decided on an individual basis.

Scalia highlighted the fact that a majority of states permitted capital punishment for people over the age of sixteen, and the federal law also allowed for sixteen- and seventeen-year-olds to be sentenced to death. He rejected the defendants' arguments that despite these legislative actions, the reluctance of juries to impose and prosecutors to seek the death penalty for juveniles proved that capital punishment for juveniles was inappropriate.

Scalia reiterated on the strands of thought that permeated his previous dissents. One, was the particular punishment considered cruel and unusual at the time the Bill of Rights was adopted? Two, was the punishment in question "contrary to the evolving standards of decency"? Scalia, as always, focused on the idea of punishment generally, rather than the specific penalty of death. He said it was important to make sure the decision reflected modern U.S. society through objective evidence.

In part of his decision, signed only by three other justices, Scalia noted that the allusion to other laws that set a line between adults and minors had no relevance. The fact that one must be eighteen to vote, drive, or drink (at that time) did not matter. He ridiculed the idea that the same maturity needed to drink, drive, or vote was needed to understand the essential wrongness of murder. If there had been one thing all seemed to agree upon in prior death penalty cases, it was that the system needed to be individualized; it needed to cater to each defendant's own particulars. To draw an absolute line, as suggested here, would destroy that idea.

Finally, executing these defendants would serve the very purposes the death penalty was meant to serve. There is no way to prove that executing juveniles such as these did not serve any deterrent effect or any of the other legitimate goals established for using the death penalty.

In the end, Scalia focused on historical notions and the need to anchor decisions in constitutional law and history. He accused the dissent and those who would use the Eighth Amendment to strike down capital punishment as having "cast loose from the historical moorings" of the Bill of Rights.

O'Connor, who had voted to suspend the execution in *Thompson*, now voted in the majority to sustain the death penalty. Using the same argument as before, because she saw no national consensus objecting to the execution of such people, she could not strike it down.

The dissent of Justices Brennan, Marshall, Blackmun, and Stevens stated categorically that to execute someone under the age of eighteen was cruel and unusual punishment and violated the Eighth Amendment. The dissent rehashed much of the same evidence the majority did, and as is evident in many death penalty cases, the decisions argued over what the statistics really meant and whether or not a national consensus had been established. Although Scalia blasted the dissent for playing the role of philosopher-kings, holding themselves above the legislature and Constitution, Brennan argued they were merely doing what they were supposed to do.

If they followed Scalia's reasoning and left the decision to legislatures and political majorities, the Court would be abdicating its responsibility. The purpose of the Bill of Rights, and hence the Court, was to protect the minority and remove certain subjects from "vicissitudes of political controversy." Their job was to place limitations on the vagaries of the political system.

Finally, age eighteen was a necessary line. Although it was an arbitrary line, it was at best a cautious guess at the line dividing maturity from adolescence. He argued that the Eighth Amendment could not support the execution of someone who lacked the full degree of responsibility. To all of a sudden reject all the assumptions made about juveniles on a daily basis, when the most horrific results would occur, was fallacious reasoning. It was turning the law topsy-turvy. If one was seeking executions to carry out certain social policies, in the case of the death penalty, retribution, and deterrence, the execution of juveniles fails to serve that purpose.

The question of juveniles was not laid to rest with *Stanford*. In light of *Atkins, Stanford* appealed again to the United States Supreme Court, which subsequently rejected the appeal. In a rare dissent from a petition for certiorari, Justice Stevens, joined by Justices Souter, Ginsburg, and Breyer, reiterated the rationale of Justice Brennan over a decade earlier. Combined with the rationale of *Atkins,* they felt it was time to rehear the argument over executing juveniles. Within two years a majority of the Court agreed and readied themselves to again look at the execution of juveniles.

Conclusion

As one looks at the cases that dot the docket in the beginning of the twenty-first century, a couple of things appear to be clear. First, the Court would seem to be entrenching the death penalty as it reasserts the constitutionality of the penalty, as it limits appeals, helps streamline the process, and at times gives the prosecutors more leeway in pursuing capital punishment.

This does not mean appeals have been cut off. A good example is an Alabama case in which the Supreme Court agreed that an Alabama death row inmate could make a last-minute appeal. Three days before his execution, David Nelson filed a civil rights lawsuit, claiming that to execute him via lethal injection would be cruel and unusual punishment because after years of drug use, his veins were so damaged. After a lower court and appeals court both rejected the claim, the Supreme Court agreed to hear the case. However, the Court took the case on narrow grounds, for the specific procedure being used, and not the death penalty per se, or even lethal injection generally.

In another case from the 1990s, *Hererra v. Collins* (1993) limited use of the federal writ of habeas corpus and declared that innocence of the crime committed was not an adequate reason to stop an execution if the defendant received a trial that did not violate the Constitution. The Court denied Hererra's petition for writ of habeas corpus, because although he had supporting evidence, which he suggested proved his innocence, a writ of habeas corpus could be granted only when individuals were imprisoned due to constitutional violations not to correct errors of fact. Chief Justice Rehnquist noted Hererra could file for clemency under Texas law, which specifically provided that pardons be granted in circumstances such as this. He saw this as a far better and more efficient mechanism than the path Hererra pursued.

Second, the Court is showing it is not static, both in its view of "evolving standards of decency" and in its desire to regularly review the death penalty. In a world that has changed radically, both in the courtroom and outside, the Court has again agreed to take up the issue of the execution of juveniles. In the first few years of the millennium, the Court has appeared to be very happy to take death penalty cases, in what would appear to be an effort to clarify and solidify the use of capital punishment. *Atkins* restricted the use of capital punishment to certain peoples, but by no means qualified it as a punishment. *Ring v. Arizona* modified the procedure to make sure that those who were executed were treated fairly. *Ring* would seem to suggest that the Court is more inclined to place the decision more firmly in the hands of a jury, rather than a judge, to better reflect society at large. In addition, it helps put the penalty phase of the trial more in line with the criminal justice system as a whole, something Justice Scalia and his wing of the Court have repeatedly emphasized.

If the Court continues to rely on "evolving standards of decency," it will create an interesting conflict with Scalia's emphasis on what was acceptable at the time of the adoption of the Eighth Amendment. What can be seen as a slim majority of jurisdictions rejecting the death penalty does not equate with a national consensus. In addition, as the war on terrorism grows and federal (as well as state) policing powers expand, the idea that the United States will turn its back on the death penalty seems remote.

Part Two

5

Documents

O'Neil v. Vermont (1892)

A noncapital, late-nineteenth century case that gave one of the rare discussions by the U.S. Supreme Court on the meaning of "cruel and unusual." It is included here because many of the late-twentieth-century cases referred in part to this case in trying to discern the exact meaning of the phrase. The majority decision did not look at the Eighth Amendment question; the dissent is included because it directly tackled what "cruel and unusual" means.

MR. JUSTICE FIELD dissenting.

The punishment imposed was one exceeding in severity, considering the offences of which the defendant was convicted, anything which I have been able to find in the records of our courts for the present century . . .[T]he defendant was . . .convicted of four hundred and fifty-seven distinct offences, and sentenced to pay . . .a fine . . .and be confined at hard labor . . .for one month, and, in case the fine and costs should not be paid on or before the expiration of this month's imprisonment, to be confined there at hard labor for the further term of twenty-eight thousand eight hundred and thirty-six days . . .This was more than seventy-nine years for selling, furnishing and giving away, as alleged, intoxicating liquor . . .

Had he been found guilty of burglary or highway robbery, he would have received less punishment than for the offences of which he was convicted. It was six times as great as any court in Vermont could have imposed for manslaughter, forgery or perjury. It was one which, in its severity, considering the offences of which he was convicted, may justly be termed both unusual and cruel. That designation, it is true, is usually applied to punishments which inflict torture, such as the rack, the thumbscrew, the iron boot, the stretching of limbs and the like, which are attended with acute pain and suffering . . .

. . .The inhibition is directed, not only against punishments of the character mentioned, but against all punishments which by their excessive length or severity are greatly disproportioned to the offences charged. The whole inhibition is against that which is excessive either in the bail required, or fine imposed, or punishment inflicted . . .

Fifty-four years' confinement at hard labor, away from one's home and relatives, and thereby prevented from giving assistance to them or receiving comfort from them, is a punishment at the severity of which, considering the offences, it is hard to believe that any man of right feeling and heart can refrain from shuddering . . .The State has the power to inflict personal chastisement, by directing whipping for petty offences—repulsive as such mode of punishment is—and should it, for each offence, inflict twenty stripes it might not be considered, as applied to a single offence, a severe punishment, but yet, if there had been three hundred and seven offences committed, the number of which the defendant was convicted in this case, and six thousand one hundred and forty stripes were to be inflicted for these accumulated offences, the judgment of mankind would be that the punishment was not only an unusual but a cruel one, and a cry of horror would rise from every civilized and Christian community of the country against it.

Weems v. United States (1910)

This was one of the first cases to test the limits and parameters of the Eighth Amendment. Although the court case took place in the Philippines, under the Philippine penal code, the U.S. Supreme Court tried to interpret what "cruel and unusual" meant under the U.S. Constitution. It pronounced in fairly broad terms that the Eighth Amendment may change as public opinion becomes "enlightened by humane justice." The dissent laid the groundwork for challenges to the death penalty in the latter half of the twentieth century.

MR. JUSTICE McKENNA delivered the opinion of the court.
. . .These provisions are attacked as infringing that provision of the bill of rights of the islands which forbids the infliction of cruel and un-

usual punishment. . . .The minimum term of imprisonment is twelve years, and that, therefore, must be imposed for 'perverting the truth' in a single item of a public record, though there be no one injured, though there be no fraud or purpose of it, no gain or desire of it. Twenty years is the maximum imprisonment . . .Its minimum degree is confinement in a penal institution for twelve years and one day, a chain at the ankle and wrist of the offender, hard and painful labor, no assistance from friend or relative, no marital authority or parental rights or rights of property, no participation even in the family council. These parts of his penalty endure for the term of imprisonment . . .

What constitutes a cruel and unusual punishment has not been exactly decided. It has been said that ordinarily the terms imply something inhuman and barbarous, torture and the like. The court, however, . . .conceded the possibility 'that imprisonment in the State prison for a long term of years might be so disproportionate to the offense as to constitute a cruel and unusual punishment.' Other cases have selected certain tyrannical acts of the English monarchs as illustrating the meaning of the clause and the extent of its prohibition.

The [Eighth Amendment] received very little debate in Congress . . .

'Punishments are cruel when they involve torture or a lingering death; but the punishment of death is not cruel, within the meaning of that word as used in the Constitution. It implies there something inhuman and barbarous, and something more than the mere extinguishment of life' . . .

[The Court proceeded to review some discussions of "cruel and unusual" punishment, including state court decisions, and commentaries by Justices Cooley and Story, among others.]

. . .[E]ven if the minimum penalty . . .had been imposed, it would have been repugnant to the bill of rights. In other words, the fault is in the law, and, as we are pointed to no other under which a sentence can be imposed, the judgment must be reversed, with directions to dismiss the proceedings.

So ordered.

MR. JUSTICE WHITE, dissenting.

. . .Turning aside, therefore, from mere emotional tendencies and guiding my judgment alone by the aid of the reason at my command, I am unable to agree with the ruling of the court. As, in my opinion, that ruling rests upon an interpretation of the cruel and unusual punishment clause of the Eighth Amendment, never before announced, which is repugnant to the natural import of the language employed in the clause, and which interpretation curtails the legislative power of Congress to define and punish crime by asserting a right of judicial supervision over the exertion of that power, in disregard of the distinction between the legislative and judicial departments of the Government, I deem it my duty to dissent and state my reasons . . .

Whatever may be the difficulty, if any, in fixing the meaning of the prohibition at its origin, it may not be doubted, and indeed is not questioned by any one, that the cruel punishments against which the bill of rights provided were the atrocious, sanguinary and inhuman punishments which had been inflicted in the past upon the persons of criminals. This being certain, the difficulty of interpretation, if any is involved, in determining what was intended by the unusual punishments referred to and which were provided against. Light, however, on this subject is at once afforded by observing that the unusual punishments provided against were responsive to and obviously considered to be the illegal punishments complained of. These complaints were, first, that customary modes of bodily punishments, such as whipping and the pillory, had, under the exercise of judicial discretion, been applied to so unusual a degree as to cause them to be illegal; and, second, that in some cases an authority to sentence to perpetual imprisonment had been exerted under the assumption that power to do so resulted from the existence of judicial discretion to sentence to imprisonment, when it was unusual, and therefore illegal, to inflict life imprisonment in the absence of express legislative authority. In other words, the prohibitions, although conjunctively stated, were really disjunctive, and embraced as follows: a, Prohibitions against a resort to the inhuman bodily punishments of the past; b, or, where certain bodily punishments were customary, a prohibition against their infliction to such an extent as to be unusual and consequently illegal; c, or the infliction, under the assumption of the exercise of judicial discretion, of unusual punishments not bodily which could not be imposed except by express statute, or which were wholly beyond the jurisdiction of the court to impose . . .

. . .Of course, it may not be doubted that the provision against cruel bodily punishment is not restricted to the mere means used in the past to accomplish the prohibited result. The prohibition being generic, embraces all methods within its intendment. Thus, if it could be conceived that to-morrow the lawmaking power, instead of providing for the infliction of the death penalty by hanging, should command its infliction by burying alive, who could doubt that the law would be repugnant to the constitutional inhibition against cruel punishment? But while this consideration is obvious, it must be equally apparent that the prohibition against the infliction of cruel bodily torture cannot be extended so as to limit legislative discretion in prescribing punishment for crime by modes and methods which are not embraced within the prohibition against cruel bodily punishment, considered even in their most generic sense, without disregarding the elementary rules of construction which have prevailed from the beginning . . .[T]his court, while never hesitating to bring within the powers granted or to restrain by the limitations created all things generically within their embrace, has also incessantly declined to allow general words to be construed so as to include subjects not within their intendment. That these great results have been accomplished through the application by the court of the familiar rule that what is generically included in the words employed in the Constitution is to be ascertained by considering their origin and their significance at the time of their adoption in the instrument may not be denied, rulings which are directly repugnant to the conception that by judicial construction constitutional limitations may be made to progress so as to ultimately include that which they were not intended to embrace, a principle with which it seems to me the ruling now made is in direct conflict . . .

I am authorized to say that MR. JUSTICE HOLMES concurs in this dissent.

Louisiana v. Resweber (1947)

What constitutes cruel and unusual punishment and whether or not the state intended for the defendant to suffer were the key issues in this case. The U.S. Supreme Court determined that although the defendant had to undergo execution more than once, that did not constitute cruel and unusual punishment. During the execution, Resweber took his place in the electric chair, the switch was thrown, and nothing happened. The defendant was returned to his cell to wait for execution yet again. The Court emphasized that establishing intent was essential in the determination of cruel and unusual punishment. Because the failure to execute was an accident, despite the fact that a shock was delivered, the state could not be said to have inflicted cruel and unusual punishment. In essence, accidents happen.

MR. JUSTICE REED announced the judgment of the Court in an opinion in which THE CHIEF JUSTICE, MR. JUSTICE BLACK and MR. JUSTICE JACKSON join . . .

We find nothing in what took place here which amounts to cruel and unusual punishment in the constitutional sense. The case before us does not call for an examination into any punishments except that of death. The traditional humanity of modern Anglo-American law forbids the infliction of unnecessary pain in the execution of the death sentence. Prohibition against the wanton infliction of pain has come into our law from the Bill of Rights of 1688. The identical words appear in our Eighth Amendment . . .

Petitioner's suggestion is that because he once underwent the psychological strain of preparation for electrocution, now to require him to undergo this preparation again subjects him to a lingering or cruel and unusual punishment. Even the fact that petitioner has already been subjected to a current of electricity does not make his subsequent execution any more cruel in the constitutional sense than any other execution. The cruelty against which the Constitution protects a convicted man is cruelty inherent in the method of punishment, not the necessary suffering involved in any method employed to extinguish life humanely. The fact that an unforeseeable accident prevented the prompt consummation of the sentence cannot, it seems to us, add an element of cruelty to a subsequent execution. There is no purpose to inflict unnecessary pain nor any unnecessary pain involved in the proposed execution. The situation of the unfortunate victim of this accident is just as though he had suffered the identical amount of mental anguish and physical pain in any other occurrence, such as, for example, a fire in the cell block. We cannot agree that the hardship imposed upon the petitioner rises to that level of hardship denounced as denial of due process because of cruelty . . .

Affirmed.

MR. JUSTICE FRANKFURTER, concurring.

. . .I cannot bring myself to believe that for Louisiana . . .to require mitigation of a sentence of death duly pronounced upon conviction for murder because a first attempt to carry it out was an innocent misadventure, offends a principle of justice 'rooted in the traditions and conscience of our people' . . .One must be on guard against finding in personal disapproval a reflection of more or less prevailing condemnation. Strongly drawn as I am to some of the sentiments expressed by my brother BURTON, I cannot rid myself of the conviction that were

I to hold that Louisiana would transgress the Due Process Clause if the State were allowed, in the precise circumstances before us, to carry out the death sentence, I would be enforcing my private view rather than that consensus of society's opinion which, for purposes of due process, is the standard enjoined by the Constitution.

The fact that I reach this conclusion does not mean that a hypothetical situation, which assumes a series of abortive attempts at electrocution or even a single, cruelly willful attempt, would not raise different questions . . . Since I cannot say that it would be 'repugnant to the conscience of mankind,' *Palko v. Connecticut*, for Louisiana to exercise the power on which she here stands, I cannot say that the Constitution withholds it.

MR. JUSTICE BURTON, with whom MR. JUSTICE DOUGLAS, MR. JUSTICE MURPHY and MR. JUSTICE RUTLEDGE concur, dissenting.

. . . The capital case before us presents an instance of the violation of constitutional due process that is more clear than would be presented by many lesser punishments prohibited by the Eighth Amendment or its state counterparts. Taking human life by unnecessarily cruel means shocks the most fundamental instincts of civilized man. It should not be possible under the constitutional procedure of a self-governing people. Abhorrence of the cruelty of ancient forms of capital punishment has increased steadily until, today, some states have prohibited capital punishment altogether. It is unthinkable that any state legislature in modern times would enact a statute expressly authorizing capital punishment by repeated applications of an electric current separated by intervals of days or hours until finally death shall result . . .

In determining whether the proposed procedure is unconstitutional, we must measure it against a lawful electrocution. The contrast is that between instantaneous death and death by installments . . . Electrocution, when instantaneous, *can* be inflicted by a state in conformity with due process of law . . . The Supreme Court of Louisiana has held that electrocution, in the manner prescribed in its statute, is more humane than hanging . . .

The all-important consideration is that the execution shall be so instantaneous and substantially painless that the punishment shall be reduced, as nearly as possible, to no more than that of death itself. Electrocution has been approved only in a form that eliminates suffering . . .

It does not provide for electrocution by interrupted or repeated applications of electric current at intervals of several days or even minutes. It does not provide for the application of electric current of an intensity less than that sufficient to cause death. It prescribes expressly and solely for the application of a current of sufficient intensity to cause death and for the *continuance* of that application until death results . . .

These considerations were emphasized when . . .an early New York statute authorizing electrocution was attacked as violative of the due process clause of the Fourteenth Amendment because prescribing a cruel and unusual punishment. In upholding that statute, this Court stressed the fact that the electric current was to cause instantaneous death . . .

If the state officials deliberately and intentionally had placed the relator in the electric chair five times and, each time, had applied electric current to his body in a manner not sufficient, until the final time, to kill him, such a form of torture would rival that of burning at the stake. Although the failure of the first attempt, in the present case, was unintended, the reapplication of the electric current will be intentional. How many deliberate and intentional reapplications of electric current does it take to produce a cruel, unusual and unconstitutional punishment? While five applications would be more cruel and unusual than one, the uniqueness of the present case demonstrates that, today, two separated applications are sufficiently 'cruel and unusual' to be prohibited . . .

Lack of intent that the first application be less than fatal is not material. The intent of the executioner cannot lessen the torture or excuse the result. It was the statutory duty of the state officials to make sure that there was no failure . . .

[Footnote 2 (Dissent): contained from copies of affidavits printed as appendices to the brief on behalf of the petitioner explicitly describing the horrible experience the condemned had faced.]

For the reasons stated, we are unable to concur in the judgment of this Court which affirms the judgment below.

Trop v. Dulles (1958)

The U.S. Supreme Court looked at whether the denial of an individual's citizenship is cruel and unusual punishment. Although not a death penalty case, Trop v. Dulles *gave a sharply divided court a chance to expound upon the basic principles embodied in the Eighth Amendment and became one of the important cases relied upon by later courts to define "cruel and unusual."*

MR. CHIEF JUSTICE WARREN announced the judgment of the Court and delivered an opinion, in which MR. JUSTICE BLACK, MR. JUSTICE DOUGLAS, and MR. JUSTICE WHITTAKER join . . .

II

. . .[W]e must face the question whether the Constitution permits the Congress to take away citizenship as a punishment for crime. If it is assumed that the power of Congress extends to divestment of citizenship, the problem still remains as to this statute whether denationalization is a cruel and unusual punishment within the meaning of the Eighth Amendment.

At the outset, let us put to one side the death penalty as an index of the constitutional limit on punishment. Whatever the arguments may be against capital punishment, both on moral grounds and in terms of accomplishing the purposes of punishment—and they are forceful—the death penalty has been employed throughout our history, and, in a day when it is still widely accepted, it cannot be said to violate the constitutional concept of cruelty. But it is equally plain that the existence of the death penalty is not a license to the Government to devise any punishment short of death within the limit of its imagination.

The exact scope of the constitutional phrase 'cruel and unusual' has not been detailed by this Court. But the basic policy reflected in these words is firmly established in the Anglo-American tradition of criminal justice. The phrase in our Constitution was taken directly from the English Declaration of Rights of 1688, and the principle it represents can be traced back to the Magna Carta. The basic concept underlying the Eighth Amendment is nothing less than the dignity of man. While the State has the power to punish, the Amendment stands to assure that this power be exercised within the limits of civilized standards. Fines, imprisonment and even execution may be imposed depending upon the enormity of the crime . . .[In *Weems v. United States,*] the Court recognized . . .that the words of the Amendment are not precise, and that their scope is not static. The Amendment must draw its meaning from the evolving standards of decency that mark the progress of a maturing society.

We believe, as did Chief Judge Clark in the court below . . .that use of denationalization as a punishment is barred by the Eighth Amendment. There may be involved no physical mistreatment, no primitive torture. There is instead the total destruction of the individual's status in organized society. It is a form of punishment more primitive than torture, for it destroys for the individual the political existence that was centuries in the development. The punishment strips the citizen of his status in the national and international political community . . .In short, the expatriate has lost the right to have rights.

This punishment is offensive to cardinal principles for which the Constitution stands. It subjects the individual to a fate of ever-increasing fear and distress. He knows not what discriminations may be established against him, what proscriptions may be directed against him, and when and for what cause his existence in his native land may be terminated. He may be subject to banishment, a fate universally decried by civilized people. He is stateless, a condition deplored in the international community of democracies. It is no answer to suggest that all the disastrous consequences of this fate may not be brought to bear on a stateless person. The threat makes the punishment obnoxious.

The civilized nations of the world are in virtual unanimity that statelessness is not to be imposed as punishment for crime . . .

Reversed and remanded.

MR. JUSTICE FRANKFURTER, whom MR. JUSTICE BURTON, MR. JUSTICE CLARK and MR. JUSTICE HARLAN join, dissenting.

. . .Loss of citizenship entails undoubtedly severe—and in particular situations even tragic—consequences . . .[T]o insist that denationalization is 'cruel and unusual' punishment is to stretch that concept beyond the breaking point. It seems scarcely arguable that loss of citizenship is within the Eighth Amendment's prohibition because [it is] disproportionate to an offense that is capital and has been so from the first year of Independence. Is constitutional dialectic so empty of reason that it can be seriously urged that loss of citizenship is a fate worse than death? The seriousness of abandoning one's country when it is in the grip of mortal conflict precludes denial to Congress of the power to terminate citizenship here, unless that power is to be denied to Congress under any circumstance. . . .In short, denationalization, when attached to the offense of wartime desertion, cannot justifiably be deemed so at variance with enlightened concepts of 'humane justice,' see *Weems v. United States,* as to be beyond the power of

Congress, because [it constitutes] a 'cruel and unusual' punishment within the meaning of the Eighth Amendment.

Rudolph v. Alabama (1963)

An important case because of Justice Goldberg's dissent from the denial of certiorari. Some historians credit his argument as the first step in the major push for the eradication of the death penalty in the United States.

Certiorari denied.

DISSENT: MR. JUSTICE GOLDBERG, with whom MR. JUSTICE DOUGLAS and MR. JUSTICE BRENNAN join, dissenting.

I would grant certiorari in this case...to consider whether the Eighth and Fourteenth Amendments to the United States Constitution permit the imposition of the death penalty on a convicted rapist who has neither taken nor endangered human life.

The following questions, *inter alia,* seem relevant and worthy of argument and consideration:

(1) In light of the trend both in this country and throughout the world against punishing rape by death[1], does the imposition of the death penalty by those States which retain it for rape violate 'evolving standards of decency that mark the progress of [our] maturing society,'[2] or 'standards of decency more or less universally accepted'[3]?

(2) Is the taking of human life to protect a value other than human life consistent with the constitutional proscription against 'punishments which by their excessive...severity are greatly disproportioned to the offenses charged'[4]?

(3) Can the permissible aims of punishment (*e.g.,* deterrence, isolation, rehabilitation)[5] be achieved as effectively by punishing rape less severely than by death (*e.g.,* by life imprisonment)[6]; if so, does the imposition of the death penalty for rape constitute 'unnecessary cruelty'[7]?

Notes

1. The United Nations recently conducted a survey on the laws, regulations and practices relating to capital punishment throughout the world...65 countries and territories responded. All but five—Nationalist China, Northern Rhodesia, Nyasaland, Republic of South Africa, and the United States—reported that their laws no longer permit the imposition of the death penalty for rape.

The following of the United States reported that their laws no longer permit the imposition of the death penalty for rape . . .

2. *Trop* v. *Dulles* (opinion of WARREN, C.J.).

3. *Francis* v. *Resweber* (Frankfurter, J., concurring). See *Weems* v. *United States*, 217 U.S. 349, 373.

4. *Weems* v. *United States* . . .quoting from the dissenting opinion of Field, J., in *O'Neil* v. *Vermont* . . .

5. See, *e.g., Williams* v. *New York*, 337 U.S. 241; *Trop* v. *Dulles* (concurring opinion of BRENNAN, J.); *Blyew* v. *United States*, 13 Wall. 581, 600.

6. The United Nations Report on Capital Punishment noted: "In Canada, rape ceased to be punishable with death in 1954: it is reported that there were 37 convictions for rape in 1950, 44 in 1953 and only 27 in 1954, the year of abolition; from 1957 to 1959 a steady decrease in convictions was noted (from 56 to 44), while in the same period the population of Canada increased by 27 per cent." United Nations, Capital Punishment, *supra*, note 1, at 54–55 . . .

7. *Weems* v. *United States*. See *Robinson* v. *California* (concurring opinion of DOUGLAS, J.).

Witherspoon v. Illinois (1968)

One of the early cases that focused on how jurors were to be selected for capital cases. In this case, during voir dire, all those who had "conscientious scruples" against the death penalty were excluded from the jury. The U.S. Supreme Court noted that this action violated Sixth Amendment guarantees of an impartial trial. The Court made a distinction between jurors who had reservations about the death penalty and those who stated that they would never apply the death penalty. It determined that the latter but not the former could be excluded from selection in capital cases. The case limited itself to these specifics and did not explore more complex juror issues.

MR. JUSTICE STEWART delivered the opinion of the Court . . .

In the present case the tone was set when the trial judge said early in the *voir dire*, 'Let's get these conscientious objectors out of the way, without wasting any time on them' . . .

The petitioner . . .maintains that such a jury, unlike one chosen at random from a cross-section of the community, must necessarily be biased in favor of conviction, for the kind of juror who would be unperturbed by the prospect of sending a man to his death, he contends, is the kind of juror who would too readily ignore the presumption of the defendant's innocence, accept the prosecution's version of the facts, and return a verdict of guilt . . .

. . .We simply cannot conclude, either on the basis of the record now before us or as a matter of judicial notice, that the exclusion of jurors opposed to capital punishment results in an unrepresentative jury on the issue of guilt or substantially increases the risk of conviction. In light of the presently available information, we are not prepared to announce a *per se* constitutional rule requiring the reversal of every conviction returned by a jury selected as this one was.

It does not follow, however, that the petitioner is entitled to no relief . . .[I]t is self-evident that, in its role as arbiter of the punishment to be imposed, this jury fell woefully short of that impartiality to which the petitioner was entitled under the Sixth and Fourteenth Amendments.

The only justification the State has offered for the jury-selection technique it employed here is that individuals who express serious reservations about capital punishment cannot be relied upon to vote for it even when the laws of the State and the instructions of the trial judge would make death the proper penalty. But in Illinois, as in other States, the jury is given broad discretion to decide whether or not death *is* 'the proper penalty' in a given case, and a juror's general views about capital punishment play an inevitable role in any such decision.

A man who opposes the death penalty, no less than one who favors it, can make the discretionary judgment entrusted to him by the State and can thus obey the oath he takes as a juror. But a jury from which all such men have been excluded cannot perform the task demanded of it . . .Culled of all who harbor doubts about the wisdom of capital punishment—of all who would be reluctant to pronounce the extreme penalty—such a jury can speak only for a distinct and dwindling minority.

If the State had excluded only those prospective jurors who stated in advance of trial that they would not even consider returning a verdict of death, it could argue that the resulting jury was simply 'neutral' with respect to penalty. But when it swept from the jury all who expressed conscientious or religious scruples against capital punishment and all who opposed it in principle, the State crossed the line of neutrality. In its quest for a jury capable of imposing the death penalty, the State produced a jury uncommonly willing to condemn a man to die.

It is, of course, settled that a State may not entrust the determination of whether a man is innocent or guilty to a tribunal 'organized to convict' . . .

Whatever else might be said of capital punishment, it is at least clear that its imposition by a hanging jury cannot be squared with the Constitution. The State of Illinois has stacked the deck against the petitioner. To execute this death sentence would deprive him of his life without due process of law.

Reversed.

MR. JUSTICE DOUGLAS.

My difficulty with the opinion of the Court is a narrow but important one . . .

I see no constitutional basis for excluding those who are so opposed to capital punishment that they would never inflict it on a defendant. Exclusion of them means the selection of jurors who are either protagonists of the death penalty or neutral concerning it. That results in a systematic exclusion of qualified groups, and the deprivation to the accused of a cross-section of the community for decision on both his guilt and his punishment . . .

. . . We can as easily assume that the absence of those opposed to capital punishment would rob the jury of certain peculiar qualities of human nature as would the exclusion of women from juries. I would not require a specific showing of a likelihood of prejudice, for I feel that we must proceed on the assumption that in many, if not most, cases of class exclusion on the basis of beliefs or attitudes some prejudice does result and many times will not be subject to precise measurement. Indeed, that prejudice 'is so subtle, so intangible, that it escapes the ordinary methods of proof.' In my view, that is the essence of the requirement that a jury be drawn from a cross-section of the community.

MR. JUSTICE BLACK, with whom MR. JUSTICE HARLAN and MR. JUSTICE WHITE join, dissenting.

. . . It is important to note that when those persons who acknowledged having 'conscientious or religious scruples against the infliction of the death penalty' were excluded from the jury, defense counsel made no attempt to show that they were nonetheless competent jurors. In fact, when the jurors finally were accepted by defense counsel, the defense still had three peremptory challenges left to exercise. In the past this has frequently been taken as an indication that the jurors who were impaneled were impartial. And it certainly amounts to a clear showing that in this case petitioner's able and distinguished counsel did not believe petitioner was being tried by a biased, much less a 'hanging,' jury . . .

As I see the issue in this case, it is a question of plain bias. A person who has conscientious or religious scruples against capital punishment will seldom if ever vote to impose the death penalty. This is just human nature, and no amount of semantic camouflage can cover it up. In the same manner, I would not dream of foisting on a criminal defendant a juror who admitted that he had conscientious or religious scruples against not inflicting the death sentence on any person convicted of murder (a juror who claims, for example, that he adheres literally to the Biblical admonition of 'an eye for an eye'). Yet the logical result of the majority's holding is that such persons must be allowed so that the 'conscience of the community' will be fully represented when it decides 'the ultimate question of life or death.' While I have always advocated that the jury be as fully representative of the community as possible, I would never carry this so far as to require that those biased against one of the critical issues in a trial should be represented on a jury . . .

It seems to me that the Court's opinion today must be read as holding just the opposite from what has been stated above. For no matter how the Court might try to hide it, the implication is inevitably in its opinion that people who do not have conscientious scruples against the death penalty are somehow callous to suffering and are, as some of the commentators cited by the Court called them, 'prosecution prone.' This conclusion represents a psychological foray into the human mind that I have considerable doubt about my ability to make, and I must confess that the two or three so-called 'studies' cited by the Court on this subject are not persuasive to me . . .

I believe that the Court's decision today goes a long way to destroying the concept of an impartial jury as we have known it . . . For this reason I dissent.

McGautha v. California (1970)

Another case that focused on jury discretion. In concert with another case Crampton v. Ohio, *the U.S. Supreme Court focused on the idea of whether there needed to be common governing standards for applying the death penalty. In dealing with this issue, the Court also looked at, for the first time, whether a unitary trial violated constitutional standards of*

122 Death Penalty on Trial

self-incrimination. In a broad statement the Court suggested that the jury has wide discretion and that bifurcated trials are no more or less fair than unitary ones. Although the Court ruled against the defendants, both issues would be raised again in Furman v. Georgia.

MR. JUSTICE HARLAN delivered the opinion of the Court . . .

III

We consider first McGautha's and Crampton's common claim: that the absence of standards to guide the jury's discretion on the punishment issue is constitutionally intolerable . . .we conclude that the courts below correctly rejected it.

. . .In light of history, experience, and the present limitations of human knowledge, we find it quite impossible to say that committing to the untrammeled discretion of the jury the power to pronounce life or death in capital cases is offensive to anything in the Constitution. The States are entitled to assume that jurors confronted with the truly awesome responsibility of decreeing death for a fellow human will act with due regard for the consequences of their decision and will consider a variety of factors, many of which will have been suggested by the evidence or by the arguments of defense counsel. For a court to attempt to catalog the appropriate factors in this elusive area could inhibit rather than expand the scope of consideration, for no list of circumstances would ever be really complete. The infinite variety of cases and facets to each case would make general standards either meaningless 'boiler-plate' or a statement of the obvious that no jury would need.

. . .The contention is that where guilt and punishment are to be determined by a jury at a single trial the desire to address the jury on punishment unduly encourages waiver of the defendant's privilege to remain silent on the issue of guilt, or, to put the matter another way, that the single-verdict procedure unlawfully compels the defendant to become a witness against himself on the issue of guilt by the threat of sentencing him to death without having heard from him. It is not contended, nor could it be successfully, that the mere force of evidence is compulsion of the sort forbidden by the privilege . . .It does no violence to the privilege that a person's choice to testify in his own behalf may open the door to otherwise inadmissible evidence which is damaging to his case . . .

It is undeniably hard to require a defendant on trial for his life and desirous of testifying on the issue of punishment to make nice calculations of the effect of his testimony on the jury's determination of guilt. The issue of cruelty thus arising, however, is less closely akin to 'the cruel trilemma of self-accusation, perjury or contempt,' . . .than to the fundamental requirements of fairness and decency embodied in the Due Process Clauses . . .We are thus constrained to reject the suggestion that a desire to speak to one's sentencer unlawfully compels a defendant in a single-verdict capital case to incriminate himself . . .We do not think that the fact that a defendant's sentence, rather than his guilt, is at issue creates a constitutionally sufficient difference from the sorts of situations we have described . . .

We conclude that the policies of the privilege against compelled self-incrimination are not offended when a defendant in a capital case yields to the pressure to testify on the issue of punishment at the risk of damaging his case on guilt. We therefore turn to the converse situation, in which a defendant remains silent on the issue of guilt and thereby loses any opportunity to address the jury personally on punishment.

. . .Petitioner's contention therefore comes down to the fact that the Ohio single-verdict trial may deter the defendant from bringing to the jury's attention evidence peculiarly within his own knowledge, and it may mean that the death verdict will be returned by a jury which never heard the sound of his voice . . .Assuming that in this case there was relevant information solely within petitioner's knowledge, we do not think the Constitution forbids a requirement that such evidence be available to the jury on all issues to which it is relevant or not at all . . .We have held that failure to ensure such personal participation in the criminal process is not necessarily a constitutional flaw in the conviction . . .

Before we conclude this opinion, it is appropriate for us to make a broader observation than the issues raised by these cases strictly call for. It may well be, as the American Law Institute and the National Commission on Reform of Federal Criminal Laws have concluded, that bifurcated trials and criteria for jury sentencing discretion are superior means of dealing with capital cases if the death penalty is to be retained at all. But the Federal Constitution, which marks the limits of our authority in these cases, does not guarantee trial procedures that are the best of all worlds, or that accord with the most enlightened ideas of students of the infant science of criminology, or even those that measure up to the individual predilections of members of this

Court . . .The Constitution requires no more than that trials be fairly conducted and that guaranteed rights of defendants be scrupulously respected. From a constitutional standpoint we cannot conclude that it is impermissible for a State to consider that the compassionate purposes of jury sentencing in capital cases are better served by having the issues of guilt and punishment determined in a single trial than by focusing the jury's attention solely on punishment after the issue of guilt has been determined.

Certainly the facts of these gruesome murders bespeak no miscarriage of justice . . .

Affirmed.

MR. JUSTICE DOUGLAS, with whom MR. JUSTICE BRENNAN and MR. JUSTICE MARSHALL concur, dissenting in No. 204.

In my view the unitary trial which Ohio provides in first-degree murder cases does not satisfy the requirements of procedural Due Process under the Fourteenth Amendment . . .

If a defendant wishes to testify in support of the defense of insanity or in mitigation of what he is charged with doing, he can do so only if he surrenders his right to be free from self-incrimination. Once he takes the stand he can be cross-examined not only as respects the crime charged but also on other misdeeds . . .

I see no way to make this unitary trial fair . . .

The Court has history on its side—but history alone. Though nations have been killing men for centuries, felony crimes increase. The vestiges of law enshrined today have roots in barbaric procedures. Barbaric procedures such as ordeal by battle that became imbedded in the law were difficult to dislodge. Though torture was used to exact confessions, felonies mounted. Once it was thought that 'sanity' was determined by ascertaining whether a person knew the difference between 'right' and 'wrong.' Once it was a capital offense to steal from the person something 'above the value of a shilling.' . . .

The unitary trial . . .has a constitutional infirmity because it is not neutral on the awesome issue of capital punishment. The rules are stacked in favor of death. It is one thing if the legislature decides that the death penalty attaches to defined crimes . . .

I would reverse this judgment of conviction.

MR. JUSTICE BRENNAN, with whom MR. JUSTICE DOUGLAS and MR. JUSTICE MARSHALL join, dissenting.

...[E]ven if I shared the Court's view that the rule of law and the power of the States to kill are in irreconcilable conflict, I would have no hesitation in concluding that the rule of law must prevail ...

We are faced with nothing more than stark legislative abdication. Not once in the history of this Court, until today, have we sustained against a due process challenge such an unguided, unbridled, unreviewable exercise of naked power...

...There is in my view no way that this Ohio capital sentencing procedure can be thought to pass muster under the Due Process Clause.

...Nothing whatsoever in the process either sets forth the basic policy considerations that Ohio believes relevant to capital sentencing, or leads towards elucidation of these considerations in the light of accumulated experience. The standard jury instruction contains at best an obscure hint. The instructions given in the present case contain none whatsoever. So far as they are concerned, the jury could have decided to impose the death penalty as a matter of simple vengeance for what it considered an atrocious crime; because it felt that imposition of the death penalty would deter other potential murderers; or because it felt that petitioner, if not himself killed, might kill or commit some other wrong in the future. The jury may have been influenced by any, all, or none of these considerations...Neither we nor the State of Ohio can know the reasoning by which this jury determined to impose the death penalty, or the facts upon which that reasoning was based. All we know is that the jury did not appear to find the question a particularly difficult one ...

...I find [California procedure] likewise defective under the Due Process Clause. Although it differs in some not insignificant respects from the procedure used in Ohio, it nevertheless is entirely bare of the fundamental safeguards required by due process.

Furman v. Georgia (1972)

*One of the longest opinions in Supreme Court history that produced nine separate opinions and allowed each justice to articulate his personal view on the death penalty. Furman was burglarizing a house and accidentally killed one of the people who lived there. This case was consolidated with two other cases (*Jackson v. Georgia *and* Branch v. Texas*). While this landmark case declared the death penalty unconstitutional,*

only Justices Brennan and Marshall were willing to declare it so under
any circumstance. The myriad of opinions focused on various aspects of
capital punishment, from its arbitrary nature, racial biases, and accept-
ability as part of the U.S. justice system. However, because only a plu-
rality were willing to declare it unconstitutional per se, all this case did
was prepare the landscape for further challenges.

PER CURIAM.

Petitioner in No. 69-5003 was convicted of murder in Georgia and
was sentenced to death pursuant to Ga. Code . . .Petitioner in No. 69-
5030 was convicted of rape in Georgia and was sentenced to death
pursuant to Ga. Code . . .Petitioner in No. 69-5031 was convicted of
rape in Texas and was sentenced to death pursuant to Tex. Penal
Code . . .Certiorari was granted limited to the following question:
'Does the imposition and carrying out of the death penalty in [these
cases] constitute cruel and unusual punishment in violation of the
Eighth and Fourteenth Amendments?' The Court holds that the imposition and carrying out of the death penalty in these cases constitute
cruel and unusual punishment in violation of the Eighth and Fourteenth Amendments. The judgment in each case is therefore reversed
insofar as it leaves undisturbed the death sentence imposed, and the
cases are remanded for further proceedings.

So ordered.

MR. JUSTICE DOUGLAS, concurring.

. . .It has been assumed in our decisions that punishment by death
is not cruel, unless the manner of execution can be said to be inhuman
and barbarous. It is also said in our opinions that the proscription of
cruel and unusual punishments 'is not fastened to the obsolete but
may acquire meaning as public opinion becomes enlightened by a humane justice.' *Weems v. United States.* A like statement was made in
Trop v. Dulles, that the Eighth Amendment 'must draw its meaning
from the evolving standards of decency that mark the progress of a
maturing society.' . . .

It would seem to be incontestable that the death penalty inflicted
on one defendant is 'unusual' if it discriminates against him by reason
of his race, religion, wealth, social position, or class, or if it is imposed
under a procedure that gives room for the play of such prejudices . . .

The words 'cruel and unusual' certainly include penalties that are
barbaric. But the words, at least when read in light of the English proscription against selective and irregular use of penalties, suggest that it

is 'cruel and unusual' to apply the death penalty—or any other penalty—selectively to minorities whose numbers are few, who are outcasts of society, and who are unpopular, but whom society is willing to see suffer though it would not countenance general application of the same penalty across the board ...

In a Nation committed to equal protection of the laws there is no permissible 'caste' aspect of law enforcement. Yet we know that the discretion of judges and juries in imposing the death penalty enables the penalty to be selectively applied, feeding prejudices against the accused if he is poor and despised, and lacking political clout, or if he is a member of a suspect or unpopular minority, and saving those who by social position may be in a more protected position ...We have, I fear ...[made] the death penalty discretionary and partially as a result of the ability of the rich to purchase the services of the most respected and most resourceful legal talent in the Nation.

The high service rendered by the 'cruel and unusual' punishment clause of the Eighth Amendment is to require legislatures to write penal laws that are evenhanded, nonselective, and nonarbitrary, and to require judges to see to it that general laws are not applied sparsely, selectively, and spottily to unpopular groups ...

A law that stated that anyone making more than $50,000 would be exempt from the death penalty would plainly fall, as would a law that in terms said that blacks, those who never went beyond the fifth grade in school, those who made less than $3,000 a year, or those who were unpopular or unstable should be the only people executed. A law which in the overall view reaches that result in practice has no more sanctity than a law which in terms provides the same.

Thus, these discretionary statutes are unconstitutional in their operation. They are pregnant with discrimination and discrimination is an ingredient not compatible with the idea of equal protection of the laws that is implicit in the ban on 'cruel and unusual' punishments.

...Whether a mandatory death penalty would otherwise be constitutional is a question I do not reach.

I concur in the judgments of the Court.

MR. JUSTICE BRENNAN, concurring.

...We have very little evidence of the Framers' intent in including the Cruel and Unusual Punishments Clause among those restraints upon the new Government enumerated in the Bill of Rights ...

Several conclusions thus emerge from the history of the adoption of the Clause. We know that the Framers' concern was directed specifically at the exercise of legislative power. They included in the Bill of Rights a prohibition upon 'cruel and unusual punishments' precisely because the legislature would otherwise have had the unfettered power to prescribe punishments for crimes. Yet we cannot now know exactly what the Framers thought 'cruel and unusual punishments' were. Certainly they intended to ban torturous punishments, but the available evidence does not support the further conclusion that only torturous punishments were to be outlawed . . .[T]he Framers were well aware that the reach of the Clause was not limited to the proscription of unspeakable atrocities. Nor did they intend simply to forbid punishments considered 'cruel and unusual' at the time. The 'import' of the Clause is, indeed, 'indefinite,' and for good reason. A constitutional provision 'is enacted, it is true, from an experience of evils, but its general language should not, therefore, be necessarily confined to the form that evil had theretofore taken. Time works changes, brings into existence new conditions and purposes . . .'

. . .The Clause, then, guards against '[t]he abuse of power' . . .

Judicial enforcement of the Clause, then, cannot be evaded by invoking the obvious truth that legislatures have the power to prescribe punishments for crimes. That is precisely the reason the Clause appears in the Bill of Rights. The difficulty arises, rather, in formulating the 'legal principles to be applied by the courts' when a legislatively prescribed punishment is challenged as 'cruel and unusual.' In formulating those constitutional principles, we must avoid the insertion of 'judicial conception[s] of . . . wisdom or propriety,' *Weems v. United States,* yet we must not, in the guise of 'judicial restraint,' abdicate our fundamental responsibility to enforce the Bill of Rights. Were we to do so, the 'constitution would indeed be as easy of application as it would be deficient in efficacy and power. Its general principles would have little value and be converted by precedent into impotent and lifeless formulas. Rights declared in words might be lost in reality.'

. . .We know 'that the words of the [Clause] are not precise, and that their scope is not static.' We know, therefore, that the Clause 'must draw its meaning from the evolving standards of decency that mark the progress of a maturing society.' That knowledge, of course, is but the beginning of the inquiry . . .

At bottom, then, the Cruel and Unusual Punishments Clause prohibits the infliction of uncivilized and inhuman punishments. The State, even as it punishes, must treat its members with respect for their intrinsic worth as human beings. A punishment is 'cruel and unusual,' therefore, if it does not comport with human dignity.

. . .[T]here are principles recognized in our cases and inherent in the Clause sufficient to permit a judicial determination whether a challenged punishment comports with human dignity.

The primary principle is that a punishment must not be so severe as to be degrading to the dignity of human beings. Pain, certainly, may be a factor in the judgment. The infliction of an extremely severe punishment will often entail physical suffering . . .

. . .The barbaric punishments condemned by history, 'punishments which inflict torture, such as the rack, the thumbscrew, the iron boot, the stretching of limbs and the like,' are, of course, 'attended with acute pain and suffering.' *O'Neil v. Vermont* (1892) (Field, J., dissenting). When we consider why they have been condemned, however, we realize that the pain involved is not the only reason. The true significance of these punishments is that they treat members of the human race as nonhumans, as objects to be toyed with and discarded. They are thus inconsistent with the fundamental premise of the Clause that even the vilest criminal remains a human being possessed of common human dignity . . .

In determining whether a punishment comports with human dignity, we are aided also by a second principle inherent in the Clause—that the State must not arbitrarily inflict a severe punishment . . .

A third principle inherent in the Clause is that a severe punishment must not be unacceptable to contemporary society. Rejection by society, of course, is a strong indication that a severe punishment does not comport with human dignity. In applying this principle, however, we must make certain that the judicial determination is as objective as possible . . .

. . .[T]he judicial task is to review the history of a challenged punishment and to examine society's present practices with respect to its use. Legislative authorization, of course, does not establish acceptance. The acceptability of a severe punishment is measured, not by its availability, for it might become so offensive to society as never to be inflicted, but by its use.

The final principle inherent in the Clause is that a severe punishment must not be excessive. A punishment is excessive under this principle if it is unnecessary: The infliction of a severe punishment by the State cannot comport with human dignity when it is nothing more than the pointless infliction of suffering. If there is a significantly less severe punishment adequate to achieve the purposes for which the punishment is inflicted . . .the punishment inflicted is unnecessary and therefore excessive . . .

There are, then, four principles by which we may determine whether a particular punishment is 'cruel and unusual.' The primary principle, which I believe supplies the essential predicate for the application of the others, is that a punishment must not by its severity be degrading to human dignity . . .

Since the Bill of Rights was adopted, this Court has adjudged only three punishments to be within the prohibition of the Clause. See *Weems v. United States* (12 years in chains at hard and painful labor); *Trop v. Dulles* (expatriation); *Robinson v. California* (imprisonment for narcotics addiction). Each punishment, of course, was degrading to human dignity, but of none could it be said conclusively that it was fatally offensive under one or the other of the principles. Rather, these 'cruel and unusual punishments' seriously implicated several of the principles, and it was the application of the principles in combination that supported the judgment. That, indeed, is not surprising. The function of these principles, after all, is simply to provide means by which a court can determine whether a challenged punishment comports with human dignity. They are, therefore, interrelated, and in most cases it will be their convergence that will justify the conclusion that a punishment is 'cruel and unusual.' The test, then, will ordinarily be a cumulative one . . .

. . .The question, then, is whether the deliberate infliction of death is today consistent with the command of the Clause that the State may not inflict punishments that do not comport with human dignity. I will analyze the punishment of death in terms of the principles set out above and the cumulative test to which they lead: It is a denial of human dignity for the State arbitrarily to subject a person to an unusually severe punishment that society has indicated it does not regard as acceptable, and that cannot be shown to serve any penal purpose more effectively than a significantly less drastic punishment. Under these principles and this test, death is today a 'cruel and unusual' punishment . . .

Death is truly an awesome punishment. The calculated killing of a human being by the State involves, by its very nature, a denial of the executed person's humanity. The contrast with the plight of a person punished by imprisonment is evident. An individual in prison does not lose 'the right to have rights.' . . .A prisoner remains a member of the human family. Moreover, he retains the right of access to the courts. His punishment is not irrevocable . . .

In comparison to all other punishments today, then, the deliberate extinguishment of human life by the State is uniquely degrading to human dignity. I would not hesitate to hold, on that ground alone, that death is today a 'cruel and unusual' punishment, were it not that death is a punishment of longstanding usage and acceptance in this country. I therefore turn to the second principle—that the State may not arbitrarily inflict an unusually severe punishment . . .

. . .[T]he history of this punishment is one of successive restriction. What was once a common punishment has become, in the context of a continuing moral debate, increasingly rare. The evolution of this punishment evidences, not that it is an inevitable part of the American scene, but that it has proved progressively more troublesome to the national conscience . . .

The question, however, is not whether death serves these supposed purposes of punishment, but whether death serves them more effectively than imprisonment . . .The assertion that death alone is a sufficiently emphatic denunciation for capital crimes suffers from the same defect. If capital crimes require the punishment of death in order to provide moral reinforcement for the basic values of the community, those values can only be undermined when death is so rarely inflicted upon the criminals who commit the crimes. Furthermore, it is certainly doubtful that the infliction of death by the State does in fact strengthen the community's moral code; if the deliberate extinguishment of human life has any effect at all, it more likely tends to lower our respect for life and brutalize our values. That, after all, is why we no longer carry out public executions . . .

There is, then, no substantial reason to believe that the punishment of death, as currently administered, is necessary for the protection of society. The only other purpose suggested, one that is independent of protection for society, is retribution. Shortly stated, retribution in this context means that criminals are put to death because they deserve it . . .

In sum, the punishment of death is inconsistent with all four principles: Death is an unusually severe and degrading punishment; there is a strong probability that it is inflicted arbitrarily; its rejection by contemporary society is virtually total; and there is no reason to believe that it serves any penal purpose more effectively than the less severe punishment of imprisonment. The function of these principles is to enable a court to determine whether a punishment comports with human dignity. Death, quite simply, does not . . .

I concur in the judgments of the Court.

MR. JUSTICE STEWART, concurring.

The penalty of death differs from all other forms of criminal punishment, not in degree but in kind. It is unique in its total irrevocability. It is unique in its rejection of rehabilitation of the convict as a basic purpose of criminal justice. And it is unique, finally, in its absolute renunciation of all that is embodied in our concept of humanity.

For these and other reasons, at least two of my Brothers have concluded that the infliction of the death penalty is constitutionally impermissible in all circumstances under the Eighth and Fourteenth Amendments. Their case is a strong one. But I find it unnecessary to reach the ultimate question they would decide . . .

. . .I would say only that I cannot agree that retribution is a constitutionally impermissible ingredient in the imposition of punishment. The instinct for retribution is part of the nature of man, and channeling that instinct in the administration of criminal justice serves an important purpose in promoting the stability of a society governed by law. When people begin to believe that organized society is unwilling or unable to impose upon criminal offenders the punishment they 'deserve,' then there are sown the seeds of anarchy—of self-help, vigilante justice, and lynch law . . .

. . .[I]t is clear that these sentences are 'cruel' in the sense that they excessively go beyond, not in degree but in kind, the punishments that the state legislatures have determined to be necessary. In the second place, it is equally clear that these sentences are 'unusual' in the sense that the penalty of death is infrequently imposed for murder, and that its imposition for rape is extraordinarily rare. But I do not rest my conclusion upon these two propositions alone.

These death sentences are cruel and unusual in the same way that being struck by lightning is cruel and unusual. For, of all the people convicted of rapes and murders in 1967 and 1968, many just as reprehensible as these, the petitioners are among a capriciously selected random handful upon whom the sentence of death has in fact been imposed. My concurring Brothers have demonstrated that, if any basis can be discerned for the selection of these few to be sentenced to die, it is the constitutionally impermissible basis of race . . .But racial discrimination has not been proved, and I put it to one side. I simply conclude that the Eighth and Fourteenth Amendments cannot tolerate the infliction of a sentence of death under legal systems that permit this unique penalty to be so wantonly and so freakishly imposed.

For these reasons I concur in the judgments of the Court.

MR. JUSTICE WHITE, concurring.

. . .In joining the Court's judgments . . .I do not at all intimate that the death penalty is unconstitutional per se or that there is no system of capital punishment that would comport with the Eighth Amendment. That question, ably argued by several of my Brethren, is not presented by these cases and need not be decided . . .

I begin with what I consider a near truism: that the death penalty could so seldom be imposed that it would cease to be a credible deterrent or measurably to contribute to any other end of punishment in the criminal justice system. . . .[W]hen imposition of the penalty reaches a certain degree of infrequency, it would be very doubtful that any existing general need for retribution would be measurably satisfied. Nor could it be said with confidence that society's need for specific deterrence justifies death for so few when for so many in like circumstances life imprisonment or shorter prison terms are judged sufficient, or that community values are measurably reinforced by authorizing a penalty so rarely invoked.

Most important, a major goal of the criminal law—to deter others by punishing the convicted criminal—would not be substantially served where the penalty is so seldom invoked that it ceases to be the credible threat essential to influence the conduct of others. For present purposes I accept the morality and utility of punishing one person to influence another. I accept also the effectiveness of punishment generally and need not reject the death penalty as a more effective deterrent than a lesser punishment. But common sense and experience tell us that seldom-enforced laws become ineffective measures for controlling human conduct and that the death penalty, unless imposed with sufficient frequency, will make little contribution to deterring those crimes for which it may be exacted.

. . .[I]ts imposition would then be the pointless and needless extinction of life with only marginal contributions to any discernible social or public purposes. A penalty with such negligible returns to the State would be patently excessive and cruel and unusual punishment violative of the Eighth Amendment . . .

I concur in the judgments of the Court.

MR. JUSTICE MARSHALL, concurring.

[In the first four parts of the decision, Justice Marshall gave a long historical discussion of the death penalty, tracing back to the Eighth Amendment's ban against cruel and unusual punishment and its roots in English law and reviewing case law.]

In order to assess whether or not death is an excessive or unnecessary penalty, it is necessary to consider the reasons why a legislature might select it as punishment for one or more offenses, and examine whether less severe penalties would satisfy the legitimate legislative wants as well as capital punishment. If they would, then the death penalty is unnecessary cruelty, and, therefore, unconstitutional.

There are six purposes conceivably served by capital punishment: retribution, deterrence, prevention of repetitive criminal acts, encouragement of guilty pleas and confessions, eugenics, and economy. These are considered seriatim below . . .

[Marshall proceeded to analyze and reject each of the above rationales for the death penalty.]

There is but one conclusion that can be drawn from all of this—i. e., the death penalty is an excessive and unnecessary punishment that violates the Eighth Amendment. The statistical evidence is not convincing beyond all doubt, but it is persuasive. It is not improper at this point to take judicial notice of the fact that for more than 200 years men have labored to demonstrate that capital punishment serves no purpose that life imprisonment could not serve equally well. And they have done so with great success. Little, if any, evidence has been adduced to prove the contrary. The point has now been reached at which deference to the legislatures is tantamount to abdication of our judicial roles . . .There is no rational basis for concluding that capital punishment is not excessive. It therefore violates the Eighth Amendment.

In addition, even if capital punishment is not excessive, it nonetheless violates the Eighth Amendment because it is morally unacceptable to the people of the United States at this time in their history.

In judging whether or not a given penalty is morally acceptable, most courts have said that the punishment is valid unless 'it shocks the conscience and sense of justice of the people.' . . .

While a public opinion poll obviously is of some assistance in indicating public acceptance or rejection of a specific penalty, its utility cannot be very great. This is because whether or not a punishment is cruel and unusual depends, not on whether its mere mention 'shocks the conscience and sense of justice of the people,' but on whether people who were fully informed as to the purposes of the penalty and its liabilities would find the penalty shocking, unjust, and unacceptable.

In other words, the question with which we must deal is not whether a substantial proportion of American citizens would today, if polled, opine that capital punishment is barbarously cruel, but whether they would find it to be so in the light of all information presently available . . .

It has often been noted that American citizens know almost nothing about capital punishment. Some of the conclusions arrived at in the preceding section and the supporting evidence would be critical to an informed judgment on the morality of the death penalty: e. g., that the death penalty is no more effective a deterrent than life imprisonment, that convicted murderers are rarely executed, but are usually sentenced to a term in prison; that convicted murderers usually are model prisoners, and that they almost always become law-abiding citizens upon their release from prison; that the costs of executing a capital offender exceed the costs of imprisoning him for life; that while in prison, a convict under sentence of death performs none of the useful functions that life prisoners perform; that no attempt is made in the sentencing process to ferret out likely recidivists for execution; and that the death penalty may actually stimulate criminal activity.

This information would almost surely convince the average citizen that the death penalty was unwise, but a problem arises as to whether it would convince him that the penalty was morally reprehensible. This problem arises from the fact that the public's desire for retribution, even though this is a goal that the legislature cannot constitutionally pursue as its sole justification for capital punishment, might influence the citizenry's view of the morality of capital punishment. The solution to the problem lies in the fact that no one has ever seriously advanced retribution as a legitimate goal of our society. Defenses of capital punishment are always mounted on deterrent or other similar theories. This should not be surprising. It is the people of this country who have urged in the past that prisons rehabilitate as well as isolate offenders, and it is the people who have injected a sense of purpose into our penology. I cannot believe that at this stage in our history, the American people would ever knowingly support purposeless vengeance. Thus, I believe that the great mass of citizens would conclude on the basis of the material already considered that the death penalty is immoral and therefore unconstitutional.

But, if this information needs supplementing, I believe that the following facts would serve to convince even the most hesitant of citizens to condemn death as a sanction: capital punishment is imposed discriminatorily against certain identifiable classes of people; there is evidence that innocent people have been executed before their innocence can be proved; and the death penalty wreaks havoc with our entire criminal justice system. Each of these facts is considered briefly below . . .

[Justice Marshall then reviewed each one of these factors that led to discrepancies in the application of the death penalty.]

Assuming knowledge of all the facts presently available regarding capital punishment, the average citizen would, in my opinion, find it shocking to his conscience and sense of justice. For this reason alone capital punishment cannot stand.

In striking down capital punishment, this Court does not malign our system of government. On the contrary, it pays homage to it. Only in a free society could right triumph in difficult times, and could civilization record its magnificent advancement. In recognizing the humanity of our fellow beings, we pay ourselves the highest tribute. We achieve 'a major milestone in the long road up from barbarism' and join the approximately 70 other jurisdictions in the world which celebrate their regard for civilization and humanity by shunning capital punishment.

I concur in the judgments of the Court.

MR. CHIEF JUSTICE BURGER, with whom MR. JUSTICE BLACKMUN, MR. JUSTICE POWELL, and MR. JUSTICE REHNQUIST join, dissenting.

. . .I conclude that the constitutional prohibition against 'cruel and unusual punishments' cannot be construed to bar the imposition of the punishment of death . . .

If we were possessed of legislative power, I would either join with MR. JUSTICE BRENNAN and MR. JUSTICE MARSHALL or, at the very least, restrict the use of capital punishment to a small category of the most heinous crimes. Our constitutional inquiry, however, must be divorced from personal feelings as to the morality and efficacy of the death penalty, and be confined to the meaning and applicability of the uncertain language of the Eighth Amendment. There is no novelty in being called upon to interpret a constitutional provision that is less than self-defining, but, of all our fundamental guarantees, the ban on 'cruel and unusual punishments' is one of the most difficult to translate into judicially manageable terms. The widely divergent views of the Amendment expressed in today's opinions reveal the haze that surrounds this constitutional command. Yet it is essential to our role as a court that we not seize upon the enigmatic character of the guarantee as an invitation to enact our personal predilections into law.

Although the Eighth Amendment literally reads as prohibiting only those punishments that are both 'cruel' and 'unusual,' history compels the conclusion that the Constitution prohibits all punishments of extreme and barbarous cruelty, regardless of how frequently or infrequently imposed . . .

From every indication, the Framers of the Eighth Amendment intended to give the phrase a meaning far different from that of its English precursor . . . There was no discussion of the interrelationship of the terms 'cruel' and 'unusual,' and there is nothing in the debates supporting the inference that the Founding Fathers would have been receptive to torturous or excessively cruel punishments even if usual in character or authorized by law . . .

There are no obvious indications that capital punishment offends the conscience of society to such a degree that our traditional deference to the legislative judgment must be abandoned. It is not a punishment such as burning at the stake that everyone would ineffably find to be repugnant to all civilized standards. Nor is it a punishment so roundly condemned that only a few aberrant legislatures have retained it on the statute books. Capital punishment is authorized by statute in 40 States, the District of Columbia, and in the federal courts for the commission of certain crimes . . .

It is argued that in those capital cases where juries have recommended mercy, they have given expression to civilized values and effectively renounced the legislative authorization for capital punishment. At the same time it is argued that where juries have made the awesome decision to send men to their deaths, they have acted arbitrarily and without sensitivity to prevailing standards of decency. This explanation for the infrequency of imposition of capital punishment is unsupported by known facts, and is inconsistent in principle with everything this Court has ever said about the functioning of juries in capital cases . . .

Capital punishment has also been attacked as violative of the Eighth Amendment on the ground that it is not needed to achieve legitimate penal aims and is thus 'unnecessarily cruel.' As a pure policy matter, this approach has much to recommend it, but it seeks to give a dimension to the Eighth Amendment that it was never intended to have and promotes a line of inquiry that this Court has never before pursued.

. . .Two of the several aims of punishment are generally associated with capital punishment—retribution and deterrence . . .[R]esponsible legal thinkers of widely varying persuasions have debated the sociological and philosophical aspects of the retribution question for generations, neither side being able to convince the other. It would be reading a great deal into the Eighth Amendment to hold that the punishments authorized by legislatures cannot constitutionally reflect a retributive purpose.

The less esoteric but no less controversial question is whether the death penalty acts as a superior deterrent . . .Yet I know of no convincing evidence that life imprisonment is a more effective deterrent than 20 years' imprisonment, or even that a $10 parking ticket is a more effective deterrent than a $5 parking ticket . . .If the States are unable to adduce convincing proof rebutting such assertions, does it then follow that all punishments are suspect as being 'cruel and unusual' within the meaning of the Constitution? On the contrary, I submit that the questions raised by the necessity approach are beyond the pale of judicial inquiry under the Eighth Amendment

. . .If today's opinions demonstrate nothing else, they starkly show that this is an area where legislatures can act far more effectively than courts . . .

The legislatures are free to eliminate capital punishment for specific crimes or to carve out limited exceptions to a general abolition of the penalty, without adherence to the conceptual strictures of the Eighth Amendment. The legislatures can and should make an assessment of the deterrent influence of capital punishment, both generally and as affecting the commission of specific types of crimes. If legislatures come to doubt the efficacy of capital punishment, they can abolish it, either completely or on a selective basis. If new evidence persuades them that they have acted unwisely, they can reverse their field and reinstate the penalty to the extent it is thought warranted. An Eighth Amendment ruling by judges cannot be made with such flexibility or discriminating precision.

The world-wide trend toward limiting the use of capital punishment, a phenomenon to which we have been urged to give great weight, hardly points the way to a judicial solution in this country under a written Constitution . . .The complete and unconditional abolition of capital punishment in this country by judicial fiat would have undermined the careful progress of the legislative trend and foreclosed further inquiry on many as yet unanswered questions in this area.

...The case against capital punishment is not the product of legal dialectic, but rests primarily on factual claims, the truth of which cannot be tested by conventional judicial processes. The five opinions in support of the judgments differ in many respects, but they share a willingness to make sweeping factual assertions, unsupported by empirical data, concerning the manner of imposition and effectiveness of capital punishment in this country. Legislatures will have the opportunity to make a more penetrating study of these claims with the familiar and effective tools available to them as they are not to us.

The highest judicial duty is to recognize the limits on judicial power and to permit the democratic processes to deal with matters falling outside of those limits. The 'hydraulic pressure[s]' that Holmes spoke of as being generated by cases of great import have propelled the Court to go beyond the limits of judicial power, while fortunately leaving some room for legislative judgment.

MR. JUSTICE BLACKMUN, dissenting.

I join the respective opinions of THE CHIEF JUSTICE, MR. JUSTICE POWELL, and MR. JUSTICE REHNQUIST, and add only the following, somewhat personal, comments.

Cases such as these provide for me an excruciating agony of the spirit. I yield to no one in the depth of my distaste, antipathy, and, indeed, abhorrence, for the death penalty, with all its aspects of physical distress and fear and of moral judgment exercised by finite minds. That distaste is buttressed by a belief that capital punishment serves no useful purpose that can be demonstrated. For me, it violates childhood's training and life's experiences, and is not compatible with the philosophical convictions I have been able to develop. It is antagonistic to any sense of 'reverence for life.' Were I a legislator, I would vote against the death penalty for the policy reasons argued by counsel for the respective petitioners and expressed and adopted in the several opinions filed by the Justices who vote to reverse these judgments...

My problem, however, as I have indicated, is the suddenness of the Court's perception of progress in the human attitude since decisions of only a short while ago.

To reverse the judgments in these cases is, of course, the easy choice. It is easier to strike the balance in favor of life and against death. It is comforting to relax in the thoughts—perhaps the rationalizations—that this is the compassionate decision for a maturing society; that this is the moral and the 'right' thing to do; that thereby we convince ourselves that we are moving down the road toward human decency; that we value life even though that life has taken another or others or has grievously scarred another or others and their families; and that we are less barbaric than we were in 1879, or in 1890, or in 1910, or in 1947, or in 1958, or in 1963, or a year ago, in 1971, when *Wilkerson, Kemmler, Weems, Francis, Trop, Rudolph,* and *McGautha* were respectively decided.

This, for me, is good argument, and it makes some sense. But it is good argument and it makes sense only in a legislative and executive way and not as a judicial expedient...The authority should not be taken over by the judiciary in the modern guise of an Eighth Amendment issue...

Although personally I may rejoice at the Court's result, I find it difficult to accept or to justify as a matter of history, of law, or of constitutional pronouncement. I fear the Court has overstepped. It has sought and has achieved an end.

MR. JUSTICE POWELL, with whom THE CHIEF JUSTICE, MR. JUSTICE BLACKMUN, and MR. JUSTICE REHNQUIST join, dissenting.

...Of course, the specific prohibitions within the Bill of Rights are limitations on the exercise of power; they are not an affirmative grant of power to the Government. I, therefore, do not read the several references to capital punishment as foreclosing this Court from considering whether the death penalty in a particular case offends the Eighth and Fourteenth Amendments. Nor are 'cruel and unusual punishments' and 'due process of law' static concepts whose meaning and scope were sealed at the time of their writing. They were designed to be dynamic and to gain meaning through application to specific circumstances, many of which were not contemplated by their authors. While flexibility in the application of these broad concepts is one of the hallmarks of our system of government, the Court is not free to read into the Constitution a meaning that is plainly at variance with its language. Both the language of the Fifth and Fourteenth Amendments and the history of the Eighth Amendment confirm beyond doubt that the death penalty was considered to be a constitutionally permissible punishment. It is, however, within the historic process of constitutional adjudication to challenge the imposition of the death penalty in some barbaric manner or as a penalty wholly disproportionate to a particular criminal act. And in making such a judgment in a case before it, a court may consider contemporary standards to the extent they are relevant. While this weighing of a punishment against the Eighth Amendment standard on a case-by-case basis is consonant with history and precedent, it is not what petitioners demand in these cases. They seek nothing less than the total abolition of capital punishment by judicial fiat . . .

Members of this Court know, from the petitions and appeals that come before us regularly, that brutish and revolting murders continue to occur with disquieting frequency. Indeed, murders are so commonplace in our society that only the most sensational receive significant and sustained publicity. It could hardly be suggested that in any of these highly publicized murder cases—the several senseless assassinations or the too numerous shocking multiple murders that have stained this country's recent history—the public has exhibited any signs of 're-vulsion' at the thought of executing the convicted murderers. The public outcry, as we all know, has been quite to the contrary. Furthermore, there is little reason to suspect that the public's reaction would differ significantly in response to other less publicized murders . . .

In pursuing the foregoing speculation, I do not suggest that it is relevant to the appropriate disposition of these cases. The purpose of the digression is to indicate that judicial decisions cannot be founded on such speculations and assumptions, however appealing they may seem . . .

I now return to the overriding question in these cases: whether this Court, acting in conformity with the Constitution, can justify its judgment to abolish capital punishment as heretofore known in this country. It is important to keep in focus the enormity of the step undertaken by the Court today. Not only does it invalidate hundreds of state and federal laws, it deprives those jurisdictions of the power to legislate with respect to capital punishment in the future, except in a manner consistent with the cloudily outlined views of those Justices who do not purport to undertake total abolition. Nothing short of an amendment to the United States Constitution can reverse the Court's judgments. Meanwhile, all flexibility is foreclosed. The normal democratic process, as well as the opportunities for the several States to respond to the will of their people expressed through ballot referenda (as in Massachusetts, Illinois, and Colorado), is now shut off . . .

With deference and respect for the views of the Justices who differ, it seems to me that all these studies—both in this country and elsewhere—suggest that, as a matter of policy and precedent, this is a classic case for the exercise of our oft-announced allegiance to judicial restraint. I know of no case in which greater gravity and delicacy have attached to the duty that this Court is called on to perform whenever legislation—state or federal—is challenged on constitutional grounds. It seems to me that the sweeping judicial action undertaken today reflects a basic lack of faith and confidence in the democratic process. Many may regret, as I do, the failure of some legislative bodies to address the capital punishment issue with greater frankness or effectiveness. Many might decry their failure either to abolish the penalty entirely or selectively, or to establish standards for its enforcement. But impatience with the slowness, and even the unresponsiveness, of legislatures is no justification for judicial intrusion upon their historic powers . . .

MR. JUSTICE REHNQUIST, with whom THE CHIEF JUSTICE, MR. JUSTICE BLACKMUN, and MR. JUSTICE POWELL join, dissenting.

The Court's judgments today strike down a penalty that our Nation's legislators have thought necessary since our country was founded . . .Whatever its precise rationale, today's holding necessarily brings into sharp relief the fundamental question of the role of judicial review in a democratic society. How can government by the elected representatives of the people co-exist with the power of the federal judiciary, whose members are constitutionally insulated from responsiveness to the popular will, to declare invalid laws duly enacted by the popular branches of government? . . .

The answer, of course, is found in Hamilton's Federalist Paper No. 78 and in Chief Justice Marshall's classic opinion in *Marbury v. Madison* . . .But just because courts in general, and this Court in particular, do have the last word, the admonition of Mr. Justice Stone dissenting in *United States v. Butler* must be constantly borne in mind:

'[W]hile unconstitutional exercise of power by the executive and legislative branches of the government is subject to judicial restraint, the only check upon our own exercise of power is our own sense of self-restraint.' . . .

Rigorous attention to the limits of this Court's authority is likewise enjoined because of the natural desire that beguiles judges along with other human beings into imposing their own views of goodness, truth, and justice upon others. Judges differ only in that they have the power, if not the authority, to enforce their desires. This is doubtless why nearly two centuries of judicial precedent from this Court counsel the sparing use of that power. The most expansive reading of the leading constitutional cases does not remotely suggest that this Court has been granted a roving commission, either by the Founding Fathers or by the framers of the Fourteenth Amendment, to strike down laws that are based upon notions of policy or morality suddenly found unacceptable by a majority of this Court . . .

A separate reason for deference to the legislative judgment is the consequence of human error on the part of the judiciary with respect to the constitutional issue before it . . .

Gregg v. Georgia (1976)

Many states, having revised their death penalty procedures in wake of Furman v. Georgia, *were looking to test the new statutes. Four years after* Furman, *the hopes that the death penalty would be permanently eradicated from America were dashed as the U.S. Supreme Court firmly noted that capital punishment was constitutional if certain guidelines were followed. In contrast to the fractured nature of* Furman, *the 7–2 decision here accepted Georgia's rationales (including deterrence) and system (a bifurcated trial) as a means to fairly and evenly apply the death penalty.*

Judgment of the Court, and opinion of MR. JUSTICE STEWART, MR. JUSTICE POWELL, and MR. JUSTICE STEVENS, announced by MR. JUSTICE STEWART.

The issue in this case is whether the imposition of the sentence of death for the crime of murder under the law of Georgia violates the Eighth and Fourteenth Amendments.

III

We address initially the basic contention that the punishment of death for the crime of murder is, under all circumstances, 'cruel and unusual' in violation of the Eighth and Fourteenth Amendments of the Constitution. In Part IV of this opinion, we will consider the sentence of death imposed under the Georgia statutes at issue in this case.

The Court on a number of occasions has both assumed and asserted the constitutionality of capital punishment. . . .

A

The history of the prohibition of 'cruel and unusual' punishment already has been reviewed at length . . .

But the Court has not confined the prohibition embodied in the Eighth Amendment to 'barbarous' methods that were generally outlawed in the 18th century. Instead, the Amendment has been interpreted in a flexible and dynamic manner. The Court early recognized that 'a principle to be vital must be capable of wider application than the mischief which gave it birth.' *Weems v. United States* (1910). Thus the Clause forbidding 'cruel and unusual' punishments 'is not fastened to the obsolete but may acquire meaning as public opinion becomes enlightened by a humane justice.' See also *Furman v. Georgia* (POWELL, J., dissenting); *Trop v. Dulles* (plurality opinion) . . .

It is clear from the foregoing precedents [*Weems, Robinson v. California, Furman*] that the Eighth Amendment has not been regarded as a static concept. As Mr. Chief Justice Warren said, in an oftquoted phrase, '[t]he Amendment must draw its meaning from the evolving standards of decency that mark the progress of a maturing society.' *Trop v. Dulles* . . .Thus, an assessment of contemporary values concerning the infliction of a challenged sanction is relevant to the application of the Eighth Amendment. As we develop below more fully this assessment does not call for a subjective judgment. It requires, rather, that we look to objective indicia that reflect the public attitude toward a given sanction.

But our cases also make clear that public perceptions of standards of decency with respect to criminal sanctions are not conclusive. A penalty also must accord with 'the dignity of man,' which is the 'basic concept underlying the Eighth Amendment.' *Trop v. Dulles* (plurality opinion). This means, at least, that the punishment not be 'excessive.' When a form of punishment in the abstract (in this case, whether capital punishment may ever be imposed as a sanction for murder) rather than in the particular (the propriety of death as a penalty to be applied to a specific defendant for a specific crime) is under consideration, the inquiry into 'excessiveness' has two aspects. First, the punishment must not involve the unnecessary and wanton infliction of pain. *Furman v. Georgia* (BURGER, C. J., dissenting). See, *Wilkerson v. Utah; Weems v. United States*. Second, the punishment must not be grossly out of proportion to the severity of the crime. *Trop v. Dulles* (plurality opinion) (dictum); *Weems v. United States*.

B

Of course, the requirements of the Eighth Amendment must be applied with an awareness of the limited role to be played by the courts.

This does not mean that judges have no role to play, for the Eighth Amendment is a restraint upon the exercise of legislative power . . .

But, while we have an obligation to insure that constitutional bounds are not overreached, we may not act as judges as we might as legislators . . .

Therefore, in assessing a punishment selected by a democratically elected legislature against the constitutional measure, we presume its validity. We may not require the legislature to select the least severe penalty possible so long as the penalty selected is not cruelly inhumane or disproportionate to the crime involved. And a heavy burden rests on those who would attack the judgment of the representatives of the people.

. . .'[I]n a democratic society legislatures, not courts, are constituted to respond to the will and consequently the moral values of the people.' *Furman v. Georgia* (BURGER, C. J., dissenting) . . .

C
. . .Four years ago, the petitioners in *Furman* and its companion cases predicated their argument primarily upon the asserted proposition that standards of decency had evolved to the point where capital punishment no longer could be tolerated . . .

The petitioners in the capital cases before the Court today renew the 'standards of decency' argument, but developments during the four years since *Furman* have undercut substantially the assumptions upon which their argument rested. Despite the continuing debate, dating back to the 19th century, over the morality and utility of capital punishment, it is now evident that a large proportion of American society continues to regard it as an appropriate and necessary criminal sanction.

The most marked indication of society's endorsement of the death penalty for murder is the legislative response to *Furman*. The legislatures of at least 35 States have enacted new statutes that provide for the death penalty for at least some crimes that result in the death of another person. And the Congress of the United States, in 1974, enacted a statute providing the death penalty for aircraft piracy that results in death. These recently adopted statutes have attempted to address the concerns expressed by the Court in *Furman* . . .

The jury also is a significant and reliable objective index of contemporary values because it is so directly involved . . .may be true that evolving standards have influenced juries in recent decades to be more discriminating in imposing the sentence of death. But the relative infrequency of jury verdicts imposing the death sentence does not indicate rejection of capital punishment per se. Rather, the reluctance of juries in many cases to impose the sentence may well reflect the humane feeling that this most irrevocable of sanctions should be reserved for a small number of extreme cases . . .

The death penalty is said to serve two principal social purposes: retribution and deterrence of capital crimes by prospective offenders.

In part, capital punishment is an expression of society's moral outrage at particularly offensive conduct. This function may be unappealing to many, but it is essential in an ordered society that asks its citizens to rely on legal processes rather than self-help to vindicate their wrongs . . .

The value of capital punishment as a deterrent of crime is a complex factual issue the resolution of which properly rests with the legislatures, which can evaluate the results of statistical studies in terms of their own local conditions and with a flexibility of approach that is not available to the courts . . .

In sum, we cannot say that the judgment of the Georgia Legislature that capital punishment may be necessary in some cases is clearly wrong. Considerations of federalism, as well as respect for the ability of a legislature to evaluate, in terms of its particular State, the moral consensus concerning the death penalty and its social utility as a sanction, require us to conclude, in the absence of more convincing evidence, that the infliction of death as a punishment for murder is not without justification and thus is not unconstitutionally severe.

IV

A

. . .In summary, the concerns expressed in *Furman* that the penalty of death not be imposed in an arbitrary or capricious manner can be met by a carefully drafted statute that ensures that the sentencing authority is given adequate information and guidance. As a general proposition these concerns are best met by a system that provides for a bifurcated proceeding at which the sentencing authority is apprised of the information relevant to the imposition of sentence and provided with standards to guide its use of the information.

We do not intend to suggest that only the above-described procedures would be permissible under *Furman* or that any sentencing system constructed along these general lines would inevitably satisfy the concerns of *Furman,* for each distinct system must be examined on an individual basis. Rather, we have embarked upon this general exposition to make clear that it is possible to construct capital-sentencing systems capable of meeting *Furman*'s constitutional concerns.

B

. . .In short, Georgia's new sentencing procedures require as a prerequisite to the imposition of the death penalty, specific jury findings as to the circumstances of the crime or the character of the defendant. Moreover, to guard further against a situation comparable to that presented in *Furman,* the Supreme Court of Georgia compares each death sentence with the sentences imposed on similarly situated defendants to ensure that the sentence of death in a particular case is not disproportionate. On their face these procedures seem to satisfy the concerns of *Furman* . . .

The petitioner contends, however, that the changes in the Georgia sentencing procedures are only cosmetic, that the arbitrariness and capriciousness condemned by *Furman* continue to exist in Georgia— both in traditional practices that still remain and in the new sentencing procedures adopted in response to *Furman* . . .

V

The basic concern of *Furman* centered on those defendants who were being condemned to death capriciously and arbitrarily. Under the procedures before the Court in that case, sentencing authorities were not directed to give attention to the nature or circumstances of the crime committed or to the character or record of the defendant. Left unguided, juries imposed the death sentence in a way that could only be called freakish. The new Georgia sentencing procedures, by contrast, focus the jury's attention on the particularized nature of the crime and the particularized characteristics of the individual defendant. While the jury is permitted to consider any aggravating or mitigating circumstances, it must find and identify at least one statutory aggravating factor before it may impose a penalty of death. In this way the jury's discretion is channeled. No longer can a jury wantonly and freakishly impose the death sentence; it is always circumscribed by the legislative guidelines. In addition, the review function of the Supreme Court of Georgia affords additional assurance that the concerns that prompted our decision in *Furman* are not present to any significant degree in the Georgia procedure applied here.

For the reasons expressed in this opinion, we hold that the statutory system under which Gregg was sentenced to death does not violate the Constitution. Accordingly, the judgment of the Georgia Supreme Court is affirmed.

It is so ordered.

MR. JUSTICE WHITE, with whom THE CHIEF JUSTICE and MR. JUSTICE REHNQUIST join, concurring in the judgment.

III

. . .[T]he petitioner argues that the death penalty will inexorably be imposed in as discriminatory, standardless, and rare a manner as it was imposed under the scheme declared invalid in *Furman*.

The argument is considerably overstated . . .The Georgia Legislature has plainly made an effort to guide the jury in the exercise of its discretion, while at the same time permitting the jury to dispense mercy on the basis of factors too intangible to write into a statute, and I cannot accept the naked assertion that the effort is bound to fail . . .[I]t can no longer be said that the penalty is being imposed wantonly and freakishly or so infrequently that it loses its usefulness as a sentencing device . . .[In addition, the Georgia Legislature] gave the Georgia Supreme Court the power and the obligation to perform precisely the task which three Justices of this Court, whose opinions were necessary to the result, performed in *Furman*: namely, the task of deciding whether in fact the death penalty was being administered for any given class of crime in a discriminatory, standardless, or rare fashion.

. . .Indeed, if the Georgia Supreme Court properly performs the task assigned to it under the Georgia statutes, death sentences imposed for discriminatory reasons or wantonly or freakishly for any given category of crime will be set aside. Petitioner has wholly failed to establish, and has not even attempted to establish, that the Georgia Supreme Court failed properly to perform its task in this case or that it is incapable of performing its task adequately in all cases; and this Court should not assume that it did not do so . . .

. . .Petitioner has argued, in effect, that no matter how effective the death penalty may be as a punishment, government, created and run as it must be by humans, is inevitably incompetent to administer it.. . . .I decline to interfere with the manner in which Georgia has chosen to enforce such laws on what is simply an assertion of lack of faith in the ability of the system of justice to operate in a fundamentally fair manner.

MR. JUSTICE BRENNAN, dissenting . . .

In *Furman v. Georgia* (concurring opinion), I read 'evolving standards of decency' as requiring focus upon the essence of the death penalty itself and not primarily or solely upon the procedures under which the determination to inflict the penalty upon a particular person was made . . .

. . .For the Clause forbidding cruel and unusual punishments under our constitutional system of government embodies in unique degree moral principles restraining the punishments that our civilized society may impose on those persons who transgress its laws . . .

This Court inescapably has the duty, as the ultimate arbiter of the meaning of our Constitution, to say whether, when individuals condemned to death stand before our Bar, 'moral concepts' require us to hold that the law has progressed to the point where we should declare that the punishment of death, like punishments on the rack, the screw, and the wheel, is no longer morally tolerable in our civilized society. My opinion in *Furman v. Georgia* concluded that our civilization and the law had progressed to this point and that therefore the punishment of death, for whatever crime and under all circumstances, is 'cruel and unusual' in violation of the Eighth and Fourteenth Amendments of the Constitution. I shall not again canvass the reasons that led to that conclusion. I emphasize only that foremost among the 'moral concepts' recognized in our cases and inherent in the Clause is the primary moral principle that the State, even as it punishes, must treat its citizens in a manner consistent with their intrinsic worth as human beings—a punishment must not be so severe as to be degrading to human dignity. A judicial determination whether the punishment of death comports with human dignity is therefore not only permitted but compelled by the Clause.

. . .Death is not only an unusually severe punishment, unusual in its pain, in its finality, and in its enormity, but it serves no penal purpose more effectively than a less severe punishment; therefore the principle inherent in the Clause that prohibits pointless infliction of excessive punishment when less severe punishment can adequately achieve the same purposes invalidates the punishment.

The fatal constitutional infirmity in the punishment of death is that it treats 'members of the human race as nonhumans, as objects to be toyed with and discarded. [It is] thus inconsistent with the fundamental premise of the Clause that even the vilest criminal remains a human being possessed of common human dignity.' As such it is a penalty that 'subjects the individual to a fate forbidden by the principle of civilized treatment guaranteed by the [Clause].' I therefore would hold, on that ground alone, that death is today a cruel and unusual punishment prohibited by the Clause. 'Justice of this kind is obviously no less shocking than the crime itself, and the new "official" murder, far from offering redress for the offense committed against society, adds instead a second defilement to the first.'

I dissent . . .

MR. JUSTICE MARSHALL, dissenting.

In *Furman v. Georgia,* I set forth at some length my views on the basic issue presented to the Court in these cases. The death penalty, I concluded, is a cruel and unusual punishment prohibited by the Eighth and Fourteenth Amendments. That continues to be my view.

I have no intention of retracing the 'long and tedious journey,' that led to my conclusion in *Furman.* My sole purposes here are to consider the suggestion that my conclusion in *Furman* has been undercut by developments since then . . .

Since the decision in *Furman,* the legislatures of 35 States have enacted new statutes authorizing the imposition of the death sentence for certain crimes, and Congress has enacted a law providing the death penalty for air piracy resulting in death . . .I would be less than candid if I did not acknowledge that these developments have a significant bearing on a realistic assessment of the moral acceptability of the death penalty to the American people. But if the constitutionality of the death penalty turns, as I have urged, on the opinion of an informed citizenry, then even the enactment of new death statutes cannot be viewed as conclusive . . .A recent study, conducted after the enactment of the post-*Furman* statutes, has confirmed that the American people know little about the death penalty, and that the opinions of an informed public would differ significantly from those of a public unaware of the consequences and effects of the death penalty.

Even assuming, however, that the post-*Furman* enactment of statutes authorizing the death penalty renders the prediction of the views of an informed citizenry an uncertain basis for a constitutional decision, the enactment of those statutes has no bearing whatsoever on the conclusion that the death penalty is unconstitutional because it is excessive. An excessive penalty is invalid under the Cruel and Unusual Punishments Clause 'even though popular sentiment may favor' it (opinion of STEWART, POWELL, and STEVENS, JJ.); *Roberts v. Louisiana* (WHITE, J., dissenting). The inquiry here, then, is simply whether the death penalty is necessary to accomplish the legitimate legislative purposes in punishment, or whether a less severe penalty—life imprisonment—would do as well.

The two purposes that sustain the death penalty as nonexcessive in the Court's view are general deterrence and retribution . . .

The available evidence, I concluded in *Furman*, was convincing that 'capital punishment is not necessary as a deterrent to crime in our society' . . .

. . .The evidence I reviewed in *Furman* remains convincing . . .The justification for the death penalty must be found elsewhere.

The other principal purpose said to be served by the death penalty is retribution. The notion that retribution can serve as a moral justification for the sanction of death finds credence in the opinion of my Brothers STEWART, POWELL, and STEVENS, and that of my Brother WHITE in *Roberts v. Louisiana*. See also *Furman v. Georgia* (BURGER, C. J., dissenting). It is this notion that I find to be the most disturbing aspect of today's unfortunate decisions.

The concept of retribution is a multifaceted one, and any discussion of its role in the criminal law must be undertaken with caution. On one level, it can be said that the notion of retribution or reprobation is the basis of our insistence that only those who have broken the law be punished, and in this sense the notion is quite obviously central to a just system of criminal sanctions. But our recognition that retribution plays a crucial role in determining who may be punished by no means requires approval of retribution as a general justification for punishment. It is the question whether retribution can provide a moral justification for punishment—in particular, capital punishment—that we must consider . . .

. . .It simply defies belief to suggest that the death penalty is necessary to prevent the American people from taking the law into their own hands.

In a related vein, it may be suggested that the expression of moral outrage through the imposition of the death penalty serves to reinforce basic moral values—that it marks some crimes as particularly offensive and therefore to be avoided. The argument is akin to a deterrence argument, but differs in that it contemplates the individual's shrinking from antisocial conduct, not because he fears punishment, but because he has been told in the strongest possible way that the conduct is wrong. This contention, like the previous one, provides no support for the death penalty. It is inconceivable that any individual concerned about conforming his conduct to what society says is 'right' would fail to realize that murder is 'wrong' if the penalty were simply life imprisonment.

The foregoing contentions . . .are essentially utilitarian in that they portray the death penalty as valuable because of its beneficial results. These justifications for the death penalty are inadequate because the penalty is, quite clearly I think, not necessary to the accomplishment of those results.

There remains for consideration, however, what might be termed the purely retributive justification for the death penalty—that the death penalty is appropriate, not because of its beneficial effect on society, but because the taking of the murderer's life is itself morally good . . .

. . .[T]he implication . . .appears to me to be . . .namely, that society's judgment that the murderer 'deserves' death must be respected not simply because the preservation of order requires it, but because it is appropriate that society make the judgment and carry it out. It is this latter notion, in particular, that I consider to be fundamentally at odds with the Eighth Amendment. See *Furman v. Georgia* (MARSHALL, J., concurring). The mere fact that the community demands the murderer's life in return for the evil he has done cannot sustain the death penalty . . .To be sustained under the Eighth Amendment, the death penalty must 'compor[t] with the basic concept of human dignity at the core of the Amendment,' *ibid.;* the objective in imposing it must be '[consistent] with our respect for the dignity of [other] men.' See *Trop v. Dulles* (plurality opinion). Under these standards, the taking of life 'because the wrongdoer deserves it' surely must fall, for such a punishment has as its very basis the total denial of the wrongdoer's dignity and worth.

The death penalty, unnecessary to promote the goal of deterrence or to further any legitimate notion of retribution, is an excessive penalty forbidden by the Eighth and Fourteenth Amendments. I respectfully dissent from the Court's judgment upholding the sentences of death imposed upon the petitioners in these cases.

Woodson v. North Carolina (1976)

Decided the same day as Gregg v. Georgia, *this case declared that sentencing procedures that made the death penalty mandatory were unconstitutional.* Woodson *established an important theme in death penalty jurisprudence—the idea of individualized justice. Because each capital case was unique in its circumstances, as well as the circumstances of the defendant, each defendant and his actions must be analyzed on a case-by-case basis. This was an important concept in future cases when the U.S. Supreme Court began to explore the importance of aggravating and mitigating circumstances.*

Judgment of the Court, and opinion of MR. JUSTICE STEWART, MR. JUSTICE POWELL, and MR. JUSTICE STEVENS, announced by MR. JUSTICE STEWART.

III

A

[The Court reviewed the history of mandatory death penalties in America]

...The history of mandatory death penalty statutes in the United States thus reveals that the practice of sentencing to death all persons convicted of a particular offense has been rejected as unduly harsh and unworkably rigid. The two crucial indicators of evolving standards of decency respecting the imposition of punishment in our society—jury determinations and legislative enactments—both point conclusively to the repudiation of automatic death sentences. At least since the Revolution, American jurors have, with some regularity, disregarded their oaths and refused to convict defendants where a death sentence was the automatic consequence of a guilty verdict. As we have seen, the initial movement to reduce the number of capital offenses and to separate murder into degrees was prompted in part by the reaction of jurors as well as by reformers who objected to the imposition of death as the penalty for any crime. Nineteenth century journalists, statesmen, and jurists repeatedly observed that jurors were often deterred from convicting palpably guilty men of first-degree murder under mandatory statutes . . ..

As we have noted today in *Gregg v. Georgia* legislative measures adopted by the people's chosen representatives weigh heavily in ascertaining contemporary standards of decency. The consistent course charted by the state legislatures and by Congress since the middle of the past century demonstrates that the aversion of jurors to mandatory death penalty statutes is shared by society at large.

Still further evidence of the incompatibility of mandatory death penalties with contemporary values is provided by the results of jury sentencing under discretionary statutes . . . Various studies indicate that even in first-degree murder cases juries with sentencing discretion do not impose the death penalty 'with any great frequency.' The actions of sentencing juries suggest that under contemporary standards of decency death is viewed as an inappropriate punishment for a substantial portion of convicted first-degree murderers . . .

Although it seems beyond dispute that, at the time of the *Furman* decision in 1972, mandatory death penalty statutes had been renounced by American juries and legislatures, there remains the question whether the mandatory statutes adopted by North Carolina and a number of other States following *Furman* evince a sudden reversal of societal values regarding the imposition of capital punishment. In view of the persistent and unswerving legislative rejection of mandatory death penalty statutes beginning in 1838 and continuing for more than 130 years until *Furman*, it seems evident that the post-*Furman* enactments reflect attempts by the States to retain the death penalty in a form consistent with the Constitution, rather than a renewed societal acceptance of mandatory death sentencing. The fact that some States have adopted mandatory measures following *Furman* while others have legislated standards to guide jury discretion appears attributable to diverse readings of this Court's multiopinioned decision in that case . . .

B

. . . [W]hen one considers the long and consistent American experience with the death penalty in first-degree murder cases, it becomes evident that mandatory statutes enacted in response to *Furman* have simply papered over the problem of unguided and unchecked jury discretion.

. . . North Carolina's mandatory death penalty statute provides no standards to guide the jury in its inevitable exercise of the power to determine which first-degree murderers shall live and which shall die. And there is no way under the North Carolina law for the judiciary to check arbitrary and capricious exercise of that power through a review of death sentences. Instead of rationalizing the sentencing process, a mandatory scheme may well exacerbate the problem identified in *Furman* by resting the penalty determination on the particular jury's willingness to act lawlessly. While a mandatory death penalty statute may reasonably be expected to increase the number of persons sentenced to death, it does not fulfill *Furman's* basic requirement by replacing arbitrary and wanton jury discretion with objective standards to guide, regularize, and make rationally reviewable the process for imposing a sentence of death.

C

A third constitutional shortcoming of the North Carolina statute is its failure to allow the particularized consideration of relevant aspects of the character and record of each convicted defendant before the imposition upon him of a sentence of death . . .A process that accords no significance to relevant facets of the character and record of the individual offender or the circumstances of the particular offense excludes from consideration in fixing the ultimate punishment of death the possibility of compassionate or mitigating factors stemming from the diverse frailties of humankind. It treats all persons convicted of a designated offense not as uniquely individual human beings, but as members of a faceless, undifferentiated mass to be subjected to the blind infliction of the penalty of death . . .

. . .While the prevailing practice of individualizing sentencing determinations generally reflects simply enlightened policy rather than a constitutional imperative, we believe that in capital cases the fundamental respect for humanity underlying the Eighth Amendment . . .requires consideration of the character and record of the individual offender and the circumstances of the particular offense as a constitutionally indispensable part of the process of inflicting the penalty of death.

This conclusion rests squarely on the predicate that the penalty of death is qualitatively different from a sentence of imprisonment, however long. Death, in its finality, differs more from life imprisonment than a 100-year prison term difference from one of only a year or two. Because of that qualitative difference, there is a corresponding difference in the need for reliability in the determination that death is the appropriate punishment in a specific case.

For the reasons stated, we conclude that the death sentences imposed upon the petitioners under North Carolina's mandatory death sentence statute violated the Eighth and Fourteenth Amendments and therefore must be set aside. . . .

MR. JUSTICE MARSHALL, concurring in the judgment.

For the reasons stated in my dissenting opinion in *Gregg v. Georgia*, I am of the view that the death penalty is a cruel and unusual punishment forbidden by the Eighth and Fourteenth Amendments. I therefore concur in the Court's judgment.

MR. JUSTICE REHNQUIST, dissenting.

II

The plurality is simply mistaken in its assertion that '[t]he history of mandatory death penalty statutes in the United States thus reveals that the practice of sentencing to death all persons convicted of a particular offense has been rejected as unduly harsh and unworkably rigid' . . .

There can be no question that the legislative and other materials discussed in the plurality's opinion show a widespread conclusion on the part of state legislatures during the 19th century that the penalty of death was being required for too broad a range of crimes, and that these legislatures proceeded to narrow the range of crimes for which such penalty could be imposed...But petitioners were convicted of first-degree murder, and there is not the slightest suggestion in the material relied upon by the plurality that there had been any turning away at all, much less any such unanimous turning away, from the death penalty as a punishment for those guilty of first-degree murder...

The second string to the plurality's analytical bow is that legislative change from mandatory to discretionary imposition of the death sentence likewise evidences societal rejection of mandatory death penalties. The plurality simply does not make out this part of its case . . .

So far as the action of juries is concerned, the fact that in some cases juries operating under the mandatory system refused to convict obviously guilty defendants does not reflect any 'turning away' from the death penalty, or the mandatory death penalty, supporting the proposition that it is 'cruel and unusual.' Given the requirement of unanimity with respect to jury verdicts in capital cases . . .it is apparent that a single juror could prevent a jury from returning a verdict of conviction. Occasional refusals to convict, therefore, may just as easily have represented the intransigence of only a small minority of 12 jurors as well as the unanimous judgment of all 12 . . .

III

The second constitutional flaw which the plurality finds in North Carolina's mandatory system is that it has simply 'papered over' the problem of unchecked jury discretion . . .

. . .The freakish and arbitrary nature of the death penalty described in the separate concurring opinions of JUSTICES STEWART and WHITE in *Furman* arose not from the perception that so many capital sentences were being imposed but from the perception that so few were being imposed. To conclude that the North Carolina system is bad because juror nullification may permit jury discretion while concluding that the Georgia and Florida systems are sound because they require this same discretion, is, as the plurality opinion demonstrates, inexplicable . . .

The plurality's insistence on 'standards' to 'guide the jury in its inevitable exercise of the power to determine which . . .murderers shall live and which shall die' is squarely contrary to the Court's opinion in *McGautha v. California* written by Mr. Justice Harlan and subscribed to by five other Members of the Court only five years ago . . .Its abandonment of stare decisis in this repudiation of *McGautha* is a far lesser mistake than its substitution of a superficial and contrived constitutional doctrine for the genuine wisdom contained in *McGautha* . . .

IV

. . .None of the cases half-heartedly cited by the plurality in Part III-C comes within a light-year of establishing the proposition that individualized consideration is a constitutional requisite for the imposition of the death penalty . . .

The plurality also relies upon the indisputable proposition that 'death is different' for the result which it reaches in Part III-C. But the respects in which death is 'different' from other punishment which may be imposed upon convicted criminals do not seem to me to establish the proposition that the Constitution requires individualized sentencing.

One of the principal reasons why death is different is because it is irreversible; an executed defendant cannot be brought back to life. This aspect of the difference between death and other penalties would undoubtedly support statutory provisions for especially careful review of the fairness of the trial, the accuracy of the factfinding process, and the fairness of the sentencing procedure where the death penalty is imposed. But none of those aspects of the death sentence is at issue here. Petitioners were found guilty of the crime of first-degree murder in a trial the constitutional validity of which is unquestioned here. And since the punishment of death is conceded by the plurality not to be a cruel and unusual punishment for such a crime, the irreversible aspect of the death penalty has no connection whatever with any requirement for individualized consideration of the sentence . . .

The plurality's insistence on individualized consideration of the sentencing, therefore, does not depend upon any traditional application of the prohibition against cruel and unusual punishment contained in the Eighth Amendment. The punishment here is concededly not cruel and unusual, and that determination has traditionally ended judicial inquiry in our cases construing the Cruel and Unusual Punishments Clause . . . What the plurality opinion has actually done is to import into the Due Process Clause of the Fourteenth Amendment what it conceives to be desirable procedural guarantees where the punishment of death, concededly not cruel and unusual for the crime of which the defendant was convicted, is to be imposed. This is squarely contrary to *McGautha*, and unsupported by any other decision of this Court . . .

Coker v. Georgia (1977)

Coker established that death was acceptable only in cases of murder. In this case, despite the horrendous crime spree and rape committed by the defendant, the U.S. Supreme Court refused to extend the death penalty to nonmurder instances. Although seven justices agreed that the death sentence violated the Eighth Amendment, a majority could not agree on why. Justice White's plurality, while acknowledging the egregious nature of the crime of rape, saw the punishment of death as a disproportionate and excessive punishment for it. The dissent argued the Court was making policy and had overstepped its bounds.

MR. JUSTICE WHITE announced the judgment of the Court and filed an opinion in which MR. JUSTICE STEWART, MR. JUSTICE BLACKMUN, and MR. JUSTICE STEVENS, joined . . .

. . . It is now settled that the death penalty is not invariably cruel and unusual punishment within the meaning of the Eighth Amendment; it is not inherently barbaric or an unacceptable mode of punishment for crime; neither is it always disproportionate to the crime for which it is imposed . . .

[The] question, with respect to rape of an adult woman, is now before us. We have concluded that a sentence of death is grossly disproportionate and excessive punishment for the crime of rape and is therefore forbidden by the Eighth Amendment as cruel and unusual punishment.

. . .In reviving death penalty laws to satisfy *Furman's* mandate, none of the States that had not previously authorized death for rape chose to include rape among capital felonies. Of the 16 States in which rape had been a capital offense, only three provided the death penalty for rape of an adult woman in their revised statutes—Georgia, North Carolina, and Louisiana . . .

The current judgment with respect to the death penalty for rape is not wholly unanimous among state legislatures, but it obviously weighs very heavily on the side of rejecting capital punishment as a suitable penalty for raping an adult woman.

B

It was also observed in *Gregg* that '[t]he jury... is a significant and reliable objective index of contemporary values because it is so directly involved,' and that it is thus important to look to the sentencing decisions that juries have made . . .

. . .Georgia juries have thus sentenced rapists to death six times since 1973. This obviously is not a negligible number; and the State argues that as a practical matter juries simply reserve the extreme sanction for extreme cases of rape and that recent experience surely does not prove that jurors consider the death penalty to be a disproportionate punishment for every conceivable instance of rape, no matter how aggravated. Nevertheless, it is true that in the vast majority of cases, at least 9 out of 10, juries have not imposed the death sentence.

These recent events evidencing the attitude of state legislatures and sentencing juries do not wholly determine this controversy, for the Constitution contemplates that in the end our own judgment will be brought to bear on the question of the acceptability of the death penalty under the Eighth Amendment. Nevertheless, the legislative rejection of capital punishment for rape strongly confirms our own judgment, which is that death is indeed a disproportionate penalty for the crime of raping an adult woman.

We do not discount the seriousness of rape as a crime. It is highly reprehensible, both in a moral sense and in its almost total contempt for the personal integrity and autonomy of the female victim and for the latter's privilege of choosing those with whom intimate relationships are to be established. Short of homicide, it is the 'ultimate violation of self.' It is also a violent crime because it normally involves force, or the threat of force or intimidation, to overcome the will and the capacity of the victim to resist. Rape is very often accompanied by physical injury to the female and can also inflict mental and psychological damage. Because it undermines the community's sense of security, there is public injury as well.

Rape is without doubt deserving of serious punishment; but in terms of moral depravity and of the injury to the person and to the public, it does not compare with murder, which does involve the unjustified taking of human life. Although it may be accompanied by another crime, rape by definition does not include the death of or even the serious injury to another person. The murderer kills; the rapist, if no more than that, does not. Life is over for the victim of the murderer; for the rape victim, life may not be nearly so happy as it was, but it is not over and normally is not beyond repair. We have the abiding conviction that the death penalty, which 'is unique in its severity and irrevocability,' *Gregg v. Georgia* is an excessive penalty for the rapist who, as such, does not take human life . . .

. . .[E]ven where the killing is deliberate, it is not punishable by death absent proof of aggravating circumstances. It is difficult to accept the notion, and we do not, that the rapist, with or without aggravating circumstances, should be punished more heavily than the deliberate killer as long as the rapist does not himself take the life of his victim. The judgment of the Georgia Supreme Court upholding the death sentence is reversed, and the case is remanded to that court for further proceedings not inconsistent with this opinion.

So ordered.

MR. JUSTICE POWELL, concurring in the judgment in part and dissenting in part . . .

Today, in a case that does not require such an expansive pronouncement, the plurality draws a bright line between murder and all rapes—regardless of the degree of brutality of the rape or the effect upon the victim. I dissent because I am not persuaded that such a bright line is appropriate . . .The deliberate viciousness of the rapist may be greater than that of the murderer. Rape is never an act committed accidentally. Rarely can it be said to be unpremeditated. There also is wide variation in the effect on the victim . . .

Thus, it may be that the death penalty is not disproportionate punishment for the crime of aggravated rape . . .But it has not been shown that society finds the penalty disproportionate for all rapes . . .

MR. CHIEF JUSTICE BURGER, with whom MR. JUSTICE REHNQUIST joins, dissenting.

. . .In striking down the death penalty imposed upon the petitioner in this case, the Court has overstepped the bounds of proper constitutional adjudication by substituting its policy judgment for that of the state legislature. I accept that the Eighth Amendment's concept of disproportionality bars the death penalty for minor crimes. But rape is not a minor crime . . .

Unlike the plurality, I would narrow the inquiry in this case to the question actually presented: Does the Eighth Amendment's ban against cruel and unusual punishment prohibit the State of Georgia from executing a person who has, within the space of three years, raped three separate women, killing one and attempting to kill another, who is serving prison terms exceeding his probable lifetime and who has not hesitated to escape confinement at the first available opportunity? Whatever one's view may be as to the State's constitutional power to impose the death penalty upon a rapist who stands before a court convicted for the first time, this case reveals a chronic rapist whose continuing danger to the community is abundantly clear.

. . .Apart from the reality that rape is inherently one of the most egregiously brutal acts one human being can inflict upon another, there is nothing in the Eighth Amendment that so narrowly limits the factors which may be considered by a state legislature in determining whether a particular punishment is grossly excessive. Surely recidivism, especially the repeated commission of heinous crimes, is a factor which may properly be weighed as an aggravating circumstance, permitting the imposition of a punishment more severe than for one isolated offense . . .As a factual matter, the plurality opinion is correct in stating that Coker's 'prior convictions do not change the fact that the instant crime being punished is a rape not involving the taking of life,' however, it cannot be disputed that the existence of these prior convictions makes Coker a substantially more serious menace to society than a first-time offender . . .

. . .[W]hen considered in light of the experience since the turn of this century, where more than one-third of American jurisdictions have consistently provided the death penalty for rape, the plurality's focus on the experience of the immediate past must be viewed as truly disingenuous. Having in mind the swift changes in positions of some Members of this Court in the short span of five years, can it rationally be considered a relevant indicator of what our society deems 'cruel and unusual' to look solely to what legislatures have *refrained* from doing under conditions of great uncertainty arising from our less than lucid holdings on the Eighth Amendment?

The question of whether the death penalty is an appropriate punishment for rape is surely an open one . . .

The subjective judgment that the death penalty is simply disproportionate to the crime of rape is even more disturbing than the 'objective' analysis discussed *supra*. The plurality's conclusion on this point is based upon the bare fact that murder necessarily results in the physical death of the victim, while rape does not. However, no Member of the Court explains why this distinction has relevance, much less constitutional significance. It is, after all, not irrational—nor constitutionally impermissible—for a legislature to make the penalty more severe than the criminal act it punishes in the hope it would deter wrongdoing . . .

Until now, the issue under the Eighth Amendment has not been the state of any particular victim after the crime, but rather whether the punishment imposed is grossly disproportionate to the evil committed by the perpetrator. As a matter of constitutional principle, that test cannot have the primitive simplicity of 'life for life, eye for eye, tooth for tooth.' Rather States must be permitted to engage in a more sophisticated weighing of values in dealing with criminal activity . . .

Rape . . . is not a crime 'light years' removed from murder in the degree of its heinousness; it certainly poses a serious potential danger to the life and safety of innocent victims—apart from the devastating psychic consequences. It would seem to follow therefore that, affording the States proper leeway under the broad standard of the Eighth Amendment, if murder is properly punishable by death, rape should be also, if that is the considered judgment of the legislators.

The Court's conclusion to the contrary is very disturbing indeed. The clear implication of today's holding appears to be that the death penalty may be properly imposed only as to crimes resulting in death of the victim. This casts serious doubt upon the constitutional validity of statutes imposing the death penalty for a variety of conduct which, though dangerous, may not necessarily result in any immediate death, *e.g.,* treason, airplane hijacking, and kidnapping . . .

Lockett v. Ohio (1978)

At issue in many death penalty cases is the kind of evidence that can be presented in making the decision on whether to execute. Lockett harkened back to the ideas of individualized justice and noted that without the opportunity to present mitigating evidence, any imposition of the death penalty was unconstitutional.

MR. CHIEF JUSTICE BURGER delivered the opinion of the Court . . .

Lockett challenges the constitutionality of Ohio's death penalty statute on a number of grounds. We find it necessary to consider only her contention that her death sentence is invalid because the statute under which it was imposed did not permit the sentencing judge to consider, as mitigating factors, her character, prior record, age, lack of specific intent to cause death, and her relatively minor part in the crime . . .

. . .The mandatory death penalty statute in *Woodson* was held invalid because it permitted *no* consideration of 'relevant facets of the character and record of the individual offender or the circumstances of the particular offense.' The plurality did not attempt to indicate, however, which facets of an offender or his offense it deemed 'relevant' in capital sentencing or what degree of consideration of 'relevant facets' it would require.

We are now faced with those questions and we conclude that the Eighth and Fourteenth Amendments require that the sentencer, in all but the rarest kind of capital case, not be precluded from considering, *as a mitigating factor,* any aspect of a defendant's character or record and any of the circumstances of the offense that the defendant proffers as a basis for a sentence less than death. We recognize that, in noncapital cases, the established practice of individualized sentences rests not on constitutional commands, but on public policy enacted into statutes. The considerations that account for the wide acceptance of individualization of sentences in noncapital cases surely cannot be thought less important in capital cases. Given that the imposition of death by public authority is so profoundly different from all other penalties, we cannot avoid the conclusion that an individualized decision is essential in capital cases. The need for treating each defendant in a capital case with that degree of respect due the uniqueness of the individual is far more important than in noncapital cases . . .

C

The Ohio death penalty statute does not permit the type of individualized consideration of mitigating factors we now hold to be required by the Eighth and Fourteenth Amendments in capital cases . . .

[In the Ohio Statute at question,] once a defendant is found guilty of aggravated murder with at least one of seven specified aggravating circumstances, the death penalty must be imposed unless, considering 'the nature and circumstances of the offense and the history, character, and condition of the offender,' the sentencing judge determines that at least one . . .mitigating circumstance is established by a preponderance of the evidence . . .

. . .We see, therefore, that once it is determined that the victim did not induce or facilitate the offense, that the defendant did not act under duress or coercion, and that the offense was not primarily the product of the defendant's mental deficiency, the Ohio statute mandates the sentence of death. The absence of direct proof that the defendant intended to cause the death of the victim is relevant for mitigating purposes only if it is determined that it sheds some light on one of the three statutory mitigating factors. Similarly, consideration of a defendant's comparatively minor role in the offense, or age, would generally not be permitted, as such, to affect the sentencing decision.

The limited range of mitigating circumstances which may be considered by the sentencer under the Ohio statute is incompatible with the Eighth and Fourteenth Amendments. To meet constitutional requirements, a death penalty statute must not preclude consideration of relevant mitigating factors

Accordingly, the judgment under review is reversed to the extent that it sustains the imposition of the death penalty, and the case is remanded for further proceedings.

MR. JUSTICE WHITE, concurring in part, dissenting in part, and concurring in the judgments of the Court.

. . .The Court has now completed its about-face since *Furman v. Georgia* . . .

With all due respect, I dissent. I continue to be of the view, for the reasons set forth in my dissenting opinion in *Roberts,* that it does not violate the Eighth Amendment for a State to impose the death penalty on a mandatory basis when the defendant has been found guilty beyond a reasonable doubt of committing a deliberate, unjustified killing. Moreover, I greatly fear that the effect of the Court's decision today will be to compel constitutionally a restoration of the state of affairs at the time *Furman* was decided, where the death penalty is imposed so erratically and the threat of execution is so attenuated for even the most atrocious murders that 'its imposition would then be the pointless and needless extinction of life with only marginal contributions to any discernible social or public purposes.' *Furman v. Georgia* (WHITE, J., concurring). By requiring as a matter of constitutional law that sentencing authorities be permitted to consider and in their discretion to act upon any and all mitigating circumstances, the Court permits them to refuse to impose the death penalty no matter what the circumstances of the crime. This invites a return to the pre-*Furman* days when the death penalty was generally reserved for those very few for whom society has least consideration . . .

II

I nevertheless concur in the judgments of the Court reversing the imposition of the death sentences because I agree with the contention of the petitioners, ignored by the plurality, that it violates the Eighth Amendment to impose the penalty of death without a finding that the defendant possessed a purpose to cause the death of the victim . . .

[T]he conclusion is unavoidable that the infliction of death upon those who had no intent to bring about the death of the victim is not only grossly out of proportion to the severity of the crime but also fails to contribute significantly to acceptable or, indeed, any perceptible goals of punishment.

MR. JUSTICE REHNQUIST, concurring in part and dissenting in part.

I join Parts I and II of THE CHIEF JUSTICE's opinion for the Court, but am unable to join Part III of his opinion or in the judgment of reversal.

I

. . .The Court has most assuredly . . .not cloven to a principled doctrine either holding the infliction of the death penalty to be unconstitutional *per se* or clearly and understandably stating the terms under which the Eighth and Fourteenth Amendments permit the death penalty to be imposed. Instead, as I believe both the opinion of THE CHIEF JUSTICE and the opinion of my Brother WHITE seem to concede, the Court has gone from pillar to post, with the result that the sort of reasonable predictability upon which legislatures, trial courts, and appellate courts must of necessity rely has been all but completely sacrificed.

. . .[I]t can scarcely be maintained that today's decision is the logical application of a coherent doctrine first espoused by the opinions leading to the Court's judgment in *Furman,* and later elaborated in the *Woodson* series of cases decided two Terms ago . . .The opinion strives manfully to appear as a logical exegesis of those opinions, but I believe that it fails in the effort. We are now told, in effect, that in order to impose a death sentence the judge or jury must receive in evidence whatever the defense attorney wishes them to hear. I do not think THE CHIEF JUSTICE's effort to trace this quite novel constitutional principle back to the plurality and lead opinions in the *Woodson* cases succeeds . . .

It seems to me indisputably clear from today's opinion that . . .the Court is scarcely faithful to what has been written before. As a practical matter, I doubt that today's opinion will make a great deal of difference in the manner in which trials in capital cases are conducted, since I would suspect that it has been the practice of most trial judges to permit a defendant to offer virtually any sort of evidence in his own defense as he wished . . .If a defendant as a matter of constitutional law is to be permitted to offer as evidence in the sentencing hearing any fact, however bizarre, which he wishes, even though the most sympathetically disposed trial judge could conceive of no basis upon which the jury might take it into account in imposing a sentence, the new constitutional doctrine will not eliminate arbitrariness or freakishness in the imposition of sentences, but will codify and institutionalize it. By encouraging defendants in capital cases, and presumably sentencing judges and juries, to take into consideration anything under the sun as a 'mitigating circumstance,' it will not guide sentencing discretion but will totally unleash it . . .

II

. . .I finally reject the proposition urged by my Brother WHITE in his separate opinion, which the plurality finds it unnecessary to reach. That claim is that the death penalty, as applied to one who participated in this murder as Lockett did, is 'disproportionate' and therefore violative of the Eighth and Fourteenth Amendments. I know of no principle embodied in those Amendments, other than perhaps one's personal notion of what is a fitting punishment for a crime, which would allow this Court to hold the death penalty imposed upon her unconstitutional because under the judge's charge to the jury the latter were not required to find that she intended to cause the death of her victim . . . Centuries of common-law doctrine establishing the felony-murder doctrine, dealing with the relationship between aiders and abettors and principals, would have to be rejected to adopt this view. Just as surely as many thoughtful moralists and penologists would reject the Biblical notion of 'an eye for an eye, a tooth for a tooth,' as a guide for minimum sentencing, there is nothing in the prohibition against cruel and unusual punishments contained in the Eighth Amendment which sets that injunction as a limitation on the maximum sentence which society may impose.

Godfrey v. Georgia (1980)

Godfrey reiterated that, despite the importance that justice be individualized, the imposition of the death penalty had to follow some type of specific standard. Here, the idea that just because a crime was "outrageously or wantonly vile, horrible and inhuman" was too vague. It provided no consistent guidance for the jury. Marshall and Brennan's concurrence noted that this paradoxical nature—individualization while simultaneously trying to make it uniform— proved the inherent arbitrary nature of the death penalty.

MR. JUSTICE STEWART announced the judgment of the Court and delivered an opinion, in which MR. JUSTICE BLACKMUN, MR. JUSTICE POWELL, and MR. JUSTICE STEVENS joined . . .

In the case before us, the Georgia Supreme Court has affirmed a sentence of death based upon no more than a finding that the offense was 'outrageously or wantonly vile, horrible and inhuman.' There is nothing in these few words, standing alone, that implies any inherent restraint on the arbitrary and capricious infliction of the death sentence. A person of ordinary sensibility could fairly characterize almost every murder as 'outrageously or wantonly vile, horrible and inhuman.' Such a view may, in fact, have been one to which the members of the jury in this case subscribed. If so, their preconceptions were not dispelled by the trial judge's sentencing instructions. These gave the jury no guidance . . .

. . .[T]he validity of the petitioner's death sentences turns on whether, in light of the facts and circumstances of the murders that he was convicted of committing, the Georgia Supreme Court can be said to have applied a constitutional construction of the phrase 'outrageously or wantonly vile, horrible or inhuman in that [they] involved . . . depravity of mind . . .' We conclude that the answer must be no. The petitioner's crimes cannot be said to have reflected a consciousness materially more 'depraved' than that of any person guilty of murder. His victims were killed instantaneously. They were members of his family who were causing him extreme emotional trauma. Shortly after the killings, he acknowledged his responsibility and the heinous nature of his crimes. These factors certainly did not remove the criminality from the petitioner's acts. But, as was said in *Gardner v. Florida,* it 'is of vital importance to the defendant and to the community that any decision to impose the death sentence be, and appear to be, based on reason rather than caprice or emotion.'

That cannot be said here. There is no principled way to distinguish this case, in which the death penalty was imposed, from the many cases in which it was not. Accordingly, the judgment of the Georgia Supreme Court insofar as it leaves standing the petitioner's death sentences is reversed, and the case is remanded to that court for further proceedings.

It is so ordered.

MR. JUSTICE MARSHALL, with whom MR. JUSTICE BRENNAN joins, concurring in the judgment . . .

I

. . . I think it necessary to emphasize that even under the prevailing view that the death penalty may, in some circumstances, constitutionally be imposed, it is not enough for a reviewing court to apply a narrowing construction to otherwise ambiguous statutory language. The jury must be instructed on the proper, narrow construction of the statute. The Court's cases make clear that it is the sentencer's discretion that must be channeled and guided by clear, objective, and specific standards. To give the jury an instruction in the form of the bare words of the statute—words that are hopelessly ambiguous and could

be understood to apply to any murder—would effectively grant it unbridled discretion to impose the death penalty . . .

For this reason, I believe that the vices of vagueness and intolerably
broad discretion are present in any case . . .

II

. . .For reasons I expressed in *Furman v. Georgia* (concurring opinion) and *Gregg v. Georgia* (dissenting opinion), I believe that the
death penalty may not constitutionally be imposed even if it were possible to do so in an evenhanded manner. But events since *Gregg* make
that possibility seem increasingly remote. Nearly every week of every
year, this Court is presented with at least one petition for certiorari
raising troubling issues of noncompliance with the strictures of *Gregg*
and its progeny. On numerous occasions since *Gregg*, the Court has
reversed decisions of State Supreme Courts upholding the imposition
of capital punishment, frequently on the ground that the sentencing
proceeding allowed undue discretion, causing dangers of arbitrariness
in violation of *Gregg* and its companion cases. These developments,
coupled with other persuasive evidence, strongly suggest that appellate courts are incapable of guaranteeing the kind of objectivity and
evenhandedness that the Court contemplated and hoped for in *Gregg*.
The disgraceful distorting effects of racial discrimination and poverty
continue to be painfully visible in the imposition of death sentences.
And while hundreds have been placed on death row in the years since
Gregg, only three persons have been executed. Two of them made no
effort to challenge their sentence and were thus permitted to commit
what I have elsewhere described as 'state-administered suicide.' . . .
The task of eliminating arbitrariness in the infliction of capital punishment is proving to be one which our criminal justice system—and perhaps any criminal justice system—is unable to perform. In short, it is
now apparent that the defects that led my Brothers DOUGLAS,
STEWART, and WHITE to concur in the judgment in *Furman* are
present as well in the statutory schemes under which defendants are
currently sentenced to death . . .

The Georgia court's inability to administer its capital punishment
statute in an evenhanded fashion is not necessarily attributable to any
bad faith on its part; it is, I believe, symptomatic of a deeper problem
that is proving to be genuinely intractable . . .

...I believe that the Court in *McGautha* was substantially correct in concluding that the task of selecting in some objective way those persons who should be condemned to die is one that remains beyond the capacities of the criminal justice system. For this reason, I remain hopeful that even if the Court is unwilling to accept the view that the death penalty is so barbaric that it is in all circumstances cruel and unusual punishment forbidden by the Eighth and Fourteenth Amendments, it may eventually conclude that the effort to eliminate arbitrariness in the infliction of that ultimate sanction is so plainly doomed to failure that it—and the death penalty—must be abandoned altogether.

MR. CHIEF JUSTICE BURGER, dissenting.

After murdering his wife and mother-in-law, petitioner informed the police that he had committed a 'hideous' crime. The dictionary defines hideous as 'morally offensive,' 'shocking,' or 'horrible.' Thus, the very curious feature of this case is that petitioner himself characterized his crime in terms equivalent to those employed in the Georgia statute. For my part, I prefer petitioner's characterization of his conduct to the plurality's effort to excuse and rationalize that conduct as just another killing. The jurors in this case, who heard all relevant mitigating evidence...obviously shared that preference; they concluded that this 'hideous' crime was 'outrageously or wantonly vile, horrible and inhuman' within the meaning of [the statute].

More troubling than the plurality's characterization of petitioner's crime is the new responsibility that it assumes with today's decision—the task of determining on a case-by-case basis whether a defendant's conduct is egregious enough to warrant a death sentence....For me, this new requirement is arbitrary and unfounded and trivializes the Constitution...

MR. JUSTICE WHITE, with whom MR. JUSTICE REHNQUIST joins, dissenting.

...As described earlier, petitioner, in a coldblooded executioner's style, murdered his wife and his mother-in-law and, in passing, struck his young daughter on the head with the barrel of his gun...

The Georgia Supreme Court held that these facts supported the jury's finding of the existence of statutory aggravating circumstance...A majority of this Court disagrees...Our role is to correct genuine errors of constitutional significance resulting from the application of Georgia's capital sentencing procedures; our role is not to peer majestically over the lower court's shoulder so that we might second-guess its interpretation of facts that quite reasonably—perhaps even quite plainly—fit within the statutory language.

Who is to say that the murders of Mrs. Godfrey and Mrs. Wilkerson were not 'vile,' or 'inhuman,' or 'horrible'? In performing his murderous chore, petitioner employed a weapon known for its disfiguring effects on targets, human or other, and he succeeded in creating a scene so macabre and revolting that, if anything, 'vile,' 'horrible,' and 'inhuman' are descriptively inadequate.

And who among us can honestly say that Mrs. Wilkerson did not feel 'torture' in her last sentient moments. Her daughter, an instant ago a living being sitting across the table from Mrs. Wilkerson, lay prone on the floor, a bloodied and mutilated corpse. The seconds ticked by; enough time for her son-in-law to reload his gun, to enter the home, and to take a gratuitous swipe at his daughter. What terror must have run through her veins as she first witnessed her daughter's hideous demise and then came to terms with the imminence of her own. Was this not torture? And if this was not torture, can it honestly be said that petitioner did not exhibit a 'depravity of mind' in carrying out this cruel drama to its mischievous and murderous conclusion? I should have thought, moreover, that the Georgia court could reasonably have deemed the scene awaiting the investigating policemen as involving 'an aggravated battery to the victim[s].'

The point is not that, in my view, petitioner's crimes were definitively vile, horrible, or inhuman, or that, as I assay the evidence, they beyond any doubt involved torture, depravity of mind, or an aggravated battery to the victims. Rather, the lesson is a much more elementary one, an instruction that, I should have thought, this Court would have taken to heart long ago. Our mandate does not extend to interfering with factfinders in state criminal proceedings or with state courts that are responsibly and consistently interpreting state law, unless that interference is predicated on a violation of the Constitution. No convincing showing of such a violation is made here . . .

Enmund v. Florida (1982)

A Florida case that rejected the death penalty for people who were by-standers and did not actually kill, attempt to kill, or intend to kill. The U.S. Supreme Court overturned the Florida Supreme Court, which ruled that the defendant was guilty of first-degree murder. Even

*though the evidence suggested that at best the defendant was in the car
waiting to help his fellow robbers escape, under Florida law anyone
who aided and abetted in a crime where a murder took place was
guilty of first-degree murder. The 5-4 decision again played out the
deep divisions in the Court over the death penalty and pulled together
many of the arguments that had highlighted previous cases such as
Gregg, Woodson, Coker, and Lockett. It is notable that only Justice
Brennan, in a short concurrence, argued that the death penalty, per se,
violated the Eighth Amendment.*

JUSTICE WHITE delivered the opinion of the Court . . .

Although the judgments of legislatures, juries, and prosecutors
weigh heavily in the balance, it is for us ultimately to judge whether
the Eighth Amendment permits imposition of the death penalty on
one such as Enmund who aids and abets a felony in the course of
which a murder is committed by others but who does not himself kill,
attempt to kill, or intend that a killing take place or that lethal force
will be employed. We have concluded, along with most legislatures
and juries, that it does not.

We have no doubt that robbery is a serious crime deserving serious
punishment. It is not, however, a crime 'so grievous an affront to humanity that the only adequate response may be the penalty of death.'
Gregg v. Georgia . . . As was said of the crime of rape in *Coker,* we
have the abiding conviction that the death penalty, which is 'unique in
its severity and irrevocability,' *Gregg v. Georgia,* is an excessive
penalty for the robber who, as such, does not take human life.

Here the robbers did commit murder; but they were subjected to
the death penalty only because they killed as well as robbed. The question before us is not the disproportionality of death as a penalty for
murder, but rather the validity of capital punishment for Enmund's
own conduct. The focus must be on *his* culpability, not on that of
those who committed the robbery and shot the victims, for we insist
on 'individualized consideration as a constitutional requirement in imposing the death sentence,' *Lockett v. Ohio,* which means that we
must focus on 'relevant facets of the character and record of the individual offender.' *Woodson v. North Carolina.* Enmund himself did not
kill or attempt to kill; and, as construed by the Florida Supreme
Court, the record before us does not warrant a finding that Enmund
had any intention of participating in or facilitating a murder. Yet under
Florida law death was an authorized penalty because Enmund aided

and abetted a robbery in the course of which murder was committed. It is fundamental that 'causing harm intentionally must be punished more severely than causing the same harm unintentionally.' Enmund did not kill or intend to kill and thus his culpability is plainly different from that of the robbers who killed; yet the State treated them alike and attributed to Enmund the culpability of those who killed the Kerseys. This was impermissible under the Eighth Amendment.

In *Gregg v. Georgia* the opinion announcing the judgment observed that '[the] death penalty is said to serve two principal social purposes: retribution and deterrence of capital crimes by prospective offenders.' Unless the death penalty when applied to those in Enmund's position measurably contributes to one or both of these goals, it 'is nothing more than the purposeless and needless imposition of pain and suffering,' and hence an unconstitutional punishment. *Coker v. Georgia.* We are quite unconvinced, however, that the threat that the death penalty will be imposed for murder will measurably deter one who does not kill and has no intention or purpose that life will be taken . . .[I]f a person does not intend that life be taken or contemplate that lethal force will be employed by others, the possibility that the death penalty will be imposed for vicarious felony murder will not 'enter into the cold calculus that precedes the decision to act.' *Gregg v. Georgia.*

JUSTICE O'CONNOR, with whom THE CHIEF JUSTICE, JUSTICE POWELL, and JUSTICE REHNQUIST join, dissenting.

. . .In *Gregg v. Georgia,* a majority of this Court concluded that the death penalty does not invariably violate the Cruel and Unusual Punishments Clause of the Eighth Amendment . . .In no case since *Gregg* and its companion cases, has this Court retreated from that position. Recognizing the constitutionality of the death penalty, however, only marks the beginning of the inquiry, for Earl Enmund was not convicted of murder as it is ordinarily envisioned—a deliberate and premeditated, unlawful killing. Rather, through the doctrine of accessorial liability, the petitioner has been convicted of two murders that he did not specifically intend. Thus, it is necessary to examine the concept of proportionality as enunciated in this Court's cases to determine whether the penalty imposed on Earl Enmund is unconstitutionally disproportionate to his crimes . . .

. . .As the petitioner acknowledges, the felony-murder doctrine, and its corresponding capital penalty, originated hundreds of years ago, and was a fixture of English common law until 1957 when Parliament declared that an unintentional killing during a felony would be classified as manslaughter. The common-law rule was transplanted to the American Colonies, and its use continued largely unabated into the 20th century, although legislative reforms often restricted capital felony murder to enumerated violent felonies.

...[I]t simply is not possible to conclude that historically this country conclusively has rejected capital punishment for homicides committed during the course of a felony...

...[I]n nearly half of the States, and in two-thirds of the States that permit the death penalty for murder, a defendant who neither killed the victim nor specifically intended that the victim die may be sentenced to death for his participation in the robbery-murder. Far from '[weighing] very heavily on the side of rejecting capital punishment as a suitable penalty for' felony murder, *Coker v. Georgia*, these legislative judgments indicate that our 'evolving standards of decency' still embrace capital punishment for this crime. For this reason, I conclude that the petitioner has failed to meet the standards in *Coker* and *Woodson* that the 'two crucial indicators of evolving standards of decency...—jury determinations and legislative enactments—*both point conclusively* to the repudiation' of capital punishment for felony murder. In short, the death penalty for felony murder does not fall short of our national 'standards of decency'...

Although the Court disingenuously seeks to characterize Enmund as only a 'robber,' it cannot be disputed that he is responsible, along with Sampson and Jeanette Armstrong, for the murders of the Kerseys. There is no dispute that their lives were unjustifiably taken, and that the petitioner, as one who aided and abetted the armed robbery, is legally liable for their deaths. Quite unlike the defendant in *Coker*, the petitioner cannot claim that the penalty imposed is 'grossly out of proportion' to the harm for which he admittedly is at least partly responsible.

The Court's holding today is especially disturbing because it makes intent a matter of federal constitutional law, requiring this Court both to review highly subjective definitional problems customarily left to state criminal law and to develop an Eighth Amendment meaning of intent...[T]he intent-to-kill requirement is crudely crafted; it fails to take into account the complex picture of the defendant's knowledge of his accomplice's intent and whether he was armed, the defendant's contribution to the planning and success of the crime, and the defendant's actual participation during the commission of the crime. Under the circumstances, the determination of the degree of blameworthiness is best left to the sentencer, who can sift through the facts unique to each case . . .

. . .[E]xamination of the qualitative factors underlying the concept of proportionality do not show that the death penalty is disproportionate as applied to Earl Enmund. In contrast to the crime in *Coker,* the petitioner's crime involves the very type of harm that this Court has held justifies the death penalty . . .

Ford v. Wainwright (1986)

Another case that focused on who could be executed. At issue here was the execution of the mentally insane. This case gave Justice Marshall a rare opportunity to write a decision in a death penalty case. Although some of the justices debated what constituted insanity, a majority acknowledged that to execute someone not cognizant of what was happening to him, and why, was cruel and unsual. While the majority focused on the substantive nature of the problem, the dissent argued this was a procedural matter, not a substantive one, that abided by traditional common law and due process dictates.

JUSTICE MARSHALL announced the judgment of the Court and delivered the opinion of the Court with respect to Parts I and II and an opinion with respect to Parts III, IV, and V, in which JUSTICE BRENNAN, JUSTICE BLACKMUN, and JUSTICE STEVENS join . . .

II

Since this Court last had occasion to consider the infliction of the death penalty upon the insane, our interpretations of the Due Process Clause and the Eighth Amendment have evolved substantially . . .Now that the Eighth Amendment has been recognized to affect significantly both the procedural and the substantive aspects of the death penalty, the question of executing the insane takes on a wholly different complexion. The adequacy of the procedures chosen by a State to determine sanity, therefore, will depend upon an issue that this Court has never addressed: whether the Constitution places a substantive restriction on the State's power to take the life of an insane prisoner.

There is now little room for doubt that the Eighth Amendment's ban on cruel and unusual punishment embraces, at a minimum, those modes or acts of punishment that had been considered cruel and unusual at the time that the Bill of Rights was adopted . . .

Moreover, the Eighth Amendment's proscriptions are not limited to those practices condemned by the common law in 1789 . . .Not bound by the sparing humanitarian concessions of our forebears, the Amendment also recognizes the 'evolving standards of decency that mark the progress of a maturing society.' *Trop v. Dulles* (plurality opinion). In addition to considering the barbarous methods generally outlawed in the 18th century, therefore, this Court takes into account objective evidence of contemporary values before determining whether a particular punishment comports with the fundamental human dignity that the Amendment protects . . .

We begin, then, with the common law. The bar against executing a prisoner who has lost his sanity bears impressive historical credentials; the practice consistently has been branded 'savage and inhuman' . . .

. . .More recent commentators opine that the community's quest for 'retribution'—the need to offset a criminal act by a punishment of equivalent 'moral quality'—is not served by execution of an insane person, which has a 'lesser value' than that of the crime for which he is to be punished. Unanimity of rationale, therefore, we do not find . . .We know of virtually no authority condoning the execution of the insane at English common law . . .

This ancestral legacy has not outlived its time. Today, no State in the Union permits the execution of the insane. It is clear that the ancient and humane limitation upon the State's ability to execute its sentences has as firm a hold upon the jurisprudence of today as it had centuries ago in England. The various reasons put forth in support of the common-law restriction have no less logical, moral, and practical force than they did when first voiced. For today, no less than before, we may seriously question the retributive value of executing a person who has no comprehension of why he has been singled out and stripped of his fundamental right to life . . .Similarly, the natural abhorrence civilized societies feel at killing one who has no capacity to come to grips with his own conscience or deity is still vivid today. And the intuition that such an execution simply offends humanity is evidently shared across this Nation. Faced with such widespread evidence of a restriction upon sovereign power, this Court is compelled to conclude that the Eighth Amendment prohibits a State from carrying out a sentence of death upon a prisoner who is insane . . .

Today we have explicitly recognized in our law a principle that has long resided there. It is no less abhorrent today than it has been for centuries to exact in penance the life of one whose mental illness prevents him from comprehending the reasons for the penalty or its implications . . .

JUSTICE REHNQUIST, with whom THE CHIEF JUSTICE joins, dissenting.

The Court today holds that the Eighth Amendment prohibits a State from carrying out a lawfully imposed sentence of death upon a person who is currently insane. This holding is based almost entirely on two unremarkable observations. First, the Court states that it 'know[s] of virtually no authority condoning the execution of the insane at English common law.' Second, it notes that '[t]oday, no State in the Union permits the execution of the insane.' Armed with these facts, and shielded by the claim that it is simply 'keep[ing] faith with our common-law heritage,' the Court proceeds to cast aside settled precedent and to significantly alter both the common-law and current practice of not executing the insane. It manages this feat by carefully ignoring the fact that the Florida scheme it finds unconstitutional, in which the Governor is assigned the ultimate responsibility of deciding whether a condemned prisoner is currently insane, is fully consistent with the 'common-law heritage' and current practice on which the Court purports to rely.

The Court places great weight on the 'impressive historical credentials' of the common-law bar against executing a prisoner who has lost his sanity. What it fails to mention, however, is the equally important and unchallenged fact that at common law it was the *executive* who passed upon the sanity of the condemned. So when the Court today creates a constitutional right to a determination of sanity outside of the executive branch, it does so not in keeping with but at the expense of 'our common-law heritage.'

. . .The Court's profession of 'faith to our common-law heritage' and 'evolving standards of decency' is thus at best a half-truth. It is Florida's scheme—which combines a prohibition against execution of the insane with executive-branch procedures for evaluating claims of insanity—that is more faithful to both traditional and modern practice.

And no matter how long-standing and universal, laws providing that the State should not execute persons the executive finds insane are not themselves sufficient to create an Eighth Amendment right that sweeps away as inadequate the procedures for determining sanity crafted by those very laws.

Since no State sanctions execution of the insane, the real battle being fought in this case is over what procedures must accompany the inquiry into sanity. The Court reaches the result it does by examining the common law, creating a constitutional right that no State seeks to violate, and then concluding that the common-law procedures are inadequate to protect the newly created but common-law based right. I find it unnecessary to 'constitutionalize' the already uniform view that the insane should not be executed, and inappropriate to 'selectively incorporate' the common-law practice. I therefore dissent.

McCleskey v. Kemp (1987)

An equal protection challenge that attempted to use statistical evidence to prove that the death penalty was unfair. Using a complex study,(the Baldus study) the defendant argued that statistical evidence showed that race played an important and often deciding factor in deciding which criminals received the death penalty. The race of the killer as well as that of the victim were important components. The resulting statistical patterns, the defendant argued, showed that blacks who killed whites were most likely to receive the death penalty. The U.S. Supreme Court acknowledged that although there was some racial disparity in death penalty convictions, that disparity was not intentional and dismissed the findings, seemingly eliminating the racial difference argument for anti–death penalty advocates.

JUSTICE POWELL delivered the opinion of the Court . . .

McCleskey . . .argues that race has infected the administration of Georgia's statute in two ways: persons who murder whites are more likely to be sentenced to death than persons who murder blacks, and black murderers are more likely to be sentenced to death than white murderers. As a black defendant who killed a white victim, McCleskey claims that the Baldus study demonstrates that he was discriminated against because of his race and because of the race of his victim. In its broadest form, McCleskey's claim of discrimination extends to every actor in the Georgia capital sentencing process, from the prosecutor who sought the death penalty and the jury that imposed the sentence, to the State itself that enacted the capital punishment statute and allows it to remain in effect despite its allegedly discriminatory application. We agree with the Court of Appeals, and every other court that has considered such a challenge, that this claim must fail.

Our analysis begins with the basic principle that a defendant who alleges an equal protection violation has the burden of proving 'the existence of purposeful discrimination' . . .A corollary to this principle is that a criminal defendant must prove that the purposeful discrimination 'had a discriminatory effect' on him . . .Thus, to prevail under the Equal Protection Clause, McCleskey must prove that the decisionmakers in his case acted with discriminatory purpose . . .Instead, he relies solely on the Baldus study. McCleskey argues that the Baldus study compels an inference that his sentence rests on purposeful discrimination . . .

Finally, McCleskey's statistical proffer must be viewed in the context of his challenge. McCleskey challenges decisions at the heart of the State's criminal justice system . . . Implementation of these laws necessarily requires discretionary judgments. Because discretion is essential to the criminal justice process, we would demand exceptionally clear proof before we would infer that the discretion has been abused. The unique nature of the decisions at issue in this case also counsels against adopting such an inference from the disparities indicated by the Baldus study. Accordingly, we hold that the Baldus study is clearly insufficient to support an inference that any of the decisionmakers in McCleskey's case acted with discriminatory purpose.

McCleskey also suggests that the Baldus study proves that the State as a whole has acted with a discriminatory purpose. He appears to argue that the State has violated the Equal Protection Clause by adopting the capital punishment statute and allowing it to remain in force despite its allegedly discriminatory application . . .For this claim to prevail, McCleskey would have to prove that the Georgia Legislature enacted or maintained the death penalty statute because of an anticipated racially discriminatory effect. In *Gregg v. Georgia* this Court found that the Georgia capital sentencing system could operate in a fair and neutral manner. There was no evidence then, and there is none now, that the Georgia Legislature enacted the capital punishment statute to further a racially discriminatory purpose . . .

In light of our precedents under the Eighth Amendment, McCleskey cannot argue successfully that his sentence is 'disproportionate to the crime in the traditional sense.' He does not deny that he committed a murder in the course of a planned robbery, a crime for which this Court has determined that the death penalty constitutionally may be imposed . . .McCleskey argues that the sentences in his case [are] disproportionate to the sentences in other murder cases.

On the one hand, he cannot base a constitutional claim on an argument that his case differs from other cases in which defendants did receive the death penalty. On automatic appeal, the Georgia Supreme Court found that McCleskey's death sentence was not disproportionate to other death sentences imposed in the State . . .

On the other hand, absent a showing that the Georgia capital punishment system operates in an arbitrary and capricious manner, McCleskey cannot prove a constitutional violation by demonstrating that other defendants who may be similarly situated did not receive the death penalty. In *Gregg*, the Court confronted the argument that 'the opportunities for discretionary action that are inherent in the processing of any murder case under Georgia law,' specifically the opportunities for discretionary leniency, rendered the capital sentences imposed arbitrary and capricious. We rejected this contention . . .

Because McCleskey's sentence was imposed under Georgia sentencing procedures that focus discretion 'on the particularized nature of the crime and the particularized characteristics of the individual defendant,' we lawfully may presume that McCleskey's death sentence was not 'wantonly and freakishly' imposed, and thus that the sentence is not disproportionate within any recognized meaning under the Eighth Amendment.

. . .Statistics at most may show only a likelihood that a particular factor entered into some decisions. There is, of course, some risk of racial prejudice influencing a jury's decision in a criminal case. There are similar risks that other kinds of prejudice will influence other criminal trials . . .McCleskey asks us to accept the likelihood allegedly shown by the Baldus study as the constitutional measure of an unacceptable risk of racial prejudice influencing capital sentencing decisions. This we decline to do . . .

At most, the Baldus study indicates a discrepancy that appears to correlate with race. Apparent disparities in sentencing are an inevitable part of our criminal justice system . . .Where the discretion that is fundamental to our criminal process is involved, we decline to assume that what is unexplained is invidious. In light of the safeguards designed to minimize racial bias in the process, the fundamental value of jury trial in our criminal justice system, and the benefits that discretion provides to criminal defendants, we hold that the Baldus study does not demonstrate a constitutionally significant risk of racial bias affecting the Georgia capital sentencing process.

Two additional concerns inform our decision in this case. First, McCleskey's claim, taken to its logical conclusion, throws into serious question the principles that underlie our entire criminal justice system. The Eighth Amendment is not limited in application to capital punishment, but applies to all penalties . . . Thus, if we accepted McCleskey's claim that racial bias has impermissibly tainted the capital sentencing decision, we could soon be faced with similar claims as to other types of penalty. Moreover, the claim that his sentence rests on the irrelevant factor of race easily could be extended to apply to claims based on unexplained discrepancies that correlate to membership in other minority groups, and even to gender. Similarly, since McCleskey's claim relates to the race of his victim, other claims could apply with equally logical force to statistical disparities that correlate with the race or sex of other actors in the criminal justice system, such as defense attorneys or judges. Also, there is no logical reason that such a claim need be limited to racial or sexual bias. If arbitrary and capricious punishment is the touchstone under the Eighth Amendment, such a claim could—at least in theory—be based upon any arbitrary variable, such as the defendant's facial characteristics, or the physical attractiveness of the defendant or the victim, that some statistical study indicates may be influential in jury decisionmaking. As these examples illustrate, there is no limiting principle to the type of challenge brought by McCleskey. The Constitution does not require that a State eliminate any demonstrable disparity that correlates with a potentially irrelevant factor in order to operate a criminal justice system that includes capital punishment. As we have stated specifically in the context of capital punishment, the Constitution does not 'plac[e] totally unrealistic conditions on its use.' *Gregg v. Georgia.*

Second, McCleskey's arguments are best presented to the legislative bodies. It is not the responsibility—or indeed even the right—of this Court to determine the appropriate punishment for particular crimes. It is the legislatures, the elected representatives of the people, that are 'constituted to respond to the will and consequently the moral values of the people.' *Furman v. Georgia* (Burger, C. J., dissenting). Legislatures also are better qualified to weigh and 'evaluate the results of statistical studies in terms of their own local conditions and with a flexibility of approach that is not available to the courts.' *Gregg v. Georgia.*

Capital punishment is now the law in more than two-thirds of our States. It is the ultimate duty of courts to determine on a case-by-case basis whether these laws are applied consistently with the Constitution. Despite McCleskey's wide-ranging arguments that basically challenge the validity of capital punishment in our multiracial society, the only question before us is whether in his case, the law of Georgia was properly applied . . .

Accordingly, we affirm the judgment of the Court of Appeals for the Eleventh Circuit.

It is so ordered.

JUSTICE BRENNAN, with whom JUSTICE MARSHALL joins, and with whom JUSTICE BLACKMUN and JUSTICE STEVENS join in all but Part I, dissenting.

I

Adhering to my view that the death penalty is in all circumstances cruel and unusual punishment forbidden by the Eighth and Fourteenth Amendments . . .

II

At some point in this case, Warren McCleskey doubtless asked his lawyer whether a jury was likely to sentence him to die. A candid reply to this question would have been disturbing. First, counsel would have to tell McCleskey that few of the details of the crime or of McCleskey's past criminal conduct were more important than the fact that his victim was white. Furthermore, counsel would feel bound to tell McCleskey that defendants charged with killing white victims in Georgia are 4.3 times as likely to be sentenced to death as defendants charged with killing blacks. In addition, frankness would compel the disclosure that it was more likely than not that the race of McCleskey's victim would determine whether he received a death sentence: 6 of every 11 defendants convicted of killing a white person would not have received the death penalty if their victims had been black, while, among defendants with aggravating and mitigating factors comparable to McCleskey's, 20 of every 34 would not have been sentenced to die if their victims had been black. Finally, the assessment would not be complete without the information that cases involving black defendants and white victims are more likely to result in a death sentence than cases featuring any other racial combination of defendant and victim. The story could be told in a variety of ways, but McCleskey could not fail to grasp its essential narrative line: there was a significant chance that race would play a prominent role in determining if he lived or died.

...The Court's evaluation of the significance of petitioner's evidence is fundamentally at odds with our consistent concern for rationality in capital sentencing, and the considerations that the majority invokes to discount that evidence cannot justify ignoring its force.

III

It is important to emphasize at the outset that the Court's observation that McCleskey cannot prove the influence of race on any particular sentencing decision is irrelevant in evaluating his Eighth Amendment claim . . .[A] death sentence must be struck down when the circumstances under which it has been imposed 'creat[e] an unacceptable risk that 'the death penalty [may have been] meted out arbitrarily or capriciously' or through 'whim or mistake' (quoting *California v. Ramos* [1983]) . . .[A] system that features a significant probability that sentencing decisions are influenced by impermissible considerations cannot be regarded as rational.

The Court assumes the statistical validity of the Baldus study, and acknowledges that McCleskey has demonstrated a risk that racial prejudice plays a role in capital sentencing in Georgia. Nonetheless, it finds the probability of prejudice insufficient to create constitutional concern . . .

This evidence shows that there is a better than even chance in Georgia that race will influence the decision to impose the death penalty: a majority of defendants in white-victim crimes would not have been sentenced to die if their victims had been black. In determining whether this risk is acceptable, our judgment must be shaped by the awareness that '[t]he risk of racial prejudice infecting a capital sentencing proceeding is especially serious in light of the complete finality of the death sentence,' . . .Surely, we should not be willing to take a person's life if the chance that his death sentence was irrationally imposed is more likely than not. In light of the gravity of the interest at stake, petitioner's statistics on their face are a powerful demonstration of the type of risk that our Eighth Amendment jurisprudence has consistently condemned.

Evaluation of McCleskey's evidence cannot rest solely on the numbers themselves. We must also ask whether the conclusion suggested by those numbers is consonant with our understanding of history and human experience. Georgia's legacy of a race-conscious criminal justice system, as well as this Court's own recognition of the persistent danger that racial attitudes may affect criminal proceedings, indicates that McCleskey's claim is not a fanciful product of mere statistical artifice.

For many years, Georgia operated openly and formally precisely the type of dual system the evidence shows is still effectively in place. The criminal law expressly differentiated between crimes committed by and against blacks and whites, distinctions whose lineage traced back to the time of slavery . . .

This Court has invalidated portions of the Georgia capital sentencing system three times over the past 15 years . . .

History and its continuing legacy thus buttress the probative force of McCleskey's statistics. Formal dual criminal laws may no longer be in effect, and intentional discrimination may no longer be prominent. Nonetheless . . . 'subtle, less consciously held racial attitudes' continue to be of concern, and the Georgia system gives such attitudes considerable room to operate. The conclusions drawn from McCleskey's statistical evidence are therefore consistent with the lessons of social experience.

The majority thus misreads our Eighth Amendment jurisprudence in concluding that McCleskey has not demonstrated a degree of risk sufficient to raise constitutional concern . . .[W]e have demanded a uniquely high degree of rationality in imposing the death penalty. A capital sentencing system in which race more likely than not plays a role does not meet this standard. It is true that every nuance of decision cannot be statistically captured, nor can any individual judgment be plumbed with absolute certainty. Yet the fact that we must always act without the illumination of complete knowledge cannot induce paralysis when we confront what is literally an issue of life and death. Sentencing data, history, and experience all counsel that Georgia has provided insufficient assurance of the heightened rationality we have required in order to take a human life.

IV

. . .Considering the race of a defendant or victim in deciding if the death penalty should be imposed is completely at odds with this concern that an individual be evaluated as a unique human being. Decisions influenced by race rest in part on a categorical assessment of the worth of human beings according to color, insensitive to whatever qualities the individuals in question may possess. Enhanced willingness to impose the death sentence on black defendants, or diminished willingness to render such a sentence when blacks are victims, reflects a devaluation of the lives of black persons . . .

In fairness, the Court's fear that McCleskey's claim is an invitation to descend a slippery slope also rests on the realization that any humanly imposed system of penalties will exhibit some imperfection. Yet to reject McCleskey's powerful evidence on this basis is to ignore both the qualitatively different character of the death penalty and the particular repugnance of racial discrimination, considerations which may properly be taken into account in determining whether various punishments are 'cruel and unusual.' Furthermore, it fails to take account of the unprecedented refinement and strength of the Baldus study.

The Court also maintains that accepting McCleskey's claim would pose a threat to all sentencing because of the prospect that a correlation might be demonstrated between sentencing outcomes and other personal characteristics. Again, such a view is indifferent to the considerations that enter into a determination whether punishment is 'cruel and unusual.' Race is a consideration whose influence is expressly constitutionally proscribed . . .That a decision to impose the death penalty could be influenced by race is thus a particularly repugnant prospect, and evidence that race may play even a modest role in levying a death sentence should be enough to characterize that sentence as 'cruel and unusual.' . . .

The Court's projection of apocalyptic consequences for criminal sentencing is thus greatly exaggerated . . .

V

. . .In more recent times, we have sought to free ourselves from the burden of . . .history. Yet it has been scarcely a generation since this Court's first decision striking down racial segregation, and barely two decades since the legislative prohibition of racial discrimination in major domains of national life. These have been honorable steps, but we cannot pretend that in three decades we have completely escaped the grip of a historical legacy spanning centuries. Warren McCleskey's evidence confronts us with the subtle and persistent influence of the past. His message is a disturbing one to a society that has formally repudiated racism, and a frustrating one to a Nation accustomed to regarding its destiny as the product of its own will. Nonetheless, we ignore him at our peril, for we remain imprisoned by the past as long as we deny its influence in the present.

It is tempting to pretend that minorities on death row share a fate in no way connected to our own, that our treatment of them sounds no echoes beyond the chambers in which they die. Such an illusion is ultimately corrosive, for the reverberations of injustice are not so easily confined. 'The destinies of the two races in this country are indissolubly linked together,' and the way in which we choose those who will die reveals the depth of moral commitment among the living ...

JUSTICE STEVENS, with whom JUSTICE BLACKMUN joins, dissenting.

 ...The Court's decision appears to be based on a fear that the acceptance of McCleskey's claim would sound the death knell for capital punishment in Georgia. If society were indeed forced to choose between a racially discriminatory death penalty (one that provides heightened protection against murder 'for whites only') and no death penalty at all, the choice mandated by the Constitution would be plain ...But the Court's fear is unfounded. One of the lessons of the Baldus study is that there exist certain categories of extremely serious crimes for which prosecutors consistently seek, and juries consistently impose, the death penalty without regard to the race of the victim or the race of the offender. If Georgia were to narrow the class of death-eligible defendants to those categories, the danger of arbitrary and discriminatory imposition of the death penalty would be significantly decreased, if not eradicated. As JUSTICE BRENNAN has demonstrated in his dissenting opinion, such a restructuring of the sentencing scheme is surely not too high a price to pay ...

Thompson v. Oklahoma (1988)

Thompson *presented the thorny question of how old is old enough to execute. In this case, a fifteen-year-old was party to the brutal murder of his brother-in-law. Although questions of competency were part of the arguments, the issue of the constitutionality of executing a fifteen-year-old per se remained. The U.S. Supreme Court focused on the cut-off age of sixteen.*

JUSTICE STEVENS announced the judgment of the Court and delivered an opinion in which JUSTICE BRENNAN, JUSTICE MARSHALL, and JUSTICE BLACKMUN join . . .

Because there is no claim that the punishment would be excessive if the crime had been committed by an adult, only a brief statement of facts is necessary. In concert with three older persons, petitioner actively participated in the brutal murder of his former brother-in-law in the early morning hours of January 23, 1983. The evidence disclosed that the victim had been shot twice, and that his throat, chest, and abdomen had been cut. He also had multiple bruises and a broken leg. His body had been chained to a concrete block and thrown into a river where it remained for almost four weeks. Each of the four participants was tried separately and each was sentenced to death . . .

III

Justice Powell has repeatedly reminded us of the importance of 'the experience of mankind, as well as the long history of our law, recognizing that there are differences which must be accommodated in determining the rights and duties of children as compared with those of adults' . . .Thus, a minor is not eligible to vote, to sit on a jury, to marry without parental consent, or to purchase alcohol or cigarettes. Like all other States, Oklahoma has developed a juvenile justice system in which most offenders under the age of 18 are not held criminally responsible. Its statutes do provide, however, that a 16- or 17-year-old charged with murder and other serious felonies shall be considered an adult . . .

The line between childhood and adulthood is drawn in different ways by various States. There is, however, complete or near unanimity among all 50 States and the District of Columbia in treating a person under 16 as a minor for several important purposes . . .Most relevant, however, is the fact that all States have enacted legislation designating the maximum age for juvenile court jurisdiction at no less than 16. All of this legislation is consistent with the experience of mankind, as well as the long history of our law, that the normal 15-year-old is not prepared to assume the full responsibilities of an adult.

Most state legislatures have not expressly confronted the question of establishing a minimum age for imposition of the death penalty . . .One might argue on the basis of this body of legislation that there is no chronological age at which the imposition of the death penalty is unconstitutional and that our current standards of decency would still tolerate the execution of 10-year-old children. We think it self-evident that such an argument is unacceptable; indeed, no such argument has been advanced in this case. If, therefore, we accept the premise that some offenders are simply too young to be put to death, it is reasonable to put this group of statutes to one side because they do not focus on the question of where the chronological age line should be drawn. When we confine our attention to the 18 States that have expressly established a minimum age in their death penalty statutes, we find that all of them require that the defendant have attained at least the age of 16 at the time of the capital offense.

The conclusion that it would offend civilized standards of decency to execute a person who was less than 16 years old at the time of his or her offense is consistent with the views that have been expressed by respected professional organizations, by other nations that share our Anglo-American heritage, and by the leading members of the Western European community . . .

IV

The second societal factor the Court has examined in determining the acceptability of capital punishment to the American sensibility is the behavior of juries. In fact, the infrequent and haphazard handing out of death sentences by capital juries was a prime factor underlying our judgment in *Furman v. Georgia* . . .

Department of Justice statistics indicate that during the years 1982 through 1986 an average of over 16,000 persons were arrested for willful criminal homicide (murder and nonnegligent manslaughter) each year. Of that group . . .1,393 were sentenced to death. Only 5 of them, including the petitioner in this case, were less than 16 years old at the time of the offense. Statistics of this kind can, of course, be interpreted in different ways, but they do suggest that these five young offenders have received sentences that are 'cruel and unusual in the same way that being struck by lightning is cruel and unusual.' *Furman v. Georgia* (Stewart, J., concurring).

V

. . .[W]e . . .ask whether the juvenile's culpability should be measured by the same standard as that of an adult, and then consider whether the application of the death penalty to this class of offenders 'measurably contributes' to the social purposes that are served by the death penalty . . .

[T]he Court has already endorsed the proposition that less culpability should attach to a crime committed by a juvenile than to a comparable crime committed by an adult . . . Inexperience, less education, and less intelligence make the teenager less able to evaluate the consequences of his or her conduct while at the same time he or she is much more apt to be motivated by mere emotion or peer pressure than is an adult. The reasons why juveniles are not trusted with the privileges and responsibilities of an adult also explain why their irresponsible conduct is not as morally reprehensible as that of an adult . . .

'The death penalty is said to serve two principal social purposes: retribution and deterrence of capital crimes by prospective offenders.' *Gregg v. Georgia* . . . Given the lesser culpability of the juvenile offender, the teenager's capacity for growth, and society's fiduciary obligations to its children, this conclusion is simply inapplicable to the execution of a 15-year-old offender.

For such a young offender, the deterrence rationale is equally unacceptable . . . The likelihood that the teenage offender has made the kind of cost-benefit analysis that attaches any weight to the possibility of execution is so remote as to be virtually nonexistent. And, even if one posits such a cold-blooded calculation by a 15-year-old, it is fanciful to believe that he would be deterred by the knowledge that a small number of persons his age have been executed during the 20th century. In short, we are not persuaded that the imposition of the death penalty for offenses committed by persons under 16 years of age has made, or can be expected to make, any measurable contribution to the goals that capital punishment is intended to achieve. It is, therefore, 'nothing more than the purposeless and needless imposition of pain and suffering,' *Coker v. Georgia* and thus an unconstitutional punishment.

VI

Petitioner's counsel and various amici curiae have asked us to 'draw a line' that would prohibit the execution of any person who was under the age of 18 at the time of the offense. Our task today, however, is to decide the case before us; we do so by concluding that the Eighth and Fourteenth Amendments prohibit the execution of a person who was under 16 years of age at the time of his or her offense . . .

JUSTICE O'CONNOR, concurring in the judgment.

The plurality and dissent agree on two fundamental propositions: that there is some age below which a juvenile's crimes can never be constitutionally punished by death, and that our precedents require us to locate this age in light of the 'evolving standards of decency that mark the progress of a maturing society.' . . .I accept both principles. The disagreements between the plurality and the dissent rest on their different evaluations of the evidence available to us about the relevant social consensus. Although I believe that a national consensus forbidding the execution of any person for a crime committed before the age of 16 very likely does exist, I am reluctant to adopt this conclusion as a matter of constitutional law without better evidence than we now possess. Because I conclude that the sentence in this case can and should be set aside on narrower grounds than those adopted by the plurality, and because the grounds on which I rest should allow us to face the more general question when better evidence is available, I concur only in the judgment of the Court . . .

JUSTICE SCALIA, with whom THE CHIEF JUSTICE and JUSTICE WHITE join, dissenting.

If the issue before us today were whether an automatic death penalty for conviction of certain crimes could be extended to individuals younger than 16 when they commit the crimes, thereby preventing individualized consideration of their maturity and moral responsibility, I would accept the plurality's conclusion that such a practice is opposed by a national consensus, sufficiently uniform and of sufficiently long standing, to render it cruel and unusual punishment within the meaning of the Eighth Amendment. We have already decided as much, and more, in *Lockett v. Ohio*. I might even agree with the plurality's conclusion if the question were whether a person under 16 when he commits a crime can be deprived of the benefit of a rebuttable presumption that he is not mature and responsible enough to be punished as an adult. The question posed here, however, is radically different from both of these. It is whether there is a national consensus that no criminal so much as one day under 16, after individuated consideration of his circumstances, including the overcoming of a presumption that he should not be tried as an adult, can possibly be deemed mature and responsible enough to be punished with death for any crime. Because there seems to me no plausible basis for answering this last question in the affirmative, I respectfully dissent.

I

[Justice Scalia restated the facts in this section, expanding upon both the heinous nature of the crime and the extent to which, in the dissent's eyes, Thompson had been a full and active participant in the murder, and therefore should stand trial as an adult.]

II

As the foregoing history of this case demonstrates, William Wayne Thompson is not a juvenile caught up in a legislative scheme that unthinkingly lumped him together with adults for purposes of determining that death was an appropriate penalty for him and for his crime. To the contrary, Oklahoma first gave careful consideration to whether, in light of his young age, he should be subjected to the normal criminal system at all. That question having been answered affirmatively, a jury then considered whether, despite his young age, his maturity and moral responsibility were sufficiently developed to justify the sentence of death. In upsetting this particularized judgment on the basis of a constitutional absolute, the plurality pronounces it to be a fundamental principle of our society that no one who is as little as one day short of his 16th birthday can have sufficient maturity and moral responsibility to be subjected to capital punishment for any crime. As a sociological and moral conclusion that is implausible; and it is doubly implausible as an interpretation of the United States Constitution.

The text of the Eighth Amendment . . .prohibits the imposition of 'cruel and unusual punishments.' The plurality does not attempt to maintain that this was originally understood to prohibit capital punishment for crimes committed by persons under the age of 16; the evidence is unusually clear and unequivocal that it was not . . .

Necessarily, therefore, the plurality seeks to rest its holding on the conclusion that Thompson's punishment as an adult is contrary to the 'evolving standards of decency that mark the progress of a maturing society' . . .Of course, the risk of assessing evolving standards is that it is all too easy to believe that evolution has culminated in one's own views. To avoid this danger we have, when making such an assessment in prior cases, looked for objective signs of how today's society views a particular punishment . . .The most reliable objective signs consist of the legislation that the society has enacted. It will rarely if ever be the case that the Members of this Court will have a better sense of the evolution in views of the American people than do their elected representatives.

It is thus significant that, only four years ago, in the Comprehensive Crime Control Act of 1984 . . .Congress expressly addressed the effect of youth upon the imposition of criminal punishment, and changed the law in precisely the opposite direction from that which the plurality's perceived evolution in social attitudes would suggest: It lowered from 16 to 15 the age at which a juvenile's case can, 'in the interest of justice,' be transferred from juvenile court to Federal District Court, enabling him to be tried and punished as an adult . . .

Turning to legislation at the state level, one observes the same trend of lowering rather than raising the age of juvenile criminal liability . . .

. . .[I]t is obviously impossible for the plurality to rely upon any evolved societal consensus discernible in legislation—or at least discernible in the legislation of this society, which is assuredly all that is relevant. Thus, the plurality falls back upon what it promises will be an examination of 'the behavior of juries.' . . .[T]he plurality examines the statistics on capital executions, which are of course substantially lower than those for capital sentences because of various factors, most notably the exercise of executive clemency. Those statistics show, unsurprisingly, that capital punishment for persons who committed crimes under the age of 16 is rare. We are not discussing whether the Constitution requires such procedures as will continue to cause it to be rare, but whether the Constitution prohibits it entirely. The plurality takes it to be persuasive evidence that social attitudes have changed to embrace such a prohibition—changed so clearly and permanently as to be irrevocably enshrined in the Constitution—that in this century all of the 18 to 20 executions of persons below 16 when they committed crimes occurred before 1948 . . .

In sum, the statistics of executions demonstrate nothing except the fact that our society has always agreed that executions of 15-year-old criminals should be rare, and in more modern times has agreed that they (like all other executions) should be even rarer still . . .

. . .It seems plain to me, in other words, that there is no clear line here, which suggests that the plurality is inappropriately acting in a legislative rather than a judicial capacity. Doubtless at some age a line does exist—as it has always existed in the common law—below which a juvenile can never be considered fully responsible for murder. The evidence that the views of our society, so steadfast and so uniform that they have become part of the agreed-upon laws that we live by, regard that absolute age to be 16 is nonexistent.

...It is assuredly 'for us ultimately to judge' what the Eighth Amendment permits, but that means it is for us to judge whether certain punishments are forbidden because, despite what the current society thinks, they were forbidden under the original understanding of 'cruel and unusual,' cf. *Brown v. Board of Education* (1954); or because they come within current understanding of what is 'cruel and unusual,' because of the 'evolving standards of decency' of our national society; but not because they are out of accord with the perceptions of decency, or of penology, or of mercy, entertained—or strongly entertained, or even held as an 'abiding conviction'—by a majority of the small and unrepresentative segment of our society that sits on this Court. On its face, the phrase 'cruel and unusual punishments' limits the evolving standards appropriate for our consideration to those entertained by the society rather than those dictated by our personal consciences . . .

For the foregoing reasons, I respectfully dissent from the judgment of the Court.

Penry v. Lynaugh (1989)

A case that showed the difficulty in drawing lines about whom the State should execute. Although the decision in Penry v. Lynaugh *was 5–4, in reality it broke down, similar to* Thompson *1–4–4. Justice O'Connor announced the decision of the U.S. Supreme Court. Justices Brennan, Stevens, and Scalia delivered separate opinions, concurring in part and dissenting in part. In* Penry *there was no question that the defendant was psychologically imbalanced. The question was to what degree was he imbalanced and was that degree large enough to release the defendant from a death sentence*

JUSTICE O'CONNOR delivered the opinion of the Court, except as to Part IV-C.

...It was well settled at common law that 'idiots,' together with 'lunatics,' were not subject to punishment for criminal acts committed under those incapacities . . .

The common law prohibition against punishing 'idiots' for their crimes suggests that it may indeed be 'cruel and unusual' punishment to execute persons who are profoundly or severely retarded and wholly lacking the capacity to appreciate the wrongfulness of their actions. Because of the protections afforded by the insanity defense today, such a person is not likely to be convicted or face the prospect of punishment . . .

. . .Penry was found competent to stand trial. In other words, he was found to have the ability to consult with his lawyer with a reasonable degree of rational understanding, and was found to have a rational as well as factual understanding of the proceedings against him . . .

In contrast, in *Ford v. Wainwright,* which held that the Eighth Amendment prohibits execution of the insane, considerably more evidence of a national consensus was available. No State permitted the execution of the insane, and 26 States had statutes explicitly requiring suspension of the execution of a capital defendant who became insane. Other States had adopted the common law prohibition against executing the insane. Moreover, in examining the objective evidence of contemporary standards of decency in *Thompson v. Oklahoma,* the plurality noted that 18 States expressly established a minimum age in their death penalty statutes, and all of them required that the defendant have attained at least the age of 16 at the time of the offense. In our view, the two state statutes prohibiting execution of the mentally retarded, even when added to the 14 States that have rejected capital punishment completely, do not provide sufficient evidence at present of a national consensus . . .

Penry argues that execution of a mentally retarded person like himself with a reasoning capacity of approximately a 7-year-old would be cruel and unusual because it is disproportionate to his degree of personal culpability. Just as the plurality in *Thompson* reasoned that a juvenile is less culpable than an adult for the same crime, Penry argues that mentally retarded people do not have the judgment, perspective, and self-control of a person of normal intelligence. In essence, Penry argues that because of his diminished ability to control his impulses, to think in long-range terms, and to learn from his mistakes, he 'is not capable of acting with the degree of culpability that can justify the ultimate penalty' . . .

On the record before the Court today, however, I cannot conclude that all mentally retarded people of Penry's ability—by virtue of their mental retardation alone, and apart from any individualized consideration of their personal responsibility—inevitably lack the cognitive, volitional, and moral capacity to act with the degree of culpability associated with the death penalty. Mentally retarded persons are individuals whose abilities and experiences can vary greatly . . .

In sum, mental retardation is a factor that may well lessen a defendant's culpability for a capital offense. But we cannot conclude today that the Eighth Amendment precludes the execution of any mentally retarded person of Penry's ability convicted of a capital offense simply by virtue of his or her mental retardation alone. So long as sentencers can consider and give effect to mitigating evidence of mental retardation in imposing sentence, an individualized determination whether 'death is the appropriate punishment' can be made in each particular case. While a national consensus against execution of the mentally retarded may someday emerge reflecting the 'evolving standards of decency that mark the progress of a maturing society,' there is insufficient evidence of such a consensus today.

Accordingly, the judgment below is affirmed in part and reversed in part, and the case is remanded for further proceedings consistent with this opinion.

It is so ordered.

JUSTICE BRENNAN, with whom JUSTICE MARSHALL joins, concurring in part and dissenting in part.

. . .I would . . .hold, however, that the Eighth Amendment prohibits the execution of offenders who are mentally retarded and who thus lack the full degree of responsibility for their crimes that is a predicate for the constitutional imposition of the death penalty . . .

I agree with JUSTICE O'CONNOR that one question to be asked in determining whether the execution of mentally retarded offenders is always unconstitutional because disproportionate is whether the mentally retarded as a class 'by virtue of their mental retardation alone, . . . inevitably lack the cognitive, volitional, and moral capacity to act with the degree of culpability associated with the death penalty.' JUSTICE O'CONNOR answers that question in the negative . . .It seems to me that the evidence compels a different conclusion . . .

In light of this clinical definition of mental retardation, I cannot agree that the undeniable fact that mentally retarded persons have 'diverse capacities and life experiences,' is of significance to the Eighth Amendment proportionality analysis we must conduct in this case . . . The impairment of a mentally retarded offender's reasoning abilities, control over impulsive behavior, and moral development in my view limits his or her culpability so that, whatever other punishment might be appropriate, the ultimate penalty of death is always and necessarily disproportionate to his or her blameworthiness and hence is unconstitutional.

Even if mental retardation alone were not invariably associated with a lack of the degree of culpability upon which death as a proportionate punishment is predicated, I would still hold the execution of the mentally retarded to be unconstitutional. If there are among the mentally retarded exceptional individuals as responsible for their actions as persons who suffer no such disability, the individualized consideration afforded at sentencing fails to ensure that they are the only mentally retarded offenders who will be picked out to receive a death sentence. The consideration of mental retardation as a mitigating factor is inadequate to guarantee, as the Constitution requires, that an individual who is not fully blameworthy for his or her crime because of a mental disability does not receive the death penalty . . .

There is second ground upon which I would conclude that the execution of mentally retarded offenders violates the Eighth Amendment: killing mentally retarded offenders does not measurably further the penal goals of either retribution or deterrence . . . Since mentally retarded offenders as a class lack the culpability that is a prerequisite to the proportionate imposition of the death penalty, it follows that execution can never be the 'just deserts' of a retarded offender, and that the punishment does not serve the retributive goal . . .

Furthermore, killing mentally retarded offenders does not measurably contribute to the goal of deterrence. It is highly unlikely that the exclusion of the mentally retarded from the class of those eligible to be sentenced to death will lessen any deterrent effect the death penalty may have for nonretarded potential offenders, for they, of course, will under present law remain at risk of execution. And the very factors that make it disproportionate and unjust to execute the mentally retarded also make the death penalty of the most minimal deterrent effect so far as retarded potential offenders are concerned . . . [T]he possibility of receiving the death penalty will not in the case of a mentally retarded person figure in some careful assessment of different courses of action . . .

Because I believe that the Eighth Amendment to the United States Constitution stands in the way of a State killing a mentally retarded person for a crime for which, as a result of his or her disability, he or she is not fully culpable, I would reverse the judgment of the Court of Appeals in its entirety.

JUSTICE SCALIA, with whom THE CHIEF JUSTICE, JUSTICE WHITE, and JUSTICE KENNEDY join, concurring in part and dissenting in part.

...Unlike JUSTICE O'CONNOR, however, I think we need go no further to resolve the Eighth Amendment issue. Part IV-C of her opinion goes on to examine whether application of the death penalty to mentally retarded offenders 'violates the Eighth Amendment because it "makes no measurable contribution to acceptable goals of punishment and hence is nothing more than the purposeless and needless imposition of pain and suffering" or because it is "grossly out of proportion to the severity of the crime"' ...'The punishment is either "cruel and unusual" (i.e.., society has set its face against it) or it is not.' If it is not unusual, that is, if an objective examination of laws and jury determinations fails to demonstrate society's disapproval of it, the punishment is not unconstitutional even if out of accord with the theories of penology favored by the Justices of this Court.

...I turn briefly to the place of today's holding within the broad scheme of our constitutional jurisprudence regarding capital sentencing, as opposed to the immediately applicable precedents. It is out of order there as well. As noted at the outset of this discussion, our law regarding capital sentencing has sought to strike a balance between complete discretion, which produces 'wholly arbitrary and capricious action,' *Gregg*, and no discretion at all, which prevents the individuating characteristics of the defendant and of the crime to be taken into account, *Woodson* ... In providing for juries to consider all mitigating circumstances insofar as they bear upon (1) deliberateness, (2) future dangerousness, and (3) provocation, it seems to me Texas had adopted a rational scheme that meets the two concerns of our Eighth Amendment jurisprudence. The Court today demands that it be replaced, however, with a scheme that simply dumps before the jury all sympathetic factors bearing upon the defendant's background and character, and the circumstances of the offense, so that the jury may decide without further guidance whether he 'lacked the moral culpability to be sentenced to death . . .did not deserve to be sentenced to death,' or 'was not sufficiently culpable to deserve the death penalty.' The Court seeks to dignify this by calling it a process that calls for a 'reasoned moral response,'—but reason has nothing to do with it, the Court having eliminated the structure that required reason. It is an unguided, emotional 'moral response' that the Court demands be allowed—an outpouring of personal reaction to all the circumstances of a defendant's life and personality, an unfocused sympathy. Not only have we never before said the Constitution requires this, but the line of cases following *Gregg* sought to eliminate precisely the unpredictability it produces . . .

. . .The decision whether to impose the death penalty is a unitary one; unguided discretion not to impose is unguided discretion to impose as well. In holding that the jury had to be free to deem Penry's mental retardation and sad childhood relevant for whatever purpose it wished, the Court has come full circle, not only permitting but requiring what Furman once condemned. 'Freakishly' and 'wantonly,' *Furman* (Stewart, J. concurring), have been rebaptized 'reasoned moral response.' I do not think the Constitution forbids what the Court imposes here, but I am certain it does not require it.

I respectfully dissent

Stanford v. Kentucky (1989)

The ongoing discussion of execution of juveniles reached to sixteen- and seventeen-year-olds in this case. Justice Scalia reiterated his viewpoint that elements such as age and mental competency were just factors to be considered in deciding whether an individual should receive the death penalty. Also very evident is Scalia's insistence on judicial restraint. Justice O'Connor continued to be the swing vote in such cases, looking at a variety of factors to discern what the national consensus was in regard to the issue. As before, she opened the door for a showing of proof.

JUSTICE SCALIA announced the judgment of the Court and delivered the opinion of the Court with respect to Parts I, II, III, and IV-A, and an opinion with respect to Parts IV-B and V, in which THE CHIEF JUSTICE, JUSTICE WHITE, and JUSTICE KENNEDY join.

These two consolidated cases require us to decide whether the imposition of capital punishment on an individual for a crime committed at 16 or 17 years of age constitutes cruel and unusual punishment under the Eighth Amendment.

II

. . .Neither petitioner asserts that his sentence constitutes one of 'those modes or acts of punishment that had been considered cruel and unusual at the time that the Bill of Rights was adopted.' Nor could they support such a contention. At that time, the common law set the rebuttable presumption of incapacity to commit any felony at the age of 14, and theoretically permitted capital punishment to be imposed on anyone over the age of 7.

Thus petitioners are left to argue that their punishment is contrary to the 'evolving standards of decency that mark the progress of a maturing society.' They are correct in asserting that this Court has 'not confined the prohibition embodied in the Eighth Amendment to "barbarous" methods that were generally outlawed in the 18th century,' but instead has interpreted the Amendment 'in a flexible and dynamic manner.' In determining what standards have 'evolved,' however, we have looked not to our own conceptions of decency, but to those of modern American society as a whole. As we have said, 'Eighth Amendment judgments should not be, or appear to be, merely the subjective views of individual Justices . . .'

III

'[F]irst' among the 'objective indicia that reflect the public attitude toward a given sanction' are statutes passed by society's elected representatives. Of the 37 States whose laws permit capital punishment, 15 decline to impose it upon 16-year-old offenders and 12 decline to impose it on 17-year-old offenders. This does not establish the degree of national consensus this Court has previously thought sufficient to label a particular punishment cruel and unusual . . .

IV

A

Wilkins and Stanford argue, however, that even if the laws themselves do not establish a settled consensus, the application of the laws does. That contemporary society views capital punishment of 16- and 17-year-old offenders as inappropriate is demonstrated, they say, by the reluctance of juries to impose, and prosecutors to seek, such sentences. Petitioners are quite correct that a far smaller number of offenders under 18 than over 18 have been sentenced to death in this country . . . Given the undisputed fact that a far smaller percentage of capital crimes are committed by persons under 18 than over 18, the discrepancy in treatment is much less than might seem. Granted, however, that a substantial discrepancy exists, that does not establish the requisite proposition that the death sentence for offenders under 18 is categorically unacceptable to prosecutors and juries. To the contrary, it is not only possible, but overwhelmingly probable, that the very considerations which induce petitioners and their supporters to believe that death should never be imposed on offenders under 18 cause prosecutors and juries to believe that it should rarely be imposed.

B

This last point suggests why there is also no relevance to the laws cited by petitioners and their amici which set 18 or more as the legal age for engaging in various activities, ranging from driving to drinking alcoholic beverages to voting. It is, to begin with, absurd to think that one must be mature enough to drive carefully, to drink responsibly, or to vote intelligently, in order to be mature enough to understand that murdering another human being is profoundly wrong, and to conform one's conduct to that most minimal of all civilized standards. But even if the requisite degrees of maturity were comparable, the age statutes in question would still not be relevant. They do not represent a social judgment that all persons under the designated ages are not responsible enough to drive, to drink, or to vote, but at most a judgment that the vast majority are not. These laws set the appropriate ages for the operation of a system that makes its determinations in gross, and that does not conduct individualized maturity tests for each driver, drinker, or voter. The criminal justice system, however, does provide individualized testing . . . The application of this particularized system to the petitioners can be declared constitutionally inadequate only if there is a consensus, not that 17 or 18 is the age at which most persons, or even almost all persons, achieve sufficient maturity to be held fully responsible for murder; but that 17 or 18 is the age before which no one can reasonably be held fully responsible. What displays society's views on this latter point are not the ages set forth in the generalized system of driving, drinking, and voting laws cited by petitioners and their amici, but the ages at which the States permit their particularized capital punishment systems to be applied.

V

Having failed to establish a consensus against capital punishment for 16- and 17-year-old offenders through state and federal statutes and the behavior of prosecutors and juries, petitioners seek to demonstrate it through other indicia, including public opinion polls, the views of interest groups, and the positions adopted by various professional associations. We decline the invitation to rest constitutional law upon such uncertain foundations. A revised national consensus so broad, so clear, and so enduring as to justify a permanent prohibition upon all units of democratic government must appear in the operative acts (laws and the application of laws) that the people have approved . . .

[I]t is not demonstrable that no 16-year-old is 'adequately responsible' or significantly deterred . . .The battle must be fought, then, on the field of the Eighth Amendment; and in that struggle socioscientific, ethicoscientific, or even purely scientific evidence is not an available weapon. The punishment is either 'cruel and unusual' (i.e., society has set its face against it) or it is not. The audience for these arguments, in other words, is not this Court but the citizenry of the United States . . .In short, we emphatically reject petitioner's suggestion that the issues in this case permit us to apply our 'own informed judgment,' regarding the desirability of permitting the death penalty for crimes by 16- and 17-year-olds . . .

. . .To say, as the dissent says, that '"it is for us ultimately to judge whether the Eighth Amendment permits imposition of the death penalty,"' quoting *Enmund v. Florida,* and to mean that as the dissent means it, i.e., that it is for us to judge, not on the basis of what we perceive the Eighth Amendment originally prohibited, or on the basis of what we perceive the society through its democratic processes now overwhelmingly disapproves, but on the basis of what we think 'proportionate' and 'measurably contributory to acceptable goals of punishment'—to say and mean that, is to replace judges of the law with a committee of philosopher-kings . . .

We discern neither a historical nor a modern societal consensus forbidding the imposition of capital punishment on any person who murders at 16 or 17 years of age. Accordingly, we conclude that such punishment does not offend the Eighth Amendment's prohibition against cruel and unusual punishment.

The judgments of the Supreme Court of Kentucky and the Supreme Court of Missouri are therefore

Affirmed.

JUSTICE O'CONNOR, concurring in part and concurring in the judgment.

. . .I conclude that the death sentences for capital murder imposed by Missouri and Kentucky on petitioners Wilkins and Stanford respectively should not be set aside because it is sufficiently clear that no national consensus forbids the imposition of capital punishment on 16- or 17-year-old capital murderers . . .

. . .I join all but Parts IV-B and V of JUSTICE SCALIA's opinion.

JUSTICE BRENNAN, with whom JUSTICE MARSHALL, JUSTICE BLACKMUN, and JUSTICE STEVENS join, dissenting.

I believe that to take the life of a person as punishment for a crime committed when below the age of 18 is cruel and unusual and hence is prohibited by the Eighth Amendment.

The method by which this Court assesses a claim that a punishment is unconstitutional because it is cruel and unusual is established by our precedents, and it bears little resemblance to the method four Members of the Court apply in this case . . .I agree . . .that a more searching inquiry is mandated by our precedents interpreting the Cruel and Unusual Punishments Clause. In my view, that inquiry must in these cases go beyond age-based statutory classifications relating to matters other than capital punishment and must also encompass what JUSTICE SCALIA calls, with evident but misplaced disdain, 'ethicoscientific' evidence. Only then can we be in a position to judge, as our cases require, whether a punishment is unconstitutionally excessive, either because it is disproportionate given the culpability of the offender, or because it serves no legitimate penal goal.

There can be no doubt at this point in our constitutional history that the Eighth Amendment forbids punishment that is wholly disproportionate to the blameworthiness of the offender . . .Indeed, this focus on a defendant's blameworthiness runs throughout our constitutional jurisprudence relating to capital sentencing . . . In my view, juveniles so generally lack the degree of responsibility for their crimes that is a predicate for the constitutional imposition of the death penalty that the Eighth Amendment forbids that they receive that punishment.

Legislative determinations distinguishing juveniles from adults abound. These age-based classifications reveal much about how our society regards juveniles as a class, and about societal beliefs regarding adolescent levels of responsibility . . .

The participation of juveniles in a substantial number of activities open to adults is either barred completely or significantly restricted by legislation . . .

...But the factors discussed above indicate that 18 is the dividing line that society has generally drawn, the point at which it is thought reasonable to assume that persons have an ability to make, and a duty to bear responsibility for their, judgments. Insofar as age 18 is a necessarily arbitrary social choice as a point at which to acknowledge a person's maturity and responsibility, given the different developmental rates of individuals, it is in fact 'a conservative estimate of the dividing line between adolescence and adulthood. Many of the psychological and emotional changes that an adolescent experiences in maturing do not actually occur until the early 20s.'

Juveniles very generally lack that degree of blameworthiness that is, in my view, a constitutional prerequisite for the imposition of capital punishment under our precedents concerning the Eighth Amendment proportionality principle...I believe that the same categorical assumption that juveniles as a class are insufficiently mature to be regarded as fully responsible that we make in so many other areas is appropriately made in determining whether minors may be subjected to the death penalty. As we noted in *Thompson,* it would be ironic if the assumptions we so readily make about minors as a class were suddenly unavailable in conducting proportionality analysis. I would hold that the Eighth Amendment prohibits the execution of any person for a crime committed below the age of 18.

Under a second strand of Eighth Amendment inquiry into whether a particular sentence is excessive and hence unconstitutional, we ask whether the sentence makes a measurable contribution to acceptable goals of punishment...Unless the death penalty applied to persons for offenses committed under 18 measurably contributes to one of these goals, the Eighth Amendment prohibits it.

I have explained...why I believe juveniles lack the culpability that makes a crime so extreme that it may warrant, according to this Court's cases, the death penalty...These same considerations persuade me that executing juveniles 'does not measurably contribute to the retributive end of ensuring that the criminal gets his just deserts.'...

Nor does the execution of juvenile offenders measurably contribute to the goal of deterrence. Excluding juveniles from the class of persons eligible to receive the death penalty will have little effect on any deterrent value capital punishment may have for potential offenders who are over 18: these adult offenders may of course remain eligible for a death sentence. The potential deterrent effect of juvenile executions on adolescent offenders is also insignificant. The deterrent value of capital punishment rests 'on the assumption that we are rational beings who always think before we act, and then base our actions on a careful calculation of the gains and losses involved.' . . .As the plurality noted in *Thompson*, '[t]he likelihood that the teenage offender has made the kind of cost-benefit analysis that attaches any weight to the possibility of execution is so remote as to be virtually nonexistent' . . . [J]uveniles have little fear of death, because they have 'a profound conviction of their own omnipotence and immortality' . . .Because imposition of the death penalty on persons for offenses committed under the age of 18 makes no measurable contribution to the goals of either retribution or deterrence, it is 'nothing more than the purposeless and needless imposition of pain and suffering,' and is thus excessive and unconstitutional.

There are strong indications that the execution of juvenile offenders violates contemporary standards of decency: a majority of States decline to permit juveniles to be sentenced to death; imposition of the sentence upon minors is very unusual even in those States that permit it; and respected organizations with expertise in relevant areas regard the execution of juveniles as unacceptable, as does international opinion. These indicators serve to confirm in my view my conclusion that the Eighth Amendment prohibits the execution of persons for offenses they committed while below the age of 18, because the death penalty is disproportionate when applied to such young offenders and fails measurably to serve the goals of capital punishment. I dissent.

Blystone v. Pennsylvania (1990)

Blystone *was part of the growing number of cases in which the U.S. Supreme Court was trying to limit the number of appeals and cut down the prolonged process that stretched from conviction to execution. The Court also wanted to give a little leeway to the states in defining their death penalty statutes.*

CHIEF JUSTICE REHNQUIST delivered the opinion of the Court.

A Pennsylvania jury sentenced petitioner Scott Wayne Blystone to death after finding him guilty of robbing and murdering a hitchhiker who was unlucky enough to have accepted a ride in his car. Petitioner challenges his sentence on the ground that the State's death penalty statute is unconstitutional because it requires the jury to impose a sentence of death if, as in this case, it finds at least one aggravating circumstance and no mitigating circumstances. We hold that the Pennsylvania death penalty statute, and petitioner's sentence under it, comport with our decisions interpreting the Eighth Amendment to the United States Constitution . . .

Petitioner was charged with and convicted of first-degree murder, robbery, criminal conspiracy to commit homicide, and criminal conspiracy to commit robbery. The same jury that convicted petitioner found as an aggravating circumstance that petitioner 'committed a killing while in the perpetration of a felony'   The jury found that no mitigating circumstances existed, and accordingly sentenced petitioner to death pursuant to the Pennsylvania death penalty statute . . .

We think that the Pennsylvania death penalty statute satisfies the requirement that a capital sentencing jury be allowed to consider and give effect to all relevant mitigating evidence. [The statute] does not limit the types of mitigating evidence which may be considered, and subsection (e) provides a jury with a nonexclusive list of mitigating factors which may be taken into account—including a 'catchall' category providing for the consideration of '[a]ny other evidence of mitigation concerning the character and record of the defendant and the circumstances of his offense.' Nor is the statute impermissibly 'mandatory' as that term was understood in *Woodson* or *Roberts*. Death is not automatically imposed upon conviction for certain types of murder. It is imposed only after a determination that the aggravating circumstances outweigh the mitigating circumstances present in the particular crime committed by the particular defendant, or that there are no such mitigating circumstances. This is sufficient under *Lockett* and *Penry* . . .

At sentencing, petitioner's jury found one aggravating circumstance present in this case—that petitioner committed a killing while in the perpetration of a robbery. No mitigating circumstances were found. Petitioner contends that the mandatory imposition of death in this situation violates the Eighth Amendment requirement of individualized sentencing since the jury was precluded from considering whether the severity of his aggravating circumstance warranted the death sentence. We reject this argument. The presence of aggravating circumstances serves the purpose of limiting the class of death-eligible defendants, and the Eighth Amendment does not require that these aggravating circumstances be further refined or weighed by a jury . . .

JUSTICE BRENNAN, with whom JUSTICE MARSHALL joins, and with whom JUSTICE BLACKMUN and JUSTICE STEVENS join except as to Part IV, dissenting.

The hallmark of our Eighth Amendment jurisprudence is that . . .capital punishment may not be imposed unless the sentencer makes an individualized determination that death is the appropriate sentence for a particular defendant. This Court has repeatedly invoked this principle to invalidate mandatory death penalty statutes for even the most egregious crimes. Today, for the first time, the Court upholds a statute containing a mandatory provision that gives the legislature rather than the jury the ultimate decision whether the death penalty is appropriate in a particular set of circumstances. Such a statute deprives the defendant of the type of individualized sentencing hearing required by the Eighth Amendment. I respectfully dissent.

. . .[T]he Court has recognized that the Eighth Amendment imposes a limit on a State's ability to 'guide' the sentencer's discretion . . .The *Woodson* plurality rejected the argument that *Furman* required removal of all discretion from the sentencer, holding that any consistency obtained by a mandatory statute would be arbitrary because the consistency would not take into account the individual circumstances of the defendant and the crime . . .A mandatory death penalty statute treats 'all persons convicted of a designated offense not as uniquely individual human beings, but as members of a faceless, undifferentiated mass to be subjected to the blind infliction of the penalty of death.' Thus, the Court held that the 'fundamental respect for humanity underlying the Eighth Amendment requires consideration of the character and record of the individual offender and the circumstances of the particular offense as a constitutionally indispensable part of the process of inflicting the penalty of death.'

Woodson and its progeny are distinguishable from this case because the Pennsylvania statute allows the jury to consider mitigating circumstances. But once a Pennsylvania jury finds that no mitigating circumstances are proved by a preponderance of the evidence, it is required to impose the death penalty . . .

. . .The mandatory language in the Pennsylvania statute [deprives] the jury of any power to make . . .an independent judgment. The jury's determination that an aggravating circumstance exists ends the decisionmaking process. In addition, whether an aggravating circumstance exists is generally a question of fact relating to either the circumstances of the offense, the status of the victim, or the defendant's criminal record. In many cases, the existence of the aggravating factor is not disputed. Finding an aggravating circumstance does not entail any moral judgment about the nature of the act or the actor, and therefore it does not give the jury an opportunity to decide whether it believes the defendant's particular offense warrants the death penalty ...[T]he mandatory language in the Pennsylvania statute deprives a defendant of an individualized sentencing hearing ...

The Court's refusal to recognize that the 'mandatory aspect' of the Pennsylvania statute deprives the defendant of an individualized sentencing hearing is contrary to reason. Rather than address the merits of petitioner's claim, the majority summarily concludes that the Eighth Amendment is 'satisfied' because the jury may consider mitigating evidence. Although our cases clearly hold that the ability to consider mitigating evidence is a constitutional requirement, it does not follow that this ability satisfies the constitutional demand for an individualized sentencing hearing. The 'weight' of an aggravating circumstance is just as relevant to the propriety of the death penalty as the 'weight' of any mitigating circumstances. The Court's unarticulated assumption that the legislature may define a group of crimes for which the death penalty is required in certain situations represents a marked departure from our previous cases. The Court's failure to provide any reasoning to reject a claim well grounded in our case law is always disturbing. An unexplained departure from fundamental principles in the death penalty context is inexcusable. I respectfully dissent.

IV

Even if I did not believe the Pennsylvania statute unconstitutionally deprives the jury of discretion to impose a life sentence, I would vacate petitioner's sentence. I adhere to my belief that the death penalty is in all circumstances cruel and unusual punishment.

Buchanan v. Angelone (1998)

By the late 1990s, two simultaneous trends seemed to be evident: the shoring up of the death penalty as generally constitutional and the attempt to limit the scope of that penalty by finding exceptions. In regard to the first, Buchanan *was another chance for Chief Justice Rehnquist to open the door to more fluid death penalty prosecutions and allow more flexibility for the states within the confines of* Furman.

CHIEF JUSTICE REHNQUIST delivered the opinion of the Court.

This case calls on us to decide whether the Eighth Amendment requires that a capital jury be instructed on the concept of mitigating evidence generally, or on particular statutory mitigating factors. We hold it does not . . .

Buchanan requested several additional jury instructions . . .Buchanan also proposed an instruction stating that, 'In addition to the mitigating factors specified in other instructions, you shall consider the circumstances surrounding the offense, the history and background of [Buchanan] and any other facts in mitigation of the offense.' The court refused to give these instructions . . .

Petitioner contends that the trial court violated his Eighth and Fourteenth Amendment right to be free from arbitrary and capricious imposition of the death penalty when it failed to provide the jury with express guidance on the concept of mitigation, and to instruct the jury on particular statutorily defined mitigating factors . . .

. . .[O]ur cases have established that the sentencer may not be precluded from considering, and may not refuse to consider, any constitutionally relevant mitigating evidence. However, the State may shape and structure the jury's consideration of mitigation so long as it does not preclude the jury from giving effect to any relevant mitigating evidence . . .

But we have never gone further and held that the state must affirmatively structure in a particular way the manner in which juries consider mitigating evidence. And indeed, our decisions suggest that complete jury discretion is constitutionally permissible . . .

The jury instruction here did not violate these constitutional principles. The instruction did not foreclose the jury's consideration of any mitigating evidence. By directing the jury to base its decision on 'all the evidence,' the instruction afforded jurors an opportunity to consider mitigating evidence. The instruction informed the jurors that if they found the aggravating factor proved beyond a reasonable doubt then they 'may fix' the penalty at death, but directed that if they believed that all the evidence justified a lesser sentence then they 'shall' impose a life sentence. The jury was thus allowed to impose a life sentence even if it found the aggravating factor proved . . .[T]he instructions here did not constrain the manner in which the jury was able to give effect to mitigation . . .

The absence of an instruction on the concept of mitigation and of instructions on particular statutorily defined mitigating factors did not violate the Eighth and Fourteenth Amendments to the United States Constitution. The judgment of the Court of Appeals is Affirmed.

JUSTICE BREYER, with whom JUSTICE STEVENS and JUSTICE GINSBURG join, dissenting.

The imposition of a penalty of death must be 'directly related to the personal culpability of the criminal defendant,' and 'reflect a reasoned *moral* response to the defendant's background, character, and crime.' . . .Consequently, a judge's instructions during penalty phase proceedings may not preclude the jury 'from considering, as a mitigating factor, any aspect of a defendant's character or record and any of the circumstances of the offense that the defendant proffers as a basis for a sentence less than death.' *Lockett v. Ohio.* The majority recognizes that 'the standard for determining whether jury instructions satisfy these principles [Is] 'whether there is a reasonable likelihood that the jury has applied the challenged instruction in a way that prevents the consideration of constitutionally relevant evidence.' In my view, the majority misapplies this standard . . .

. . .[T]he *presentation* of evidence does not tell the jury that the evidence presented is relevant and can be taken into account . . .I also realize that the defense attorney told the jury the evidence was relevant, and the prosecution conceded the point. But a jury may well consider such advice from a defense attorney to be advocacy which it should ignore or discount. And the jury here might have lost the significance of the prosecution's concession, for that concession made a brief appearance in lengthy opening and closing arguments, the basic point of which was that the evidence did not sufficiently mitigate the crime but warranted death.

. . .The jury will look to the judge, not to counsel, for authoritative direction about what it is to do with the evidence that it hears . . .For the reasons I have mentioned, taking the instructions and the context together, the judge's instructions created a 'reasonable likelihood' that the jury 'applied the challenged instruction in a way that prevents the consideration of constitutionally relevant evidence.' To uphold the instructions given here is to 'risk that the death penalty will be imposed in spite of factors which may call for a less severe penalty.' *Lockett.* To do so therefore breaks the promise made in *Brown* that the imposition of the punishment of death will 'reflect a reasoned moral response to the defendant's background, character, and crime.'

For these reasons, I dissent.

Atkins v. Virginia (2002)

After his conviction for abduction, armed robbery, and capital murder, Daryl Atkins relied on a forensic psychologist for mitigating evidence at the penalty phase of the trial. The psychologist's testimony that Atkins was mildly retarded was later rebutted by the prosecution. The jury returned a sentence of death. On appeal, Atkins challenged the holding in Penry v. Lynaugh *that mental retardation was just a mitigating circumstance. The 6–3 decision noted that "evolving notions of decency" had reached a point where such executions now (unlike previously in* Penry) *were deemed unacceptable by most states. The case incorporated what was becoming a common debate over statistical information and how to interpret it. It also included a particularly virulent dissent from Justice Scalia.*

JUSTICE STEVENS delivered the opinion of the Court.

Those mentally retarded persons who meet the law's requirements for criminal responsibility should be tried and punished when they commit crimes. Because of their disabilities in areas of reasoning, judgment, and control of their impulses, however, they do not act with the level of moral culpability that characterizes the most serious adult criminal conduct. Moreover, their impairments can jeopardize the reliability and fairness of capital proceedings against mentally retarded defendants. Presumably for these reasons, in the 13 years since we decided *Penry v. Lynaugh,* the American public, legislators, scholars, and judges have deliberated over the question whether the death penalty should ever be imposed on a mentally retarded criminal. The consensus reflected in those deliberations informs our answer to the question presented by this case: whether such executions are 'cruel and unusual punishments' prohibited by the Eighth Amendment to the Federal Constitution.

The Eighth Amendment succinctly prohibits 'excessive' sanctions...We have repeatedly applied this proportionality precept in...cases interpreting the Eighth Amendment...As Justice Stewart explained in *Robinson:* 'Even one day in prison would be a cruel and unusual punishment for the "crime" of having a common cold.'

A claim that punishment is excessive is judged not by the standards that prevailed in 1685 when Lord Jeffreys presided over the 'Bloody Assizes' or when the Bill of Rights was adopted, but rather by those that currently prevail. As Chief Justice Warren explained in his opinion in *Trop v. Dulles:* 'The basic concept underlying the Eighth Amendment is nothing less than the dignity of man . . .The Amendment must draw its meaning from the evolving standards of decency that mark the progress of a maturing society' . . .

. . .Much has changed since [*Penry*] . . .[T]he large number of States prohibiting the execution of mentally retarded persons (and the complete absence of States passing legislation reinstating the power to conduct such executions) provides powerful evidence that today our society views mentally retarded offenders as categorically less culpable than the average criminal. The evidence carries even greater force when it is noted that the legislatures that have addressed the issue have voted overwhelmingly in favor of the prohibition. Moreover, even in those States that allow the execution of mentally retarded offenders, the practice is uncommon . . .The practice . . .has become truly unusual, and it is fair to say that a national consensus has developed against it . . .

This consensus unquestionably reflects widespread judgment about the relative culpability of mentally retarded offenders, and the relationship between mental retardation and the penological purposes served by the death penalty. Additionally, it suggests that some characteristics of mental retardation undermine the strength of the procedural protections that our capital jurisprudence steadfastly guards.

. . .Mentally retarded persons frequently know the difference between right and wrong and are competent to stand trial. Because of their impairments, however, by definition they have diminished capacities to understand and process information, to communicate, to abstract from mistakes and learn from experience, to engage in logical reasoning, to control impulses, and to understand the reactions of others. There is no evidence that they are more likely to engage in criminal conduct than others, but there is abundant evidence that they often act on impulse rather than pursuant to a premeditated plan, and that in group settings they are followers rather than leaders. Their deficiencies do not warrant an exemption from criminal sanctions, but they do diminish their personal culpability.

In light of these deficiencies, our death penalty jurisprudence provides two reasons consistent with the legislative consensus that the mentally retarded should be categorically excluded from execution. First, there is a serious question as to whether either justification that we have recognized as a basis for the death penalty applies to mentally retarded offenders . . .Unless the imposition of the death penalty on a mentally retarded person 'measurably contributes to one or both of these goals, it "is nothing more than the purposeless and needless imposition of pain and suffering," and hence an unconstitutional punishment.' *Enmund.*

With respect to retribution—the interest in seeing that the offender gets his 'just deserts'—the severity of the appropriate punishment necessarily depends on the culpability of the offender . . .If the culpability of the average murderer is insufficient to justify the most extreme sanction available to the State, the lesser culpability of the mentally retarded offender surely does not merit that form of retribution. Thus, pursuant to our narrowing jurisprudence, which seeks to ensure that only the most deserving of execution are put to death, an exclusion for the mentally retarded is appropriate.

. . .The theory of deterrence in capital sentencing is predicated upon the notion that the increased severity of the punishment will inhibit criminal actors from carrying out murderous conduct. Yet it is the same cognitive and behavioral impairments that make these defendants less morally culpable—for example, the diminished ability to understand and process information, to learn from experience, to engage in logical reasoning, or to control impulses—that also make it less likely that they can process the information of the possibility of execution as a penalty and, as a result, control their conduct based upon that information. Nor will exempting the mentally retarded from execution lessen the deterrent effect of the death penalty with respect to offenders who are not mentally retarded. Such individuals are unprotected by the exemption and will continue to face the threat of execution. Thus, executing the mentally retarded will not measurably further the goal of deterrence.

The reduced capacity of mentally retarded offenders provides a second justification for a categorical rule making such offenders ineligible for the death penalty. The risk 'that the death penalty will be imposed in spite of factors which may call for a less severe penalty,' *Lockett v. Ohio,* is enhanced, not only by the possibility of false confessions, but also by the lesser ability of mentally retarded defendants to make a persuasive showing of mitigation in the face of prosecutorial evidence of one or more aggravating factors. Mentally retarded defendants may be less able to give meaningful assistance to their counsel and are typically poor witnesses, and their demeanor may create an unwarranted impression of lack of remorse for their crimes. As *Penry* demonstrated, moreover, reliance on mental retardation as a mitigating factor can be a two-edged sword that may enhance the likelihood that the aggravating factor of future dangerousness will be found by the jury. Mentally retarded defendants in the aggregate face a special risk of wrongful execution.

Our independent evaluation of the issue reveals no reason to disagree with the judgment of 'the legislatures that have recently addressed the matter' and concluded that death is not a suitable punishment for a mentally retarded criminal . . .Construing and applying the Eighth Amendment in the light of our 'evolving standards of decency,' we therefore conclude that such punishment is excessive and that the Constitution 'places a substantive restriction on the State's power to take the life' of a mentally retarded offender. *Ford.*

The judgment of the Virginia Supreme Court is reversed and the case is remanded for further proceedings not inconsistent with this opinion.

It is so ordered.

JUSTICE SCALIA, with whom the CHIEF JUSTICE and JUSTICE THOMAS join, dissenting.

Today's decision is the pinnacle of our Eighth Amendment death-is-different jurisprudence. Not only does it, like all of that jurisprudence, find no support in the text or history of the Eighth Amendment, it does not even have support in current social attitudes regarding the conditions that render an otherwise just death penalty inappropriate. Seldom has an opinion of this Court rested so obviously upon nothing but the personal views of its members.

. . .[P]etitioner's mental retardation was a *central issue* at sentencing. The jury concluded, however, that his alleged retardation was not a compelling reason to exempt him from the death penalty in light of the brutality of his crime and his long demonstrated propensity for violence . . .

The Court makes no pretense that execution of the mildly mentally retarded would have been considered 'cruel and unusual' in 1791. Only the *severely* or *profoundly* mentally retarded, commonly known as 'idiots,' enjoyed any special status under the law at that time. They, like lunatics, suffered a 'deficiency in will' rendering them unable to tell right from wrong . . .Due to their incompetence, idiots were 'excuse[d] from the guilt, and of course from the punishment, of any criminal action committed under such deprivation of the senses.' 4 *Blackstone* 25. Instead, they were often committed to civil confinement or made wards of the State, thereby preventing them from 'go[ing] loose, to the terror of the king's subjects.' 4 *Blackstone* 25. Mentally retarded offenders with less severe impairments—those who were not 'idiots'—suffered criminal prosecution and punishment, including capital punishment . . .

The Court is left to argue, therefore, that execution of the mildly retarded is inconsistent with the 'evolving standards of decency that mark the progress of a maturing society.' *Trop v. Dulles,* Before today, our opinions consistently emphasized that Eighth Amendment judgments regarding the existence of social 'standards' 'should be informed by objective factors to the maximum possible extent' and 'should not be, or appear to be, merely the subjective views of individual Justices.' *Coker v. Georgia* . . .

The Court pays lipservice to these precedents as it miraculously extracts a 'national consensus' forbidding execution of the mentally retarded . . .If one is to say, as the Court does today, that *all* executions of the mentally retarded are so morally repugnant as to violate our national 'standards of decency,' surely the 'consensus' it points to must be one that has set its righteous face against *all* such executions . . .

But let us accept, for the sake of argument, the Court's faulty count. That bare number of States alone—*18*—should be enough to convince any reasonable person that no 'national consensus' exists. How is it possible that agreement among 47% of the death penalty jurisdictions amounts to 'consensus'? . . .

The Court attempts to bolster its embarrassingly feeble evidence of 'consensus' with the following: 'It is not so much the number of these States that is significant, but the *consistency* of the direction of change.' But in what *other* direction *could we possibly* see change? Given that 14 years ago *all* the death penalty statutes included the mentally retarded, *any* change (except precipitate undoing of what had just been done) was *bound to be* in the one direction the Court finds significant enough to overcome the lack of real consensus. That is to say, to be accurate the Court's '*consistency*-of-the-direction-of-change' point should be recast into the following unimpressive observation: 'No State has yet undone its exemption of the mentally retarded, one for as long as 14 whole years.' In any event, reliance upon 'trends,' even those of much longer duration than a mere 14 years, is a perilous basis for constitutional adjudication . . .

Even less compelling (if possible) is the Court's argument, that evidence of 'national consensus' is to be found in the infrequency with which retarded persons are executed in States that do not bar their execution . . .It is not at all clear that execution of the mentally retarded is 'uncommon' . . .*If,* however, execution of the mentally retarded *is* 'uncommon'; and if it is not a sufficient explanation of this that the retarded comprise a tiny fraction of society; then surely the explanation is that mental retardation is a constitutionally mandated mitigating factor at sentencing . . .

But the Prize for the Court's Most Feeble Effort to fabricate 'national consensus' must go to its appeal (deservedly relegated to a footnote) to the views of assorted professional and religious organizations, members of the so-called 'world community,' and respondents to opinion polls . . .'[W]here there is not first a settled consensus among our own people, the views of other nations, however enlightened the Justices of this Court may think them to be, cannot be imposed upon Americans through the Constitution.' *Thompson* (Scalia, J., dissenting).

Beyond the empty talk of a 'national consensus,' the Court gives us a brief glimpse of what really underlies today's decision: pretension to a power confined *neither* by the moral sentiments originally enshrined in the Eighth Amendment (its original meaning) *nor even* by the current moral sentiments of the American people. '[T]he Constitution,' the Court says, 'contemplates that in the end *our own judgment* will be brought to bear on the question of the acceptability of the death penalty under the Eighth Amendment.' (The unexpressed reason for this unexpressed 'contemplation' of the Constitution is presumably that really good lawyers have moral sentiments superior to those of the common herd, whether in 1791 or today.) The arrogance of this assumption of power takes one's breath away. And it explains, of course, why the Court can be so cavalier about the evidence of consensus. It is just a game, after all . . .

. . .The Court's analysis rests on two fundamental assumptions: (1) that the Eighth Amendment prohibits excessive punishments, and (2) that sentencing juries or judges are unable to account properly for the 'diminished capacities' of the retarded. The first assumption is wrong . . .The Eighth Amendment is addressed to always-and-everywhere 'cruel' punishments, such as the rack and the thumbscrew . . .The second assumption—inability of judges or juries to take proper account of mental retardation—is not only unsubstantiated, but contradicts the immemorial belief, here and in England, that they play an *indispensable* role in such matters . . .

Proceeding from these faulty assumptions, the Court gives two reasons why the death penalty is an excessive punishment for all mentally retarded offenders. First, the 'diminished capacities' of the mentally retarded raise a 'serious question' whether their execution contributes to the 'social purposes' of the death penalty, viz., retribution and deterrence. (The Court conveniently ignores a third 'social purpose' of the death penalty—'incapacitation of dangerous criminals and the consequent prevention of crimes that they may otherwise commit in the future,' *Gregg v. Georgia* (joint opinion of Stewart, Powell, and Stevens, JJ.). But never mind; its discussion of even the other two does not bear analysis . . . Is there an established correlation between mental acuity and the ability to conform one's conduct to the law in such a rudimentary matter as murder? Are the mentally retarded really more disposed (and hence more likely) to commit willfully cruel and serious crime than others? In my experience, the opposite is true: being child-like generally suggests innocence rather than brutality.

Assuming, however, that there is a direct connection between diminished intelligence and the inability to refrain from murder, what scientific analysis can possibly show that a mildly retarded individual who commits an exquisite torture-killing is 'no more culpable' than the 'average' murderer in a holdup-gone-wrong or a domestic dispute? Or a moderately retarded individual who commits a series of 20 exquisite torture-killings? Surely culpability, and deservedness of the most severe retribution, depends not merely (if at all) upon the mental capacity of the criminal (above the level where he is able to distinguish right from wrong) but also upon the depravity of the crime—which is precisely why this sort of question has traditionally been thought answerable not by a categorical rule of the sort the Court today imposes upon all trials, but rather by the sentencer's weighing of the circumstances (both degree of retardation and depravity of crime) in the particular case. The fact that juries continue to sentence mentally retarded offenders to death for extreme crimes shows that society's moral outrage sometimes demands execution of retarded offenders . . . Once the Court admits (as it does) that mental retardation does not render the offender morally *blameless,* there is no basis for saying that the death penalty is *never* appropriate retribution, no matter *how* heinous the crime . . .

As for the other social purpose of the death penalty that the Court discusses, deterrence . . . [S]urely the deterrent effect of a penalty is adequately vindicated if it successfully deters many, but not all, of the target class . . . I am not sure that a murderer is somehow less blameworthy if (though he knew his act was wrong) he did not fully appre-

ciate that he could die for it; but if so, we should treat a mentally retarded murderer the way we treat an offender who may be 'less likely'
to respond to the death penalty because he was abused as a child. We
do not hold him immune from capital punishment, but require his
background to be considered by the sentencer as a mitigating factor.
Eddings v. Oklahoma.

The Court throws one last factor into its grab bag of reasons why
execution of the retarded is 'excessive' in all cases: Mentally retarded
offenders 'face a special risk of wrongful execution' . . . 'Special risk' is
pretty flabby language (even flabbier than 'less likely')—and I suppose
a similar 'special risk' could be said to exist for just plain stupid people, inarticulate people, even ugly people . . .

Today's opinion adds one more to the long list of substantive and
procedural requirements impeding imposition of the death penalty
imposed under this Court's assumed power to invent a death-is-different jurisprudence. None of those requirements existed when the
Eighth Amendment was adopted, and some of them were not even
supported by current moral consensus . . . There is something to be
said for popular abolition of the death penalty; there is nothing to be
said for its incremental abolition by this Court.

This newest invention promises to be more effective than any of the
others in turning the process of capital trial into a game. One need
only read the definitions of mental retardation adopted by the American Association of Mental Retardation and the American Psychiatric
Association (set forth in the Court's opinion) to realize that the symp-
toms of this condition can readily be feigned. And whereas the capital
defendant who feigns insanity risks commitment to a mental institution until he can be cured (and then tried and executed), the capital defendant who feigns mental retardation risks nothing at all. The mere
pendency of the present case has brought us petitions by death row inmates claiming for the first time, after multiple habeas petitions, that
they are retarded . . .

I respectfully dissent.

In Re Kevin Nigel Stanford (2002)

*One of the rare dissents from a denial of certiorari. This case was
brought to the U.S. Supreme Court post-*Atkins. *Stanford argued that
because* Atkins *created an exception to the death penalty for the mentally retarded, the applicabilitly of the death penalty for all those un-*

der the age of 18 should be reviewed. The Court's opinion here mirrored the rationale of Atkins. The justices took a two-track approach: first, in recent years, a national consensus against executing 18-year-olds had been established; second, that the execution of juveniles did not serve the professed purposes of the death penalty.

JUSTICE STEVENS, with whom JUSTICE SOUTER, JUSTICE GINSBURG, and JUSTICE BREYER join, dissenting.

Petitioner has filed an application for an original writ of habeas corpus asking us to hold that his execution would be unconstitutional because he was under the age of 18 when he committed his offense. A bare majority of the Court rejected that submission 13 years ago. *Stanford v. Kentucky* (1989). There are no valid procedural objections to our reconsideration of the issue now, and, given our recent decision in *Atkins v. Virginia* we certainly should do so.

In *Atkins,* we held that the Constitution prohibits the application of the death penalty to mentally retarded persons. The reasons supporting that holding, with one exception, apply with equal or greater force to the execution of juvenile offenders. The exception—the number of States expressly forbidding the execution of juvenile offenders (28) is slightly fewer than the number forbidding the execution of the mentally retarded (30)—does not justify disparate treatment of the two classes . . .

Rather than repeating the reasoning in our opinion in *Atkins,* I think it appropriate to quote the following comments from Justice Brennan's dissenting opinion in *Stanford v. Kentucky* which I joined in 1989 . . .*[quote omitted]*

. . .[W]hen determining what legal obligations and responsibilities juveniles will be allowed to take on, the trend tends to require individuals to be older, rather than younger . . .Neuroscientific evidence of the last few years has revealed that adolescent brains are not fully developed, which often leads to erratic behaviors and thought processes in that age group. Scientific advances such as the use of functional magnetic resonance imaging—MRI scans— have provided valuable data that serve to make the case even stronger that adolescents 'are more vulnerable, more impulsive, and less self-disciplined than adults' *Stanford v. Kentucky.*

Moreover, in the last 13 years, a national consensus has developed that juvenile offenders should not be executed . . .The majority of Americans, when asked in 2001, indicated that the death penalty should not apply to juvenile offenders.

All of this leads me to conclude that offenses committed by juveniles under the age of 18 do not merit the death penalty. The practice of executing such offenders is a relic of the past and is inconsistent with evolving standards of decency in a civilized society. We should put an end to this shameful practice.

I would set the application for an original writ for argument and respectfully dissent from the Court's refusal to do so.

Ring v. Arizona (2002)

A 2000 New Jersey case, Apprendi v. New Jersey, *raised Sixth Amendment issues challenging the methodology used to apply the death penalty in many districts and overruled* Walton v. Arizona. *In* Walton *the U.S. Supreme Court ruled that in the penalty phase of any trial, a defendant cannot receive "a penalty exceeding the maximum he would receive if punished according to the facts reflected in the jury verdict alone." Judges often found aggravating circumstances after the jury had concluded its work, and the Court ruled that this procedure compromised the Sixth Amendment right to trial by jury by shifting fact-finding to the judge. Some states, in this case Arizona, had such a system in place. In* Ring, *additional testimony at the sentencing phase—that is, new facts—upped the ante and made Ring eligible for the death penalty, which he was subsequently given. In striking down any death penalty procedure that excluded the jury from the sentencing decision after it had convicted the defendant, the Court reinforced the notion of capital punishment and simultaneously bolstered anti–capital punishment advocates.*

JUSTICE GINSBURG delivered the opinion of the Court.

Based solely on the jury's verdict finding Ring guilty of first-degree felony murder, the maximum punishment he could have received was life imprisonment. The question presented is whether that aggravating factor may be found by the judge, as Arizona law specifies, or whether the Sixth Amendment's jury trial guarantee, made applicable to the States by the Fourteenth Amendment, requires that the aggravating factor determination be entrusted to the jury . . .

[In *Apprendi v. New Jersey* (2000)] . . .we said . . .[if] a State makes an increase in a defendant's authorized punishment contingent on the finding of a fact, that fact—no matter how the State labels it—must be found by a jury beyond a reasonable doubt. A defendant may not be 'exposed . . .to a penalty *exceeding* the maximum he would receive if punished according to the facts reflected in the jury verdict alone.' *Apprendi* (SCALIA, J., concurring) . . .

In an effort to reconcile its capital sentencing system with the Sixth Amendment as interpreted by *Apprendi,* Arizona first restates the *Apprendi* majority's portrayal of Arizona's system: Ring was convicted of first-degree murder, for which Arizona law specifies 'death or life imprisonment' as the only sentencing options; Ring was therefore sentenced within the range of punishment authorized by the jury verdict. This argument overlooks *Apprendi*'s instruction that 'the relevant inquiry is one not of form, but of effect.' In effect, 'the required finding [of an aggravated circumstance] exposed [Ring] to a greater punishment than that authorized by the jury's guilty verdict.' . . .

Apart from the Eighth Amendment provenance of aggravating factors, Arizona presents 'no specific reason for excepting capital defendants from the constitutional protections . . .extended to defendants generally, and none is readily apparent.' [*Apprendi*], (O'CONNOR, J., dissenting) . . .

Arizona suggests that judicial authority over the finding of aggravating factors 'may . . .be a better way to guarantee against the arbitrary imposition of the death penalty.' The Sixth Amendment jury trial right, however, does not turn on the relative rationality, fairness, or efficiency of potential factfinders . . .

For the reasons stated, we hold that *Walton* and *Apprendi* are irreconcilable; our Sixth Amendment jurisprudence cannot be home to both. Accordingly, we overrule *Walton* to the extent that it allows a sentencing judge, sitting without a jury, to find an aggravating circumstance necessary for imposition of the death penalty. Because Arizona's enumerated aggravating factors operate as 'the functional equivalent of an element of a greater offense,' *Apprendi,* the Sixth Amendment requires that they be found by a jury.

The right to trial by jury guaranteed by the Sixth Amendment would be senselessly diminished if it encompassed the factfinding necessary to increase a defendant's sentence by two years, but not the factfinding necessary to put him to death. We hold that the Sixth Amendment applies to both. The judgment of the Arizona Supreme Court is therefore reversed, and the case is remanded for further proceedings not inconsistent with this opinion.

It is so ordered.

JUSTICE SCALIA, with whom JUSTICE THOMAS joins, concurring . . .

. . .What compelled Arizona (and many other States) to specify particular 'aggravating factors' that must be found before the death penalty can be imposed was the line of this Court's cases beginning with *Furman v. Georgia.* In my view, that line of decisions had no proper foundation in the Constitution . . .I am therefore reluctant to magnify the burdens that our *Furman* jurisprudence imposes on the States . . .

On the other hand, . . .as I reaffirmed by joining the opinion for the Court in *Apprendi,* I believe that the fundamental meaning of the jury-trial guarantee of the Sixth Amendment is that all facts essential to imposition of the level of punishment that the defendant receives—whether the statute calls them elements of the offense, sentencing factors, or Mary Jane—must be found by the jury beyond a reasonable doubt . . .

. . .[O]bserving over the past 12 years the accelerating propensity of both state and federal legislatures to adopt 'sentencing factors' determined by judges that increase punishment beyond what is authorized by the jury's verdict, and my witnessing the belief of a near majority of my colleagues that this novel practice is perfectly OK . . .cause me to believe that our people's traditional belief in the right of trial by jury is in perilous decline. That decline is bound to be confirmed, and indeed accelerated, by the repeated spectacle of a man's going to his death because *a judge* found that an aggravating factor existed. We cannot preserve our veneration for the protection of the jury in criminal cases if we render ourselves callous to the need for that protection by regularly imposing the death penalty without it . . .

I add one further point, lest the holding of today's decision be confused by the separate concurrence. JUSTICE BREYER, who refuses to accept *Apprendi* . . .nonetheless concurs in today's judgment because he 'believes that jury sentencing in capital cases is mandated by the Eighth Amendment.' While I am, as always, pleased to travel in JUSTICE BREYER's company, the unfortunate fact is that today's judgment has nothing to do with jury sentencing. What today's decision says is that the jury must find the existence of the *fact* that an aggravating factor existed. Those States that leave the ultimate life-or-death decision to the judge may continue to do so . . .

JUSTICE BREYER, concurring in the judgment.

Given my views in *Apprendi v. New Jersey* . . . I cannot join the Court's opinion. I concur in the judgment, however, because I believe that jury sentencing in capital cases is mandated by the Eighth Amendment.

This Court has held that the Eighth Amendment requires States to apply special procedural safeguards when they seek the death penalty . . . I therefore conclude that the Eighth Amendment requires that a jury, not a judge, make the decision to sentence a defendant to death . . .

. . . Leaving questions of arbitrariness aside . . . diversity argues strongly for procedures that will help assure that, in a particular case, the community indeed believes application of the death penalty is appropriate, not 'cruel,' 'unusual,' or otherwise unwarranted.

. . . And I conclude that the Eighth Amendment requires individual jurors to make, and to take responsibility for, a decision to sentence a person to death.

JUSTICE O'CONNOR, with whom the CHIEF JUSTICE joins, dissenting.

I understand why the Court holds that the reasoning of *Apprendi v. New Jersey* is irreconcilable with *Walton v. Arizona.* Yet in choosing which to overrule, I would choose *Apprendi,* not *Walton.*

Not only was the decision in *Apprendi* unjustified in my view, but it has also had a severely destabilizing effect on our criminal justice system . . .

The decision today is only going to add to these already serious effects. The Court effectively declares five States' capital sentencing schemes unconstitutional . . . There are 168 prisoners on death row in these States.

United States of America v. Alan Quinones (2002)

[New York Federal District Court, Reversed on Appeal]
A New York Federal District Court case that took the radical step of declaring the federal death penalty statue unconstitutional. Judge Jed S. Rakoff allowed the government to present its argument again. In a subsequent case after reargument, Rakoff reaffirmed his holding from the earlier case and expanded some of the reasoning. His judgment boiled down to the idea that because there is a possibility that an innocent person could be executed, the death penalty is inherently cruel and unusual.

Although his decision was overturned on appeal, and the death penalty reinstated, the case provided strong arguments against capital punishment and provided more fuel for the death penalty debate.

JED S. RAKOFF, U.S.D.J.

The Federal Death Penalty Act serves deterrent and retributive functions, or so Congress could reasonably have concluded when it passed the Act in 1994. But despite the important goals, and undoubted popularity, of this federal act and similar state statutes, legislatures and courts have always been queasy about the possibility that an innocent person, mistakenly convicted and sentenced to death under such a statute, might be executed before he could vindicate his innocence—an event difficult to square with basic constitutional guarantees, let alone simple justice . . .

. . .[T]he possibility that an innocent person might be executed pursuant to a death penalty statute seemed remote . . . While recognizing that no system of justice is infallible, the majority in *Herrera* implicitly assumed that the high standard of proof and numerous procedural protections required in criminal cases, coupled with judicial review, post-conviction remedies, and, when all else failed, the possibility of executive clemency, rendered it highly unlikely that an executed person would subsequently be discovered to be innocent.

That assumption no longer seems tenable. In just the few years since *Herrera*, evidence has emerged that clearly indicates that, despite all the aforementioned safeguards, innocent people—mostly of color—are convicted of capital crimes they never committed, their convictions affirmed, and their collateral remedies denied, with a frequency far greater than previously supposed.

Most striking are the results obtained through the use of post-conviction testing with deoxyribonucleic acid ('DNA') . . . DNA testing has established the factual innocence of no fewer than 12 inmates on death row . . .

. . .[T]he inference is unmistakable that numerous innocent people have been executed whose innocence might otherwise have been similarly established, whether by newly-developed scientific techniques, newly-discovered evidence, or simply renewed attention to their cases . . .

Just as there is typically no statute of limitations for first-degree murder—for the obvious reason that it would be intolerable to let a cold-blooded murderer escape justice through the mere passage of time—so too one may ask whether it is tolerable to put a time limit on when someone wrongly convicted of murder must prove his innocence or face extinction. In constitutional terms, the issue is whether—now that we know the fallibility of our system in capital cases—capital punishment is unconstitutional because it creates an undue risk that a meaningful number of innocent persons, by being put to death before the emergence of the techniques or evidence that will establish their innocence, are thereby effectively deprived of the opportunity to prove their innocence—and thus deprived of the process that is reasonably due them in these circumstances under the Fifth Amendment . . .

The issue—not addressed by *Herrera* or, so far as appears, anywhere else—boils down to this. We now know, in a way almost unthinkable even a decade ago, that our system of criminal justice, for all its protections, is sufficiently fallible that innocent people are convicted of capital crimes with some frequency. Fortunately, as DNA testing illustrates, scientific developments and other innovative measures (including some not yet even known) may enable us not only to prevent future mistakes but also to rectify past ones by releasing wrongfully-convicted persons—but only if such persons are still alive to be released. If, instead, we sanction execution, with full recognition that the probable result will be the state-sponsored death of a meaningful number of innocent people, have we not thereby deprived these people of the process that is their due? Unless we accept—as seemingly a majority of the Supreme Court in *Herrera* was unwilling to accept—that considerations of deterrence and retribution can constitutionally justify the knowing execution of innocent persons, the answer must be that the federal death penalty statute is unconstitutional.

Consequently, if the Court were compelled to decide the issue today, it would, for the foregoing reasons, grant the defendants' motion to dismiss all death penalty aspects of this case on the ground that the federal death penalty statute is unconstitutional . . .

So ordered.

Key People,
Laws, and Concepts

Beccaria, Cesare (1738–1794)

Italian jurist, economist, and philosopher. He wrote one of the early works attacking the death penalty. His *Essay on Crimes and Punishments,* published in 1764 (anonymously), is considered one of the seminal works on criminal justice in Western history. It provided fodder for Enlightenment thinkers who challenged at times the method of execution as well as execution itself. The book radically influenced criminal justice throughout the Western world, resulting in reform of criminal law throughout Western Europe.

Black, Hugo (1886–1971)

Justice of the Supreme Court from 1937 to 1971. Black was acclaimed for his "literal" reading of the Constitution. This strict approach to the Constitution produced a justice who, while being a staunch advocate for civil liberties, would not extend the Constitution to include the right to privacy. Born in Alabama, he was elected to the Senate in 1926. Part of his political career included being an active member of the Ku Klux Klan, although he always denied any participation in their violent activities. He was a staunch support of F.D.R. and the New Deal. Black quickly disassociated himself from his Klan past by becoming an advocate of the Court's expansion of criminal due process rights, often being in the lead, writing the majority opinion in

Gideon v. Wainright (1963), the case that guaranteed the right to counsel for all criminal defendants. His absolutist approach to the text of the Constitution resulted in very expansive readings of the First Amendment and protection of religious freedom and free speech, but failed to gain his support in either declaring a right to privacy in *Griswold v. Connecticut* (1965) (because there was no right of privacy explicit in the words of the Constitution) or in ruling the death penalty unconstitutional. In historical retrospect, it is difficult to classify Black as either a liberal or a conservative because of this literalist approach.

Blackmun, Harry A. (1908–1999)

A graduate of Harvard Law School, Blackmun was a Nixon appointee. Originally appealing because he was a compromise candidate to the Court as well as being seen as a clone of Chief Justice Burger, with whom he was good friends, Blackmun rapidly developed his own philosophy and style, especially after he authored the majority opinion in *Roe v. Wade* (1973), which recognized a woman's constitutionally guaranteed right to abortion. He originally supported the imposition of the death penalty. Blackmun was one of the stalwarts on the Court who began to reject the death penalty as a viable penalty. As his tenure on the Court grew, so did his objection to capital punishment. By the time he retired in 1994, he was steadfastly opposed to execution. He repeated this admonition prior to his death in a series of interviews. Blackmun always argued that his positions never changed and rather than his growing more liberal, it was the Court that had shifted to the right.

Bloody Code

The list of crimes for which people could be executed in England. At its height, there were approximately 220 different crimes that were punishable by death. The crimes included "being in the company of gypsies for one month," "strong evidence of malice in a child aged 7–14 years of age," and "blacking the face or using a disguise whilst committing a crime." Although execution for many of these crimes was rare, major crimes on the list, such as murder, burglary, and robbery, regularly called for a death sentence.

Brennan, William J. (1906–1997)

One of the advocates of the absolutist approach that argued the Eighth Amendment prohibited capital punishment, per se, because no matter the form or reason, it is cruel and unusual punishment. A graduate of Harvard Law School, he began his career on the bench as a justice of the New Jersey Supreme Court in 1952. He was appointed to the United States Supreme Court by President Eisenhower in 1956. Appointed as a conservative justice, he quickly proved Eisenhower wrong and became one of the great liberal justices on the Court. He wrote many important opinions that focused on criminal procedure, freedom of expression, reapportionment, and voting rights. He left the Court in 1990.

Burger, Warren Earl (1907–1995)

Warren Burger succeeded Earl Warren as chief justice of the United States Supreme Court in 1969. Although it was expected that under his tenure the Court would reverse many of the Warren Court decisions, the conservative backlash did not happen, and more "liberal" decisions, such as *Roe v. Wade* (1973) (guaranteeing a woman's constitutional right to abortion), were produced. Burger strongly supported separation of powers and ruled that President Nixon had to turn over the Watergate tapes, despite Nixon's claim of executive privilege. Burger oversaw the transition of the Court from its liberal Warren Court days to the more conservative Rehnquist Court.

Camus, Albert (1913–1960)

A French existentialist writer born in Algiers. Camus was an actor, playwright, teacher, and journalist. He was very active with the French resistance during World War II. He coedited *Combate,* a left-wing newspaper after the war, and won the Nobel Prize for literature in 1957. He wrote a biting critique of the death penalty in "Reflections on a Guillotine."

Capital Crime

Crime warranting the death penalty.

Capital Punishment

Punishing persons convicted of crimes that warrant the death penalty.

Chessman, Caryl (1921–1960)

The Red-Light Bandit who was convicted of kidnapping and robbery and was sentenced to death in 1948 in California. He was on death row for twelve years, during which time he spurred a large anti–death penalty movement on the strength of three books he wrote that argued against capital punishment: *Cell 2455, Death Row* (1954), *Trial by Ordeal* (1955), and *The Face of Justice* (1957).

Cruel and Unusual

Phrase in the Eighth Amendment, which establishes the framework by which criminal punishments are to be judged. Some justices (such as Scalia) argue that it is meant purely to forbid those acts that are designed to inflict pain and degradation, such as torture. Questions about the death penalty often center on whether the method and process fit within the definition, which varies.

Darrow, Clarence (1857–1938)

One of America's most famous defense lawyers, Darrow spent most of his life in labor and criminal law. A small-town lawyer in Ohio, he began his rise to notoriety with a friendship with John Altgeld, who eventually became governor of Ohio and was instrumental in pardoning several of the men convicted in the Haymarker Riot of 1886. Darrow questioned the treatment of both those who were caught in the criminal justice system, which he saw as unfair, and the workers who were trying to organize. Among Darrow's most famous cases were the defense of Eugene Debs during the Pullman strike, Big Bill Haywood, and the Scopes Monkey Trial. His turn to criminal law came later in life, and his most famous case was the Leopold-Loeb trial. It was the only time in Darrow's career that he asked his clients to plead guilty. He saved the two from the death penalty through the introduction of psychiatric evidence.

Deterrence

One of the justifications for the death penalty. Proponents argue the death penalty inhibits people who would otherwise commit capital crimes. Opponents of the death penalty contend it does no such thing and it is impossible to prove that it has such an effect.

Douglas, William O. (1898–1980)

Known as one of the most liberal justices in Supreme Court history, who regularly voted against the death penalty. A graduate of Columbia Law School, he taught there as well as Yale before becoming a member of the Securities and Exchange Commission in 1936. He was nominated to the Supreme Court in 1939 by Franklin Roosevelt. Considered a very young justice, he served thirty-six years on the Court. He authored numerous controversial opinions, was a staunch advocate of civil liberties, interpreted the Bill of Rights in a broad manner, and advocated the broad use of the Court's powers.

Due Process

Phrase found in both the Fifth and Fourteenth Amendments of the United States Constitution. The phrase demands that a criminal defendant be given his or her "day in court," and means that one must get a fair trial and a fair hearing and certain procedures must be followed along the way to produce that.

Electric Chair

Method of execution first developed in the early twentieth century in the United States. It was considered, at the time, to be a more humane way to execute prisoners than hanging. It works by delivering a lethal dose of electrical current.

Equal Protection

Part of the Fourteenth Amendment of the United States Constitution. Equal protection demands that all those in like circumstances are treated in a like manner. It is usually the source for challenges that the government's actions were racially discriminatory.

Frankfurter, Felix (1882–1965)

Graduate of Harvard Law School, he helped found the American Civil Liberties Union in 1920. During the 1920s he joined in the effort to save Sacco and Vanzetti, writing one of the seminal articles against their execution. He was appointed to the Supreme Court in 1939 and served until 1962. Despite his obvious liberal leanings outside the Court, once he became a justice, Frankfurter became a very outspoken supporter of judicial restraint and one of the major conservative voices on the Court. He regularly conceded authority to the executive and legislative branches as long as their actions did not seriously offend. Although he did join *Brown v. Board of Education* (1954) (outlawing segregation in public schools), he often dissented from Warren Court decisions.

Furman v. Georgia

Case in 1972 that declared the death penalty, as then applied, unconstitutional. Only a plurality ruled the death penalty was unconstitutional per se. Because there was no clear majority, it left the status of the death penalty open.

Goldberg, Arthur (1908–1990)

Although he only served on the Court for three years, he offered some unique interpretations of the Constitution and authored an important memorandum against the death penalty that many historians note as an important catalyst for modern death penalty litigation. In addition to time as a justice, he served as secretary of labor in the Kennedy administration and as United States ambassador to the United Nations under Lyndon Johnson. Goldberg's decidedly liberal views and broad construction of constitutional rights helped shift the Court to the left.

Gregg v. Georgia

1976 case that ruled the death penalty, when properly applied, did not violate the Eighth Amendment's prohibition against "cruel and unusual punishment."

Guillotine

Developed in France in the eighteenth century as a more humane way to execute criminal defendants. The guillotine became a symbol of the French Revolution and egalitarianism, because, for the first time, all guilty parties, not just the rich, would be executed by decapitation (seen as a privilege of the wealthy prior to this).

Habeus Corpus

Known as the "great writ." It means literally "you have the body." An important mechanism in the criminal process by which a prisoner challenges his detainment as being illegal. The challenger must allege his imprisonment is the result of a constitutional violation. Since the early 1990s, the U.S. Supreme Court has limited the ability of death row inmates to use this writ.

Hammurabi's Code

One of the earliest written legal codes, promulgated by Hammurabi, who ruled over the Babylonian Empire from 1728 to 1686 B.C.E.

Hanging

Until the 1890s the preferred method of execution in the United States. The last hanging to take place in the United States was in 1986 in Delaware.

Kennedy, Anthony (1936–)

Appointed in 1988, Kennedy was confirmed in the wake of the disastrous attempts to appoint Robert Bork (rejected for his stark conservatism) and Douglas Ginsburg (whose admissions to smoking marijuana derailed his nomination) by Ronald Reagan. He proves to be throughout his tenure one of the swing votes on the Court. Although he tends to vote conservative, voting in favor of states' rights and the death penalty, and against affirmative action, he has also made "liberal" votes, writing the majority decision that outlawed homosexual sodomy in *Lawrence v. Texas* (2003), and joined the plurality in *Planned Parenthood v. Casey* (1992), reaffirming *Roe v. Wade* (1973).

Lethal Injection

Latest method to execute prisoners. Developed in response to problems with the electric chair and gas chamber, which seemed to make the condemned suffer. Under lethal injection, a prisoner is usually bound to a gurney. A member of the execution team inserts two needles. The needles are connected to intravenous drips. The first drip is a saline solution, which is harmless. This drip starts immediately. When the warden gives the signal, the witnesses are permitted to see the condemned. Witnesses sit in a separate room and view the defendant through a window. While the witnesses watch, the condemned prisoner is put to sleep through a second injection. Finally, as the prisoner falls asleep, a third substance is introduced that paralyzes the muscle system and stops the breathing. Finally, the heart is stopped. Death results from respiratory and cardiac arrest while the condemned is unconscious.

Marshall, Thurgood (1908–1993)

Appointed in 1967, Marshall was the first black justice appointed to the Supreme Court. He was a strong advocate for civil rights and believed the death penalty was unconstitutional. Marshall applied to the University of Maryland Law School and was rejected because of its segregationist policy, and he attended Howard Law School instead. A year after graduation in 1933, he began working for the NAACP, eventually becoming chief counsel in 1940. He argued major cases before the United States Supreme Court, including *Brown v. Board of Education* (1954). Marshall was appointed to the Second Circuit Court of Appeals by Kennedy and served as solicitor general under President Lyndon Johnson. Marshall's twenty-four-year tenure on the Court marked a consistently liberal voting record that included protection of all individual rights, especially those involving criminal due process. He was the spokesperson on the Court for civil rights and a strong advocate against the death penalty (along with Justice Brennan), consistently arguing that poor and minorities were affected disproportionately.

Model Penal Code

Attempt to create uniform laws through the fifty states. Although not accepted by all states, many base their criminal code and procedures on the standards established in the code.

O'Connor, Sandra Day (1930–)

The first woman appointed to the Supreme Court. Although originally seen as a key member of the conservative wing of the Court, in her later years she was seen as a moderate voice and swing vote. Oftentimes she was a swing vote on death penalty cases in the 1990s. She is one of the justices who are willing to vote for abolition of the death penalty if a strong case can be made that society now believes that execution of a certain group of individuals is against social policy or the national conscience.

Old Sparky

The name given to the Florida electric chair, it often serves as the symbol of why the death penalty is cruel and unusual. The name derives from the fact that several times in its history, the chair has not worked in a quick and efficient manner, and flames shot out of the victims' bodies.

Per Curiam

When a member of the Court speaks as the Court, rather than as a specific justice giving an opinion. *Furman v. Georgia* (1972), produced a short per curiam opinion, only to be followed by nine concurring and dissenting opinions.

Plurality

When the majority of the Court can agree on the judgment but not the opinion. The main published opinion is not signed by a majority of the justices and has less value as a precedent.

Powell, Lewis (1907–1998)

A Nixon appointee, he took the place of Hugo Black and took his seat in 1972 with William Rehnquist. One of the stalwart moderates on the Court, he often became a deciding vote in crucial cases dealing with affirmative action and abortion. Powell wrote the lone decision in *Regents of the University of California v. Bakke* (1978), which no other justice joined in its entirety, but because four joined the reasoning and four joined the judgment, it became the benchmark for affirmative action until two rulings in 2004 concerning the University of Michigan and the University of Michigan Law School. Powell dissented in *Furman v. Georgia* (1972) and was a key element in producing the compromise that reinstated the death penalty in *Gregg v. Georgia* (1976).

Progressive Movement

Movement at the beginning of the twentieth century that focused on the problems in the United States, including corruption in government, need for social justice, rights of the underclass, and so on. Many Progressives focused on the plight of the human condition as a result of nurture not nature and felt that criminal behavior was a product of environment and criminals could be rehabilitated.

Rehnquist, William H. (1924–)

Graduate of Stanford Law School in 1950. Clerked for Supreme Court Justice Robert Jackson. His tenure with Jackson did not moderate his views, and he became a staunch advocate of conservatism both on and off the Court. He campaigned for Barry Goldwater in 1964 and served as deputy attorney general in the Justice Department's Office of Legal Counsel in the Nixon administration. He was nominated to replace Justice John Harlan in 1971, and a Democratic Senate readily confirmed him. Rehnquist became an advocate for the reinvigoration of the Tenth Amendment, reaffirmation of states' rights and the curtailment of federal authority. Through numerous dissents, he laid the groundwork for his ascendancy to the position of chief justice in 1986. He was confirmed despite rabid opposition from many Democratic senators. As chief justice, he has continued his conservative agenda, writing the majority opinion in *United*

States v. Lopez, striking down a federal law as being beyond the power of the Congress under the commerce clause, and *Zelman v. Simmons-Harris* (2002), conceding more authority to the state to aid religion, validating school voucher programs for parochial schools.

Retribution

Another word for revenge. Death penalty advocates argue this is a legitimate reason for executing those found guilty of capital crimes. It gives the victims' families closure and enables society as well as the individual to exact compensatory satisfaction. Follows from the "eye-for-an-eye" approach to criminal justice.

Rosenbergs

They were the only Americans to be executed during the Cold War for conspiracy to commit espionage. Julius and Ethel Rosenberg were convicted of spying for the Russians and getting them the secrets for creating the atomic bomb. Amid much controversy and Red Scare hysteria, both were executed for their crimes. There was tremendous question at the time as to their guilt, and it was felt that even if they were not guilty of espionage, they were guilty of selling the secrets for creating the bomb, and their acts warranted death. Reportedly, Julius died immediately after the first jolt of electricity, but Ethel needed three charges before she could be pronounced dead. The result was an outcry that helped stir up anti–death penalty feelings.

Rush, Benjamin (1745–1830)

A prominent Philadelphia physician, who argued for the abolition of the death penalty. He felt that it was inhumane, did not act as a deterrent, and had a "coarsening effect on the public." An important figure in the American Revolution and signer of the Declaration of Independence.

Sacco and Vanzetti (1927)

One of the early twentieth-century cases that helped stir up protest against the death penalty. Nicola Sacco and Bartolomeo Vanzetti were Italian immigrants who were self-described anarchists who spoke broken English. They were found guilty of committing a payroll robbery, during which two people were killed. Although at the trial numerous witnesses exonerated them, it did not matter. Key prosecution witnesses who initially said they could not identify them, at trial changed their minds. Their conviction resulted from the nativist hysteria and Red Scare that enveloped the 1920s. During the seven years between their conviction and execution, additional information became available, including a confession by another man, which if not exonerating them raised serious questions as to their guilt. Felix Frankfurter wrote a monstrous article for *The Atlantic Monthly* defending them. Their execution stirred up protests not only in the United States, but also across the world.

Warren, Earl (1891–1974)

Appointed as chief justice by Eisenhower, the president considered it one of the gravest mistakes he ever made as president. The Warren Court is known for revolutionizing constitutional jurisprudence with rulings on racial segregation, civil rights, free speech, separation of church and state, police arrest procedure, criminal rights, and more. Warren was elected governor of California in the 1940s, during which time he supported the internment of Japanese-Americans during World War II. In addition to his liberal record on the Supreme Court, Warren chaired the famous "Warren Commission," which investigated the assassination of President John F. Kennedy.

Chronology

1608	First recorded execution in America (in Virginia).
1612	"Divine, Moral and Martial Laws" passes in Virginia. Rigid code that provides for death penalty for a host of both petty and major crimes.
1622	First definitive legal execution in America.
1764	Cesare Beccaria's *Essays on Crime and Punishment* is published.
1791	Ratification of the American Bill of Rights, including the Eighth Amendment. In France, Dr. Joseph Ignace-Guillotin's invention, the guillotine, is used for all French citizens who have committed a capital crime, in the name of equality and humanitarianism.
1833	New York and Rhode Island stop public executions.
1888	New York establishes electrocution as the state's method of execution.
1890	William Kemmler is executed in the electric chair. The execution is not perfect, and Kemmler failed to die. A second current is applied with death the result.
1892	*O'Neil v. Vermont:* Early state case that takes up the issue of "cruel and unusual" punishment, although it is a noncapital case.
1910	*Weems v. United States:* Defining "cruel and unusual" punishment, one of first cases to test the limits of the Eighth Amendment.
1924	Introduction of cyanide gas as form of execution.
1927	Execution of Sacco and Vanzetti.
1932	Execution of Bruno Hauptmann.

1936	Last public execution in the United States. Rainey Bethea is hanged in front of 20,000 people in Kentucky.
1941	Forty-two of forty-eight states have the death penalty.
1947	*Lousiana v. Resweber:* Execution by electrocution that fails multiple times, ruled not cruel and unusual punishment.
1953	Execution of the Rosenbergs.
1957	Publication of Nobel Prize–winner Albert Camus's "Reflections on a Guillotine."
1958	*Trop v. Dulles:* non–death penalty case that looks at the scope of the Eighth Amendment's prohibition against cruel and unusual punishment in *modern* society.
1960	Execution of Caryl Chessman.
1962	Model Penal Code passed.
1963	*Rudolph v. Alabama:* Denial of certiorari noted for Goldberg's eloquent dissent argued against the imposition of the death penalty.
1967	*United States v. Jackson:* Declaring Federal Kidnapping Statute's procedure for imposition of the death penalty unconstitutional.
1968	*Witherspoon v. Illinois:* Narrow decision overturning the application of the death penalty in the specific case because of improprieties in jury selection.
1969	Chief Justice Warren retires. Warren Burger becomes the chief justice.
1971	*McGautha v. California:* Challenge to unitary schemes where defendant is convicted and sentenced at the same time. Does not overturn such schemes.
1972	*Furman v. Georgia:* The Supreme Court declares the death penalty as unconstitutional.
1976	*Gregg v. Georgia:* Court reinstates the death penalty.
1976	*Woodson v. North Carolina:* Decided same day as *Gregg;* establishes that mandatory death penalty schemes are unconstitutional, emphasizing the importance of bifurcated trials and individualized justice.
1977	*Coker v. Georgia:* The Court declares the death penalty as cruel and unusual for the crime of rape, limiting the death penalty to only cases involving the taking of another human life.

1977	Oklahoma becomes the first state to adopt lethal injection as means of execution.
1978	*Lockett v. Ohio:* Sentencer (jury or judge) must be able to consider all mitigating factors and cannot be limited to a specific list. The result is the release of ninety-nine prisoners from death row in Ohio.
1982	*Eddings v. Oklahoma:* Failure of the Court to consider defendant's background, including his mental retardation, declared unconstitutional.
1982	First person executed by use of lethal injection.
1982	*Enmund v. Florida:* Compromised the ability of the government to execute people who were guilty for felony-murder generally. Defendant, who was an accomplice to a robbery and did not intend, attempt, or actually kill the victim, could not receive the death penalty.
1984	Velma Barfield is the first woman executed since the reinstatement of the death penalty.
1986	*Ford v. Wainwright:* Deems it is unconstitutional to execute a person who is insane.
1987	*McCleskey v. Kemp:* Rejects that the death penalty was applied in a racially discriminatory manner, although proportionally more blacks than whites have been executed.
1988	*Thompson v. Oklahoma:* Decides juveniles, who are younger than sixteen at the time of the murder, cannot be executed.
1989	*Penry v. Lynaugh:* The Court rules it is not unconstitutional, per se, to execute a mentally retarded person. Although mental retardation can be a mitigating factor, it does not preclude considering the death penalty.
1989	*Stanford v. Kentucky:* Reaffirms the decision in *Thompson.* However, there is a growing trend of states determining what is the lowest age at which they will execute juveniles.
1993	*Herrera v. Collins:* The Court holds that, in the absence of other constitutional violations, new evidence of innocence is no reason for federal courts to order a new trial. The Court also holds that an innocent inmate can seek to prevent his execution through the clemency process,

which, historically, has been "the 'fail safe' in our justice system." Herrera is not granted clemency and is executed in 1993.

1994   President Clinton signs the Violent Crime Control and Law Enforcement Act, expanding the federal death penalty.

1996   President Clinton signs the Anti-Terrorism and Effective Death Penalty Act, restricting review in federal courts.

1997   Declaration of moratorium against the death penalty in Ohio.

2000   Due to possible discrepancies in the conviction of prisoners on death row, Illinois Governor George Ryan declares a moratorium on executions and appoints a blue-ribbon Commission on Capital Punishment to study the issue.

2002   *Atkins v. Virginia:* Court rules that the mentally retarded, as a matter of law, cannot be executed, because it violates the dictates of the Eighth Amendment.

2002   *Ring v. Arizona:* In a jury trial, allowing the judge when deciding the sentence to find aggravating circumstances not determined by the jury, violates the Sixth Amendment's right to trial by jury.

2002   *United States of America v. Alan Quinones:* United States District Court holds the death penalty is unconstitutional, per se, because it poses a substantial risk of innocent defendants being executed. Upon appeal, the Second Circuit Court of Appeals reverses.

2003   Governor George Ryan grants clemency to all of Illinois' death row inmates (167) because of improprieties in the system that led to their convictions and sentences.

2004   *Roper v. Simmons:* Supreme Court confronts the question, again, of whether the Eighth Amendment prohibits the execution of minors, all those under the age of eighteen.

Table of Cases

Annotated Bibliography

Acker, James R., Robert M. Bohm, and Charles S. Lanier. 1998. *America's Experiment with Capital Punishment: Reflections on the Past, Present, and Future of the Ultimate Penal Sanction.* Durham, NC: Carolina Academic Press.

An extremely comprehensive work, that is composed of twenty-three chapters, each one written by a different author, who are among leading social science and legal scholars. This covers a wide range of topics, from public opinion toward capital punishment, victims' issues, costs, methodology, and so on.

Baird, Robert, and Stuart Rosenbaum, eds. 1995. *Punishment and the Death Penalty: The Current Debate.* Amherst, NY: Prometheus Books.

The first half of the book deals generally with the idea of punishment. The second half of the book focuses on the issue of the death penalty, presenting opposite viewpoints, some written in response to each other. Included are two statements by Justices Blackmun and Scalia from the case of *Collins v. Collins,* especially notable for the completion of Blackmun's transition to being an anti–death penalty advocate.

Baldus, David C., George C. Woodworth, and Charles A. Pulaski. 1990. *Equal Justice and the Death Penalty: A Legal and Empirical Analysis.* Boston, MA: Northeastern University Press.

The book that contains the empirical evidence and argument used in *McCleskey v. Kemp,* stating that the death penalty discriminated on the basis of race.

Banner, Stuart. 2003. *The Death Penalty: An American History.* Cambridge, MA: Harvard University Press.

A wide-ranging history of capital punishment in the United States. It traces the legal, philosophical, and religious arguments from the seventeenth century on. It provides a good historical background, although somewhat slanted toward an anti–death penalty viewpoint. The book helps explain the changes that have taken place in both the method of application of the death penalty as well as the whys and hows.

Bedau, Hugo Adams. 1997. *The Courts, the Constitution and Capital Punishment.* Lexington, MA: Lexington Books.

Collection of essays formerly printed in different journals. Although the volume is somewhat dated, it provides a good overview of how death penalty arguments have evolved. In the case of Bedau, one can see the shifts in how he phrased the argument, while the essential argument remained the same.

———. 1997. *The Death Penalty in America: Current Controversies.* New York: Oxford University Press.

Bedau is one of the premier authors on the death penalty. While each of his books covers some of the same territory, each one stands on its own, with unique insight and approaches.

This book includes thirty essays that cover the wide range of issues that crop up in death penalty debates. Although purporting to be a balanced discussion of the issue, this really is an anti–death penalty collection. Death penalty advocates can find some support for their argument, but it is very limited. The book does include a good bibliography and some Supreme Court opinions.

———. 2004. *Debating the Death Penalty: Should America Have Capital Punishment: The Experts on Both Sides Make Their Best Cases.* New York: Oxford University Press.

Perhaps the most evenhanded of Bedau's books. Each side gets a fair shake.

———. 2004. *Killing as Punishment: Reflections on the Death Penalty in America.* Boston, MA: Northeastern University Press.

Collection of articles covering a wide range of disciplines, including law, history, sociology, theology, and philosophy, that reviews a wide range of issues. Again in this text, Bedau tends to swing toward the opposition side.

Berger, Raoul. 1982. *Death Penalties: The Supreme Court's Obstacle Course.* Cambridge, MA: Harvard University Press.

Looks at the death penalty in a historical context. Berger, keeping with his general approach to constitutional issues and how the Court should interpret the Constitution, argues here, once again, that the Court has overstepped its bounds and is dictating social policy. This is an example of those who criticize the Court for its death penalty jurisprudence, not on the grounds that the death penalty is or is not constitutional, rather that it is outside the function of the Court to determine constitutionality.

Berns, Walter. 1979. *For Capital Punishment: Crime and the Morality of the Death Penalty.* New York: Basic Books.

Pro–death penalty book that argues that the idea of rehabilitating criminals, especially those who commit capital crimes, is foolish. It provides good arguments for death penalty advocates as to why capital punishment is effective, why it is a moral and just punishment in modern society, and finally why it is an integral cog in the modern justice system wheel.

Bessler, John D. 2003. *Kiss of Death: America's Love Affair With the Death Penalty.* Boston, MA: Northeastern University Press.

Very anti–death penalty book. John Bessler is someone who has been affected by the death penalty personally, and that plays out in this book. As a result, it is more a collection of personal memory mixed with his interpretations of that memory and the stories of those who sit on death row or have been executed. Part of his argument revolves around the idea that the death penalty is merely one aspect of a violent society. Until the United States works toward decreasing violence generally, capital punishment will never disappear.

Bohm, Robert. 1999. *Deathquest: An Introduction to the Theory and Practice of Capital Punishment in the United States.* Cincinnati: Anderson Publishing Co.

This is really a textbook on the death penalty and is advertised as the "first true textbook" on capital punishment. Although it is devised for a classroom setting (questions at the end of each chapter), it does provide a good overview of the history and issues. The author's bias (anti–death penalty) does not intrude on the presentation.

Bosco, Antoinette. 2001. *Choosing Mercy: A Mother of Murder Victims Pleads to End the Death Penalty.* Maryknoll, NY: Orbis Books.

Fascinating book by a journalist whose son and daughter-in-law were murdered in their home by, it turned out, the son of the people they had bought their home from. It is an interesting example of principle meeting reality as Bosco, a sworn anti–death penalty advocate, became that much more against capital punishment in the wake of her own personal tragedy. The book does not focus just on her own story, as fascinating as that is, but on others as well, and how their stories speak strongly against capital punishment. The book includes a good appendix of anti–death penalty sources.

Bowers, William J. 1984. *Legal Homicide: Death as Punishment in America, 1864–1982.* Boston, MA: Northeastern University Press.

Anti–death penalty book that argues the pre-*Furman* errors, which apparently had been fixed by *Gregg,* failed. The discrepancies and inconsistencies that *Furman* said had to be fixed, have not been. Using the Court's criteria, established in *Gregg,* Bowers tries to establish that the history of the death penalty is such that those criteria never have been and never will be met.

Camus, Albert. 1961. *Resistance, Rebellion, and Death.* Trans. J. O'Brien. New York: Vintage International.

This book contains the famous essay "Reflections on a Guillotine," Camus's powerful anti–death penalty statement that argued only without capital punishment can society move forward. Without abolition there can never be true peace.

Chessman, Caryl. 1954. *Cell 2455, Death Row.* Englewood Cliffs, NJ: Prentice Hall.

This and the next two books were produced by the celebrated prisoner during his twelve years on death row. They provide a rare insight into life on death row. Chessman, in writing these books, provided anti–death penalty advocates strong material for showing that capital prisoners were not all "worthy" of execution, what it was like to live on death row, and raised questions that only one sitting there could ask. Written under the shadow of execution, it has a certain urgency that adds to its appeal.

———. 1955. *Trial by Ordeal.* Englewood Cliffs, NJ: Prentice Hall.

Lengthy personal indictment of the death penalty. Some critics argue that if not for Chessman's notoriety, the book would never have been published; however, it is still noteworthy because of the circumstances under which it was written.

———. 1957. *The Face of Justice.* Englewood Cliffs, NJ: Prentice Hall.

Final book of the trilogy, written longhand, and in secret. More reminiscent of the first book. More a discussion of himself, and how he was a victim of a bad system.

Day, Nancy. 2000. *The Death Penalty for Teens: A Pro/Con Issue (Hot Pro/Con Issues).* Berkeley Heights, NJ: Enslow.

Good book for juveniles. In a very few pages it lays out the debate over capital punishment, specifically as it relates to teenage criminals.

Diaz, Joseph D. 2003. *The Execution of a Serial Killer: One Man's Experience Witnessing the Death Penalty.* Morrison, CO: Poncha Press.

Very disturbing book that focuses on one death penalty case by following the life of Edward Castro. Castro was a serial killer in Florida, whose execution the author witnessed. The book is interesting, because it does not preach (although Diaz is anti–death penalty) but rather presents the dilemmas that one must face when taking either a pro– or anti–death penalty stance. A good book for both pro– and anti–death penalty advocates.

Dicks, Shirley. 1995. *Congregation of the Condemned: Voices against the Death Penalty.* Reprint edition. Amherst, NY: Prometheus Books.

A virulently anti–death penalty collection, this book includes a series of essays. The author's own son sits on death row, so her bias is obvious. The book gives a good insight into the emotional arguments against the death penalty, but tends to be devoid of any balance or measured discussion of the issue. It includes statements from death row inmates and their views on capital punishment.

Drimmer, Frederick. 1990. *Until You Are Dead: The Book of Executions in America.* New York: Windsor Publishing Company.

An extensive survey of executions in America from colonial times to the execution of Ted Bundy. Describes the development of hanging, firing squad, electric chair, gas, and lethal injection as forms of execution.

Flanders, Stephen A. 2000. *Capital Punishment.* New York: Facts on File.

Part of the "Library in a Book" series that contains a wide range of sources for research on the death penalty, focusing on legal and ethical issues.

Fleury-Steiner, Benjamin Doy. 2004. *Jurors' Stories of Death: How America's Death Penalty Invests in Inequality (Law, Meaning, and Violence).* Ann Arbor: University of Michigan Press.

Anti–death penalty tome that surveys jurors who have sentenced people to death. The book focuses on how race and class play into decisions to execute, supporting the viewpoint that the death penalty is applied in an arbitrary and capricious manner and should be eliminated.

Foley, Michael A. 2003. *Arbitrary and Capricious: The Supreme Court, the Constitution and the Death Penalty.* Westport, CT: Praeger.

Analysis of Supreme Court opinions that indirectly argues against the death penalty. Shows the difficulty the Court has in coming up with a coherent, consistent approach to death penalty jurisprudence. Broad review of the constitutional issues raised by death penalty cases.

Galliher, John F. 2002. *America without the Death Penalty: States Leading the Way.* Boston, MA: Northeastern University Press.

A sociological analysis of the death penalty. The book focuses on nine states and different factors that influence capital punishment in those states.

Garvey, Stephen P. 2003. *Beyond Repair?: America's Death Penalty (Constitutional Conflicts).* Durham, NC: Duke University Press.

Seven essays that try to approach the death penalty in novel ways. Although not a decidedly anti–death penalty book, it slants that way, especially in the final essay. It is an interesting collection that tries to answer old questions in new ways and asks some new questions as well. The book includes some commentary on the United States and its relationship to the international debate.

Gottfried, Ted. 1997. *Capital Punishment: The Death Penalty Debate.* Springfield, NJ: Enslow Publishers.

High school–level book that presents arguments for and against the death penalty. Notes a variety of arguments from both sides and includes some basic statistics.

Grossman, Mark, and Mike Dixon-Kennedy. 1998. *Encyclopedia of Capital Punishment.* Santa Barbara, CA: ABC-CLIO.

High school–level book that has an outstanding range of materials without notable bias. A good series of appendices, including a chronology of the death penalty and a solid index of materials.

Henson, Burt M., et al. 1996. **Furman v. Georgia:** *The Death Penalty and the Constitution (Historic Supreme Court Cases).* London: Franklin Watts.

High school–level book that discusses the history of the death penalty prior to *Furman* and the implications of that historic case. Book focuses on *Furman v. Georgia.*

King, Rachel. 1997. *Don't Kill in Our Names: Families of Murder Victims Speak out against the Death Penalty.* Lanham, MD: University Presses of America.

This book opposes the death penalty. It profiles ten people, all of whom have had family members murdered. Each of the families is adamantly anti–death penalty. This is the type of book that is useful in constructing an argument against the revenge or vengeance type arguments used by death penalty advocates. Although the compassion and forgiveness these people exhibit is astounding, those who favor capital punishment will find this book a fascinating, and sometimes shocking, discussion from the opposite viewpoint.

Latzer, Barry. 2002. *Death Penalty Cases, Second Edition.* Amsterdam: Butterworth-Heinemann.

Nonbiased presentation of twenty-five U.S. Supreme Court cases dealing with the death penalty. Included with the edited versions of the cases are introductory materials, statistical data, statutes, and quality analysis and interpretation.

Lifton, Robert J., and Greg Mitchell. 2000. *Who Owns Death? Capital Punishment, the American Conscience, and the End of the Death Penalty.* New York: Morrow.

The basic premise of this book is that the death penalty is on the way out in the United States. The authors talk to the various people involved in executions, from the executioners to those sentenced to execution and all those in between, and provide various statistics to reach this conclusion. Despite the growing number of executions, Lifton and Mitchell conclude Americans are seriously conflicted over capital punishment and in the end will resign themselves to eradicating it.

Martinez, J. Michael, William D. Richardson, and D. Brandon Hornsby, eds. 2002. *The Leviathan's Choice: Capital Punishment in the Twenty-First Century.* Lanham, MD: Rowman and Littlefield.

Series of essays that comment on the death penalty by focusing on different aspects like race, social science data, religious orientation, and so forth. Although the majority of the articles are anti–death penalty, some argue the pro position. The book contains a good cross section of commentary.

Mello, Michael. 1996. *Against the Death Penalty: The Relentless Dissents of Justices Brennan and Marshall.* Boston, MA: Northeastern University Press.

Good overview and explanation of two of the key justices who helped frame the anti–death penalty jurisprudence during the last half of the twentieth century. It generally discusses not only their dissents but looks at the approaches each justice took and how they framed their arguments.

Mitchell, Hayley R. 2001. *The Death Penalty (Contemporary Issues Companion).* San Diego, CA: Greenhaven Press.

High school–level book that is written at a bit higher level. Although it tries to present the material in a straightforward manner, and includes a variety of articles, it has a definite anti–death penalty bias. The book contains a good index, bibliography, and list of organizations.

Nathanson, Stephen. 1988. *An Eye for an Eye? The Morality of Punishing by Death.* Lanham, MD: Rowman and Littlefield.

This book examines arguments for and against capital punishment on both philosophical and moral grounds and concludes that the death penalty is immoral.

Nelson, Lane, and Burk Foster. 2000. *Death Watch: A Death Penalty Anthology.* Englewood Cliffs, NJ: Prentice Hall.

Straightforward anthology that covers a wide range of topics, including the history of how the death penalty has been imposed, final words of the condemned, problems in executing women and juveniles, and the ethics of the death penalty.

Palmer, Louis J., Jr. 2001. *Encyclopedia of Capital Punishment in the United States.* Jefferson, NC: McFarland.

This is a good comprehensive resource that is organized alphabetically and that contains statistical material and extensive summaries of Supreme Court cases, which include facts, issues, holdings, and opinions. The book includes a short bibliography.

Prejean, Helen. 1997. *Dead Man Walking.* New York: Newmarket Press.

Maybe THE book arguing against the death penalty. This is the story of Sister Helen Prejean, who took on the role of spiritual advisor to men who were on death row at Louisiana's Angola State Prison. This book tells the story of two of those men. In addition to the story of those men and how her interaction with them solidifies her feeling about the death penalty, it gives a good background and history of capital punishment in a very nonjudgmental manner. However, in the end it is a powerful denunciation of capital punishment.

Radelet, Michael, and Margaret Vandiver. 1988. *Capital Punishment in America: An Annotated Bibliography.* New York: Garland.

While somewhat dated, it is an extensive bibliography that includes not just books but articles, congressional publications, pamphlets, and Supreme Court opinions. Provides a good starting point to do death penalty research, as well as a way to expand one's knowledge of specific aspects of capital punishment.

Radelet, Michael L., ed. 1989. *Facing the Death Penalty: Essays on a Cruel and Unusual Punishment.* Philadelphia, PA: Temple University Press.

This book is a series of essays that argue against the death penalty. The writers come from a variety of disciplines, including law, history, sociology, and theology. Also, three of the essays are written by death row prisoners.

Randa, Laura E., ed. 1997. *Society's Final Solution: A History and Discussion of the Death Penalty.* Lanham, MD: University Presses of America.

This book offers a solid, balanced discussion of the death penalty. It presents both sides of the argument and gives a good extensive history. Biases are not obvious, so it is a good source for those on either side of the debate.

Roberston, Diane P. 2002. *Tears from Heaven Voices from Hell: The Pros and Cons of the Death Penalty As Seen through the Eyes of the Victims of Violent Crime and Death Row Inmates throughout America.* Lincoln, NE: Writers Club Press.

A unique book that presents both sides of the argument from the points of view of both the victims and the perpetrators.

Sarat, Austin. 2001. *When the State Kills: Capital Punishment and the American Condition.* Princeton, NJ: Princeton University Press.

Philosophical work that delves into what the death penalty says about U.S. society. A critique of how the United States imposes the death penalty and the implications that imposition has on U.S. democracy and the culture at large. Most importantly, the author argues that capital punishment diminishes the United States and what it stands for.

Sarat, Austin, ed. 1999. *The Killing State: Capital Punishment in Law, Politics and Culture.* New York: Oxford University Press.

This book is a collection of essays that argue against the death penalty. Much of the work stresses the symbolic nature of the death penalty and how that symbolism plays out in modern U.S. society.

Schonebaum, Stephen E., ed. 1998. *Does Capital Punishment Deter Crime?* San Diego, CA: Greenhaven Press.

Written for a high school audience, this book presents a good discussion of the deterrence argument from both sides.

Steelwater, Eliza. 2003. *The Hangman's Knot: Lynching, Legal Execution and America's Struggle with the Death Penalty.* Boulder, CO: Westview Press.

This book connects the legal and illegal aspects (i.e., lynching) of the death penalty in trying to explain how capital punishment is as much a part of the political structure and economic system as it is a reflection of cultural and social elements in U.S. society. The author claims it has nothing to do with vengeance, deterrence, or any of the other arguments often given for maintaining capital punishment.

Steffans, Bradley, et al. 2001. **Furman v. Georgia:** *Fairness and the Death Penalty.* San Diego, CA: Lucent Press.

This book was written for young adults. It is a study of the landmark Supreme Court case, *Furman v. Georgia.*

Stewart, Gail, ed. 1998. *The Death Penalty.* San Diego, CA: Greenhaven Press.

Written for young adults, this book reviews the arguments for and against the death penalty.

Streib, Victor L. 2003. *Death Penalty in a Nutshell.* St. Paul, MN: Thomson/ West.

Part of a series on the law, this book provides a good overview of all aspects of the death penalty, from basic constitutional challenges and limitations, to substantive criminal law issues, trial issues, sentencing issues, the appeals process, post-conviction challenges, clemency problems, defense counsel issues, and problems of race, gender, class, and other biases.

Index

About the Author

Gary P. Gershman, Ph.D., is assistant professor of history and legal studies in the Division of Humanities at Nova Southeastern University, Fort Lauderdale, Florida.